CONTINUITY AND CHANGE IN HOUSE ELECTIONS

CONTRIBUTORS

Stephen Ansolabehere
David W. Brady
Charles S. Bullock III
Brandice Canes-Wrone
John F. Cogan
Melissa P. Collie
Robert D'Onofrio
David Epstein
Robert S. Erikson
Morris P. Fiorina
Frederick M. Hess
John R. Hibbing
Gary C. Jacobson
David L. Leal
John Lyman Mason
Sharyn O'Halloran
James M. Snyder Jr.
Eric Tiritilli
Gerald C. Wright

CONTINUITY AND CHANGE IN HOUSE ELECTIONS

Edited by

DAVID W. BRADY, JOHN F. COGAN,
AND MORRIS P. FIORINA

STANFORD UNIVERSITY PRESS • HOOVER INSTITUTION PRESS

Stanford, California

2000

Stanford University Press
Stanford, California
© 2000 by the Board of Trustees of the Leland Stanford
Junior University
Printed in the United States of America

Library of Congress Cataloging-in-Publication Data

Continuity and change in House elections / edited by
David W. Brady, John F. Cogan, and Morris P. Fiorina.
    p.   cm.
  Includes bibliographical references and index.
  ISBN 0-8047-3737-1 (alk. paper)—
  ISBN 0-8047-3739-8 (pbk. : alk. paper)
  1. United States. Congress. House—Elections.
2. Elections—United States—History—20th century.
3. United States—Politics and government—1989–
4. United States—Politics and government—1945–
1989. I. Brady, David W. II. Cogan, John F.
III. Fiorina, Morris P.

JK1965.C578 2000
324.973′0929—dc21

                          00-039488

CONTENTS

Stephen Ansolabehere is a professor of political science at the Massachusetts Institute of Technology.

David W. Brady is the Bowen H. and Janice Arthur McCoy Professor of Business and a professor of political science at Stanford University, and a senior fellow at the Hoover Institution.

Charles S. Bullock III is the Richard Russell Professor of Political Science at the University of Georgia.

Brandice Canes-Wrone is an assistant professor of political science at the Massachusetts Institute of Technology.

John F. Cogan is a senior fellow at the Hoover Institution.

Melissa P. Collie is a professor of political science at the University of Texas at Austin.

Robert D'Onofrio is a graduate student in political science at Stanford University.

David Epstein is an associate professor of political science at Columbia University.

Robert S. Erikson is a professor of political science at Columbia University.

Morris P. Fiorina is a professor of political science at Stanford University and a senior fellow at the Hoover Institution.

Frederick M. Hess is an assistant professor of political science and education at the University of Virginia.

John R. Hibbing is a professor of political science at the University of Nebraska at Lincoln.

Gary C. Jacobson is a professor of political science at the University of California at San Diego.

David L. Leal is an assistant professor of political science at the State University of New York at Buffalo.

John Lyman Mason is a graduate student in political science at the University of Texas at Austin.

Sharyn O'Halloran is an associate professor of public policy and political science at Columbia University.

James M. Snyder Jr. is a professor of political science and economics at the Massachusetts Institute of Technology.

Eric Tiritilli is a graduate student in political science at the University of Nebraska at Lincoln.

Gerald C. Wright is a professor of political science at Indiana University.

TABLES

CONTINUITY AND CHANGE IN HOUSE ELECTIONS

Chapter 1

An Introduction to
Continuity and Change in House Elections

DAVID W. BRADY, JOHN F. COGAN,

AND MORRIS P. FIORINA

In the period prior to and immediately after World War II, a focus on American congressional elections would not have furthered a political scientist's career. From 1946 through the 1950s only a handful of published articles had anything to do with U.S. House elections. To the extent that such elections were mentioned at all, it was largely in connection with normative claims about how safe districts, historical alliances, and other aspects of the party system inhibited the development of responsible political parties (Schattschneider 1950). The normative view that parties should set priorities and enact policies to which voters should react was the main thesis of Schattschneider's party responsibility report. The skeptical responses of Julius Turner (1951), Austin Ranney (1951), and Ranney and Willmoore Kendall (1954) arguing that party did matter, although not in the British style, set the early postwar agenda for political scientists interested in elections. Articles about levels of party voting in the House, presidential versus congressional factions within parties, and issues of party leadership dominated the literature of the time. Congressional elections as important objects of analysis in themselves were not featured. From 1946 to 1960 only two articles dealing with congressional elections appeared in the nine leading political science journals.[1]

The decade following the publication of the Schattschneider report, demonstrating that party in some sense did matter, slowly confirmed the findings of Turner and Ranney that American parties were "not respon-

1

sible" in the British sense of the term. In the 1950s, V. O. Key Jr. published his classic articles on realigning elections (1955, 1959) and Walter Dean Burnham (1965) began his studies of American electoral behavior. The early studies of presidential elections by Paul Lazarsfeld, Bernard Berelson, and their collaborators (Lazarsfeld et al. 1948; Berelson et al. 1954) introduced survey research techniques to the study of elections. And in the 1950s, the University of Michigan put together a team of scholars—Angus Campbell, Philip Converse, Warren Miller, and Donald Stokes—whose monumental study, *The American Voter* (1960), and subsequent articles (1966) provided the dominant frame for explaining American elections.

Briefly, the Michigan model posited that the vote in any particular election could be explained by a linear combination of a long-term force, party identification, and the effects of two short-term (election specific) forces, the candidates and the issues. Minority party victories, such as Dwight Eisenhower's in 1952, were explainable by the candidate's personal popularity and by his advantage on issues like the Korean War, which together overrode the Democrats' advantage in party identification. Party identification was the key variable because it established the baseline vote for each party and the *ceteris paribus* prediction that the majority party would win given generic candidates and issues. On the basis of these three variables, specific election results such as those of 1972 (Miller et al. 1976) or 1968 (Converse et al. 1969) were seen as the result of the normal party vote plus or minus candidate and issue effects. Thus, for example, Lyndon Johnson's 1964 landslide victory (Converse et al. 1965) was the result of the Democrats' baseline party advantage, plus the issues that favored the Democrats (peace and civil rights), plus Johnson's candidate advantage over Barry Goldwater.

The authors of *The American Voter* went further, classifying all presidential elections into four categories: The first consisted of realigning elections, where the baseline vote shifted, as in 1932 or 1896. Second were maintaining elections, where the electorate continued as the majority party in office, as in 1944 and 1948. Deviating elections occurred when short-term factors like candidate appeal (Eisenhower in 1952 and 1956) put the minority party in the presidency. Finally, in reinstating elections, which came after deviating elections, the electorate returned the party with the normal vote advantage to the presidency (1920, 1960).

Note that House elections were not relevant to classifying elections, although careful analysis of House elections might have raised some questions about the classification scheme. Eisenhower (who represents a two-term deviating presidency) served six of his eight years with a House controlled by the other party, whereas Woodrow Wilson (who also held office over a two-term deviating presidency) served six of his eight years with a House in the hands of his own party. Moreover, the Democratic takeover of the House in 1910 (deviating) signaled a Democratic victory in the 1912 presidential election, while the Democratic House victories in 1950 and 1954 (also deviating) did not presage Republican presidential victories in 1952 and 1956.

House elections according to the Michigan model were low salience events compared to presidential elections. House elections were low information, party-line affairs, in which voters knew little about the potential short-term forces—issues and candidates—thereby leaving party identification as the major determinant of the vote. Off-year congressional elections were the least salient of all, and thus the most partisan. During a presidential election year, voter turnout increased and the president's party carried some House candidates to victory. The midterm loss phenomenon was a predictable result of the fact that in the off-year election the party vote returned to normal and the president's party lost the seats it had gained from the president's coattails. If the president's coattails were short, as in the election of John Kennedy in 1960, then the loss in the subsequent midterm election was lower (4 seats); conversely, if the coattails were long, as in 1964, the midterm loss was greater, as in 1966 (47 seats).

In sum, the Michigan explanation for House elections focused on voter traits such as political interest and party identification that left individual congressional candidates little responsibility for their own fates. Candidates live and die electorally according to the distribution of partisan supporters in their districts, the popularity of the presidential candidates at the top of their tickets, and fluctuations in turnout caused by national forces. In a pair of classic articles, Miller and Stokes (1962, 1963) showed just how little individual citizens knew about the House candidates: roll-call voting records, in particular, were esoteric bits of information among the electorate-at-large. Little in the empirical record lent any support to the now-quaint party responsibility notion that voters hold members of the congressional parties accountable for their votes.

If the early post–World War II period did not see many articles on congressional elections, the three decades following publication of the seminal works of Campbell, Converse, Miller, and Stokes witnessed the growth of a congressional election cottage industry. The beginning was gradual enough. A perusal of the nine major political science journals mentioned above shows a series of articles from 1960 to 1970 on congressional elections, most of which either follow the Michigan model or argue about estimates of various parts of the model. Only a few works outside the Michigan model can be found (e.g., Hinckley 1967). In the next decade, however, interest in congressional elections began to take off. Robert Erikson's (1971, 1972a) articles on incumbency advantage, David Mayhew's (1974b) classic article on the disappearing marginals, Thomas Mann's *Unsafe at Any Margin* (1978), and Gerry Kramer's (1971) aggregate time series analysis revealed the inadequacies of the dominant Michigan model and confirmed the renewed interest in House elections.

One of the driving forces behind this outpouring of research was the insufficiency of *The American Voters* to explain American elections. House elections appeared to reflect the Democratic edge in party identification but Republicans were repeatedly winning presidential elections. If the explanation was short-term forces at the presidential election level, then how many Republican presidents in a row had to be elected before we concluded that the forces might not be so short-term after all? And why did the short-term forces stop working at the level of House elections? The Democrats held the House for all but four years (1947–49, 1953–55) during the postwar period until 1994, and from the 1954 elections until 1994 Democrats won twenty consecutive House majorities. Scholars were fascinated by the clear indications of change in elections, but their initial work was severely constrained by data availability: aggregate data and surveys designed to study presidential elections were all that was at hand. Recognizing the growing ferment in the subfield, the reconstituted National Election Studies (NES) in 1978 turned its focus to House elections. This and later studies made possible an impressive new research effort that produced a new model, one we describe in our conclusion as an equilibrium of "incumbency and insulation."

Relative to the older Michigan account, the new model of congressional elections was micro rather than macro, and endogenous, not exogenous. Members of the House of Representatives were no longer ciphers operated on by party identification and presidential coattails; rather, they were strategic actors who created their own campaign organizations, knew their districts, took positions, advertised, and claimed credit. In general, incumbents won reelection not because they were "safe" by some outside standard; rather, they were safe because they understood their districts, tailored their campaigns to the district, performed nonpartisan constituent services, and rather than lose, they strategically retired when losing seemed a likely prospect. Whatever changes occurred in House elections occurred in the open seats where no incumbent was running.

Of course, just as the anomalies of the party responsibility and Michigan models led to new research, the "new" model also had anomalies. Most obviously, why did the Democrats control the House continuously after 1954? Some argued that the rise of the incumbency advantage had serendipitously conferred the advantage on the Democrats. Others argued that the 1962–66 series of Supreme Court cases led to a redistricting that, given the magnitude of Goldwater's loss, benefited Democrats. Jacobson (1991) argued that Democrats were better local candidates since, unlike Republicans, they could more easily promise to bring home goods and services useful to local constituents. Others argued that Republicans retired earlier than Democrats because minority seats were worth less than majority seats. There was little emphasis, however, on issues or policy outcomes in the revisionist literature. Incumbents had name recognition, performed neutral constituent service, publicized themselves, claimed credit, raised money from political action committees (PACs) sufficient to scare off good challengers, and so on. Indeed, the dominant book on Congress, Mayhew's *Congress: The Electoral Connection* (1974), held that members cared about their individual positions vis-à-vis district sentiment, but were unconcerned about policy outcomes. Economists who looked at the House talked about "slack," the freedom of members to vote as they wished without fear of voter retribution. While there were important unanswered questions about congressional elections (for example, how exactly did money affect House elections?), the dominant picture was one of incumbent-driven success where endogenous choices by members greatly enhanced their reelection prospects.

The 1994 House elections shook the foundations of the post-Michigan incumbency consensus. No model of congressional elections came close to predicting the House results. How had the Republicans captured the House? Surely they could not keep it in 1996 with President Bill Clinton assured of a sizable victory. The Republicans' win in 1994 and their subsequent maintenance of a majority in spite of Clinton's near-landslide victory stimulated the Hoover Institution to sponsor a conference on Change and Continuity in House Elections early in 1997. We invited a distinguished group of scholars, many of whom had contributed to the revisionist literature now called into question by the developments of 1994 and 1996. We also asked Nelson Polsby and Raymond Wolfinger of the University of California, Berkeley and Thomas Edsall of the *Washington Post* to comment on the papers. The results are what one would expect from such a distinguished group—an interesting and insightful set of papers that, we hope, will help set the agenda for the study of congressional elections.

In the introductory chapter, Gary Jacobson provides an overview of the major electoral trends that led to the "reversal of partisan fortunes" in the 1994 midterm elections. Over the past forty years, there has been a decline in the incumbency advantage, an increase in the number of contested House races, a greater congruence between House and presidential voting, and an increase in the uniformity of interrelation vote swings. These patterns worked in combination with an increase in the quality of Republican challengers and a higher rate of strategic Democratic retirements to provide the GOP with its first House majority in forty years. Jacobson notes further that although the partisan makeup is now reversed, divided government persists despite a brief two-year hiatus. Extending earlier work on the subject, Jacobson claims that the current pattern of split control reflects a reversal of institutional roles, but questions the stability of this unusual partisan division.

The first section of the book focuses on some particular aspects of change in recent House elections. Charles Bullock notes that the largest seat gains for the Republicans came in the South. He shows that the key to these southern gains was the GOP's ability finally to capture swing white voters who previously voted Democratic in congressional elections but Republican in presidential elections. The Republicans' breakthrough in the South is impressive: in 1996 they won a majority of the seats that were less than 40 percent black, driving the Democrats back to their strongholds. In sum, the Republican takeover in 1994 was the result of voting patterns long evident in presidential elections finally appearing farther down the ticket.

Steve Ansolabehere and Jim Snyder analyze recent trends in campaign finance and their contribution to incumbency advantage in the House. Since 1980, incumbent spending has doubled in real terms, compared with only a 40 percent increase in challenger spending. Ansolabehere and Snyder estimate that, on average, this trend has added about 5 percentage points to an incumbent's electoral margin. The disparity between incumbent and challenger spending is mainly fueled by the greater rate of PAC contributions to those who are currently in office. To illustrate this, the authors estimate that the "sophomore surge" in PAC receipts is nearly $200,000, which constitutes 70 percent of the monetary advantage such incumbents enjoy over their challengers. In addition to simply holding office, being in a position of power in Congress allows a member to reap even greater financial benefits. Ansolabehere and Snyder conclude that the incumbency advantage in campaign finance has grown over the past twenty years because interest group activity has grown over the same period.

Turning to the electoral impact of majority-minority redistricting, David Epstein and Sharyn O'Halloran examine the contribution of such seats to the Republican midterm victory in 1994 and examine the representational consequences of creating such districts. They argue that while concentrated minority districts have surely had an impact on congressional elections, it is not easy to characterize that effect. On one hand, majority-minority districts have increased *descriptive* minority representation, that is, the number of House seats held by minorities. However, the authors claim, this increase may have come at the expense of *substantive* minority representation. By concentrating minorities in a few majority-minority seats, members of the House not representing such districts may feel little obligation to further policies important to minorities, thus hindering the advancement of such legislation. The net result has been the weakening of the moderate bipartisan coalition that formed in the 1960s and 1970s for the advancement of minority interests.

In the next chapter, John Hibbing and Eric Tiritilli focus on recent changes in the nature of public opinion about Congress. For decades scholars have noted the public disdain for the legislative branch as a whole, yet most congressional elections resulted in minimal turnover. The implication the authors draw from this familiar pattern is that voters rarely hold a particular group of members accountable for the institutional shortcomings that cause them to dislike Congress. They argue, however, that 1994 was one of those rare instances when public disapproval and electoral outcomes were related. Although surveys usually reveal an electorate generally unable to correctly pick the majority party in Congress, in 1994 voters were unusually aware that the Democrats controlled a unified government, an awareness aided by aggressive minority party leaders who publicly and regularly placed blame on the majority party. Since this connection of disapproval with electoral fates was only observable in districts with running Democratic incumbents, the authors conclude that this was a significant causal factor in the Republican takeover.

In concluding the first section of the book, David Brady, Robert D'Onofrio, and Morris Fiorina review the often-discussed notion of nationalization. Many political observers claimed that part of the Republicans' successes in 1994 were due to their success in nationalizing the election, in contrast to the usual picture of congressional elections as purely local affairs. The authors examine the concept of nationalization and show with simple indicators that the national component of the House vote has indeed been increasing while the local component has been constant or declining since the late 1960s. According to their estimates, the 1994 midterm election was the most nationalized election since 1954, with national concerns equally as important as local influences. The chapter concludes with a brief analysis of some possible causes of this change, including the decline in incumbency advantage and recent changes in southern congressional elections.

The second section of the book focuses specifically on how issues, partisanship, and ideology affect House members' reelection prospects. Robert

Erikson and Gerald Wright provide preliminary evidence that there is a strong causal connection between a member's ideological position and the position of the district he or she represents. Conservative districts tend to elect Republicans, whereas liberal districts tend to put Democrats in office. Moderate districts favor moderate candidates of either party, but all three types of districts punish members who stray too far from the district's ideological position. In addition, party polarization in the House has been increasing in such a way that these observed effects of constituency ideology are even stronger. The implication of these findings is that in addition to the usual nonpolicy factors such as name visibility and constituency service, members' roll-call voting behavior plays an important role in determining their electoral fates.

David Brady, Brandice Canes-Wrone, and John Cogan demonstrate that this connection of issues with electoral success has been a feature of most House elections since 1952. In addition to providing an explanation for the Republican victories in 1994, the authors show that most incumbent defeats during this period can be attributed to the member straying too far from the district's ideal ideological position. Naturally, this begs the question of why a rational member would engage in such risky behavior. One possibility considered by the authors is the notion of *presidential pull*, whereby the current president pulls members of his party away from district opinion toward supporting his position in exchange for political favors. In the next House election, the members who have been pulled in such a manner stand a greater chance of losing their bid for reelection, but for those who survive the political payoffs make the earlier risk worthwhile.

In a case study of the 1994 elections, David Leal and Rick Hess analyze the impact of issue emphasis on electoral results at the micro level. Using the results of surveys of 42 House challengers in Mid-Atlantic and New England states, the authors find that Democrats were less likely than Republicans to discuss specific issues during the campaigns, regardless of their actual position on those issues. The issues discussed most often by the Republican challengers were crime and the federal deficit; both of these issues turned out to be fruitful at the polls. Challengers who focused on these two issues got significantly larger vote shares than those who did not. Thus, for challengers as well as incumbents, there seems to be a connection between policy issues and electoral success.

In the penultimate chapter, Melissa Collie and John Mason examine the relationship between changes in the constituency bases of the two major parties and changes in the behavior of the legislative parties. The past two decades have witnessed a resurgence of partisan voting behavior and polarization in the House, particularly within the Democratic party, so that members of the same party vote together in opposition to the other party at historically high rates. One possible explanation for this trend is that the electoral bases for members of both parties have themselves become more homogenous and differentiated, so that the voting patterns observed in Congress are simply reflections of these changes at the district level. Surprisingly, however, the authors find that changes in the ideological and policy positions of the electorate have been minimal. Collie and Mason suggest that small shifts in constituency sentiments are translated into greater shifts within the legislature via the single-member district system used to elect House members.

Finally, in our concluding chapter the coeditors examine the 1998 election results in light of the research findings presented in the preceding articles. One clear conclusion is that any explanation of recent House elections must give a prominent place to national issues and policies and the members' stands on them. This represents a noteworthy shift from the emphasis on nonprogrammatic aspects of incumbency that dominated the congressional elections literature from 1974 to 1994.

Scholars working in the area of elections to the United States House of Representatives are an unusually cooperative group of scholars. The result is that data on House elections is widely and freely shared. Gary Jacobson is clearly the person who has shared his data the most, especially his variables on previous political experience. Others, including the contributors to this book and in particular Stephen Ansolabehere and James Snyder of the Massachusetts Institute of Technology, have shared their data on ADA scores and presidential voting in the House district. (An important positive result of this collaboration is that if a scholar were to make a mistake in calculating a statistic, such as swing, he or she would be notified of the mistake because everyone else is working from the same basic data set.) For this book that means that, unless information has been otherwise attributed, the data sets used by all the scholars (regarding vote percentages by party ADA scores, etc.) are jointly created and do not have any one official source.

The authors owe a special debt of gratitude to Stanford political science graduate students Louis Ayala and Jeremy Pope for services beyond the call of duty.

Chapter 2

Reversal of Fortune: The Transformation of U.S. House Elections in the 1990s

GARY C. JACOBSON

The idea that the Democrats could win the White House by more than eight million votes without winning a majority in the House of Representatives would have been unthinkable only a few years ago. Yet by the time it happened, no one was particularly surprised; indeed, the unthinkable had become the predictable (Jacobson and Kim 1996). Despite Bill Clinton's easy reelection, Democrats gained only 9 House seats in 1996, leaving them with 207, only 3 more than they had won in 1994.[1] The 1996 elections confirmed in unmistakable terms that the competitive balance in House elections has shifted sharply and durably to the Republicans in the 1990s.[2] One purpose of this essay is to document and explain this reversal of partisan fortune.

The 1996 elections also extended a broader set of trends that distinguished House elections in the 1990s from those of the previous two decades. These trends deserve examination and explanation as well, for the electoral behavior that preserved a Democratic president and a Republican Congress in 1996 was not a simple inversion of the voting habits that had produced Republican presidents and Democratic Congresses for much of the postwar period. Despite the electorate's endorsement of divided government and continuing expressed indifference, if not hostility, to political parties, electoral coherence has risen sharply in the 1990s, while the incumbency advantage, along with the electoral idiosyncrasy associated with it, have diminished. The second purpose of this essay is to examine these changes and consider what they portend for future congressional elections.

The Republican House Majority

The Republican takeover of the House in 1994, shocking as it was after more than 40 years of Democratic rule, marked neither a transient aberration nor a sudden partisan realignment. It represented, rather, the payoff to congressional Republicans from electoral changes that had been accumulating for years. The question is not so much why the Republicans finally won the House in 1994 but why it took them so long to do so.

Republicans have dominated presidential voting since Richard Nixon's first victory in 1968. Only Jimmy Carter's narrow win in 1976 interrupted the string of Republican victories from 1968 through 1988. Even with Bill Clinton's pluralities in 1992 and 1996, Republican presidential candidates have run, on average, about 6 percentage points ahead of their Democratic opponents over the last eight elections.

Moreover, the electorate became significantly more Republican during the period of Republican presidential ascendancy. Three separate time series measuring the electorate's party identification—from the Gallup Polls, the CBS News/*New York Times* Polls, and the National Election Studies—uniformly find substantial increases in the proportion calling themselves Republicans during the 1980s. Furthermore, all three series show an abrupt and sustained swing toward the Republicans (from 5 to 6 percent) among party identifiers around the time of the 1984 election, with no further subsequent trend.[3] The Republican takeover of the House in 1994 was not accompanied by a sustained increase in Republican party identification;[4] rather, the party finally cashed in on favorable changes in party identification that had raised Republicans to near parity with the Democrats ten years earlier.

Why did it take so long for House Republicans to reap the rewards of the far more congenial political climate that emerged in the late 1970s and early 1980s? Why were they finally able to reap those rewards in 1994? My summary answer to the first question, defended at length in earlier work (Jacobson 1990b, 1990c, 1991), was that "Republicans . . . failed to advance in the House because they . . . fielded inferior candidates on the wrong side of issues important to voters in House elections and because voters find it difficult to assign blame or credit when control of government is divided between the parties" (Jacobson 1990a: 3). My short answer to the second question derived directly from the answer to the first: "In 1994, the Republicans won the House by fielding (modestly) superior candidates who were on the right side of the issues that were important to voters in House elections and by persuading voters to blame a unified Democratic government for government's failures" (Jacobson 1996c: 2).

Clinton's victory in 1992 broke the logjam. Government divided between a Republican president and a Democratic Congress had offered little leverage to Republican congressional candidates. Voters might punish the president's party in bad times, but credit for good times was shared with the other party's congressional majority. It is hard to convince voters to throw the rascals of either party out when they are satisfied with government's performance. Only under a unified Democratic government could congressional Democrats be saddled with wholesale blame for government's failures, as they were in 1994 (Jacobson 1996a), finally enabling House Republican candidates to profit from the more Republican electorate that had emerged a decade earlier.

Not all of the action took place in 1994. Republicans actually got their initial boost toward majority status in 1992 from the reallocation of House seats that followed the 1990 census. The states in the South and West that gained seats were, on average, considerably more Republican in their presidential voting habits than the states in the Northeast and Midwest that lost seats.[5] The drawing of majority-minority districts also helped Republicans by packing overwhelmingly Democratic African-American voters into minority districts, leaving neighboring districts relatively more Republican (Hill 1995). Moreover, the usual dislocations that follow redistricting were compounded in 1992 by the House bank scandal, which contributed to a huge turnover in House membership that year (Jacobson and Dimock 1994). The shift in the competitive balance in favor of Republicans brought about by redistricting was easy to overlook in 1992, when George Bush's dismal showing dragged down the entire Republican ticket. But even then, the Republicans' pickup of ten House seats despite the loss of the White House signaled that the competitive balance between the parties had undergone a fundamental change.

We can get a rough estimate of the magnitude of that change by examining a standard regression model of Republican House victories in postwar elections. The first equation in Table 2.1 estimates the Republicans' total number of House victories as a function of the economy's performance (measured as the change in real income per capita in the election year) and presidential approval (percent approving of the president's performance in the last Gallup Poll prior to the election). Both variables are multiplied by -1 under Democratic administrations, requiring an administration dummy

Table 2.1
Effects of National Conditions on Republican Share of House Seats, 1946–1996

	1946–1990	1946–1996		
	1[a]	2	3	4
Intercept	263.7***	251.1***	263.7***	265.8***
	(16.5)	(18.7)	(16.5)	(14.9)
Democratic administration	−176.8***	−138.0***	−176.8***	−183.7***
	(36.7)	(40.2)	(36.7)	(33.1)
Change in real income, %	3.2*	4.5*	3.2*	3.1*
	(1.6)	(1.9)	(1.6)	(1.5)
Presidential approval, %	1.5***	1.0*	1.5***	1.5***
	(0.4)	(0.4)	(0.4)	(0.3)
1992			32.8	
			(18.5)	
1994			45.9*	
			(16.8)	
1996			44.0*	
			(17.3)	
1992–96				41.3***
				(10.4)
Adjusted R^2	.59	.46	.65	.68
N	23	26	26	26

SOURCE: Unless otherwise stated, all data for tables and figures in Chapter 2 are taken from the author's data set.

NOTE: The dependent variable is the number of House seats won by Republicans; see text for description of independent variables. Standard errors are in parentheses.

[a]Numbers at head of columns represent different equations, as discussed in text.

*$p < .05$, two-tailed test.

***$p < .001$, two-tailed test.

(1 if a Republican sits in the White House, 0 otherwise) to be included as a control.

The results for the 1946–90 period are typical of such models (Tufte 1973 presents the original; see also Jacobson 1997b). Notice that when the period is extended to include the elections of the 1990s (equation 2), the fit of the equation declines sharply (the adjusted R^2 falls from .59 to .46). The reason is apparent from equation 3, which includes separate variables representing each of the past three elections. Notice that in 1992 as well as in 1994 and 1996, House Republicans did much better than they would have prior to the 1990s, other things being equal.[6] The fourth equation shows that in elections since 1992, Republicans have won about 41 more House seats than they would have under the same conditions during the 1946–90 period. During that earlier era, they won an average of 180 seats; adding 41 seats raises their "expected" contingent to 221, a narrow majority close to their current House strength of 227.[7]

Redistricting does not, by itself, explain all of the Republican gains in the 1990s. At least as important is the rise in congruity between presidential and House voting in congressional districts. Most of the House seats Republicans have picked up in the 1990s have been in districts that had been leaning Republican at the presidential level. The end of divided government in 1992 and the policies of the Clinton administration heightened the partisan component of the 1994 elections, sharply increasing the proportion of voters who cast House votes consistent with their usual presidential votes (Jacobson 1996c). As a result, Republicans took over by winning House seats where their party already had a strong base of support.

A serviceable measure of a district's presidential leanings in the 1990s can be computed by taking the average division of its two-party vote for president in 1988 and 1992 (Jacobson 1997a). Its mean for all districts is 49.9 percent Democratic; its median, 48.3 percent Democratic. Table 2.2 divides House districts into three categories, depending on whether the district's average vote for the presidential candidate of the member's party was below 48 percent, between 48 and 52 percent, or over 52 percent. The first category represents districts where, by the evidence of presidential voting habits, members are at greatest electoral risk, the second, districts where the risk is more moderate, and the third, districts where the member should be most secure.

Mark the changes between 1992 and 1996. More than three-quarters of the net Democratic losses (39 of 51) have come in districts where Democratic presidential candidates have done poorly. Which is to say, more than three-quarters of the Republican gains have come in districts where Republican presidential candidates have run strongly. Yet even after these shifts, Democrats have more seats at high risk than Republicans (36 compared with 19), while Republicans hold more seats where their party has a comfortable base of support (179 compared with 143). Given the kind of districts Democrats lost in 1994, it is not surprising that they won back only a handful in

Table 2.2
At-Risk and Safe House Seats by Party, 1992–1996

Average district presidential vote for winner's party 1988–1992	*1992*	*1994*	*1996*	*Change 1992–1996*
Less than 48%				
Democrats	75	38	36	−39
Republicans	16	21	19	+3
TOTAL	91	59	55	−36
48%–52%				
Democrats	37	25	28	−9
Republicans	20	32	29	+9
TOTAL	57	57	57	0
More than 52%				
Democrats	146	141	143	−3
Republicans	140	177	179	+39
TOTAL	286	318	322	+36

1996. Of the 56 seats newly taken by Republicans in 1994, Democrats retook a mere 10, only 2 of them in districts clearly favoring Republican presidential candidates. Observe also that the total number of members representing unfriendly territory has fallen by 40 percent in the 1990s (from 91 to 55); I will have more to say about the increasing congruity of presidential and House voting at the district level after reviewing the special case of the South.

The South

It is no secret that Republicans have made their greatest advances in the 1990s in the South,[8] where, after lagging for decades, Republican House (and Senate) candidates have finally begun to catch up with their presidential candidates' electoral performance (Frymer 1996). Table 2.3 recapitulates Table 2.2 for southern House districts. It shows how thoroughly Republican gains in the South have been concentrated in districts that favor Republican presidential candidates, underlining how difficult it will be for Democrats to recapture those districts, especially now that the logic of electing conservative Democrats rather than Republicans to protect local interests no

Table 2.3

At–Risk and Safe House Seats in the South, by Party, 1992–1996

Average district presidential vote for winner's party 1988–1992	1992	1994	1996	Change 1992–1996
Less than 48%				
Democrats	40	24	18	−22
Republicans	3	2	2	−1
TOTAL	43	26	20	−23
48%–52%				
Democrats	6	5	4	−2
Republicans	3	4	5	+2
TOTAL	9	9	9	0
More than 52%				
Democrats	31	32	32	+1
Republicans	42	58	64	+22
TOTAL	73	90	96	+23

longer prevails now that Democrats have lost the clout conferred by majority status.

The growth of Republican House strength in the South during the 1990s represents the sharp acceleration of a trend, displayed in Figure 2.1, that has been going on since the 1950s. In the 1940s, Republicans held only 2 of the region's 105 seats. After making substantial gains in the 1960s, Republicans made only modest further progress until the 1990s. In the 1994 election, they won a majority of southern seats for the first time ever. And in 1996, they increased their share to 57 percent even while they were losing seats elsewhere.[9] Whereas 50 years ago southerners made up only a trace fraction of the Republican House contingent, now almost a third of the Republicans are from the South.

There is nothing mysterious about this trend. It is a direct if occasionally delayed response to the growing Republican allegiance among white southerners. Figure 2.2 illustrates the connection. The dotted line traces the growth in the Republican share of House seats, while the solid line traces the growth in the share of white southern party identifiers (including partisan leaners) who label themselves Republicans. The trends track closely, although with seats occasionally lagging party identification. In 1994 and

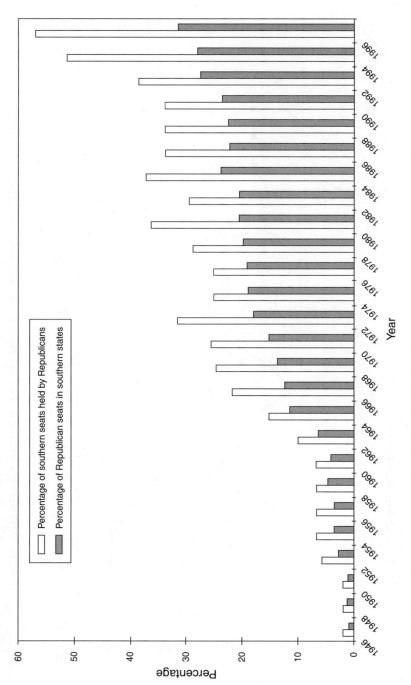

Figure 2.1. Republican House strength in the South, 1946–1996.

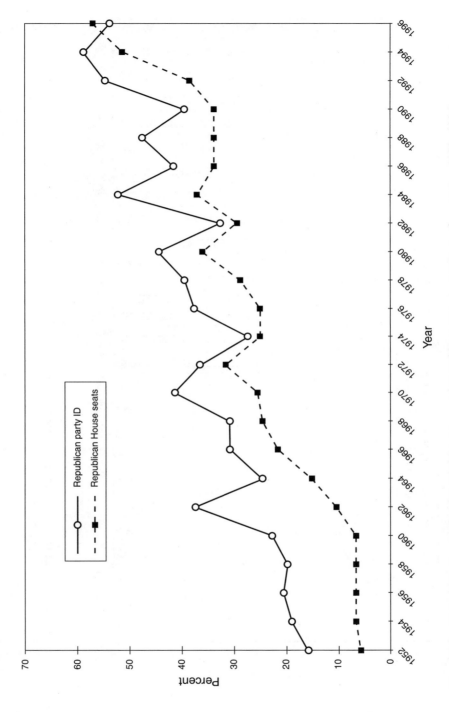

Figure 2.2. Republican party ID among white voters and Republican House seats in southern states, 1952–1996.

SOURCE: NES. Data include only those respondents who reported voting in House elections.

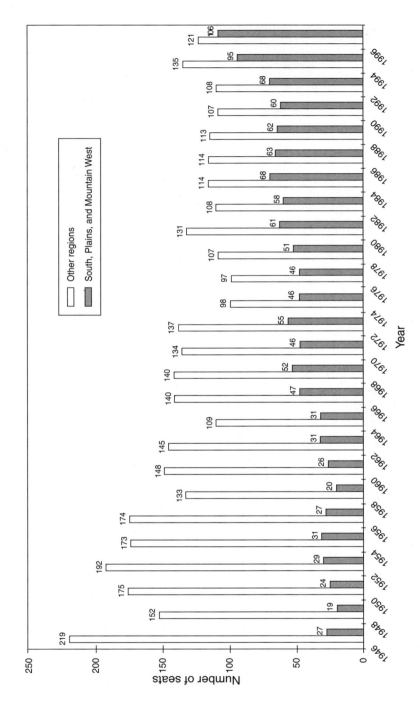

Figure 2.3. Republican strength in House, by region, 1946–1996.

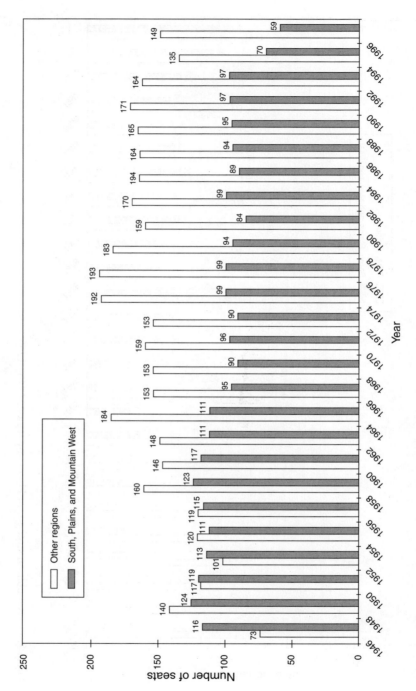

Figure 2.4. Democratic strength in House, by region, 1946–1996.

1996, Republicans finally exploited this regional realignment in a major way, and they have by no means exhausted their potential for further growth. Note from Table 2.3 that, by the criteria of presidential voting, Democrats still have eighteen seats at risk in the South, while the Republicans have but two. The Republican party is on its way to building the kind of strong congressional base in the South that once gave the Democrats a formidable head start in the battle to control the House and Senate.

The swing to Republicans in the South is actually part of a longer, broader regional realignment in Congress. Figures 2.3 and 2.4 show how each party's regional strength in the House has changed over the postwar period. The Republican majority of the 1990s is the product of dramatic gains in the western plains and Mountain States as well as the South.[10] Over the longer haul, the parties have gradually exchanged regional hegemony at the House level, with Republicans now strongest where Democrats once predominated, and to a lesser extent, vice versa.

The Resurgence of Electoral Coherence

It is scarcely a coincidence that Republican House representation has grown in just those states in which the party's cultural conservatism and anti-tax, antiwelfare, anti–big government, and progun themes resonate most strongly. They are the same states where Bob Dole ran strongly in the 1996 presidential election. Indeed, the growing congruity of House and presidential election results is one of the most intriguing features of elections in the 1990s. Figure 2.5 traces changes in the correlations between district-level House and presidential voting from 1952 through 1996. My choice of measures for the district-level presidential vote for each election was nakedly empirical; I simply used the measure of presidential vote from whatever concurrent or adjacent presidential elections, or combination thereof, produced the largest correlation with the House vote.[11] The idea was to accord the presidential vote its maximum explanatory power for every election year.

The growing dissociation of presidential and House voting, a well-documented feature of electoral politics from the 1950s to the 1980s (Jacobson 1990a), is clearly evident in the chart. Not surprisingly, the correlations fell most steeply in the South, where Democrats held onto most of the House seats for several decades after the region began preferring Republican presidents. But the same downward trend, though shallower, showed up outside the South as well. The trend reversed in the 1990s as the correlations between presidential and House voting rose steeply, reaching levels in 1996

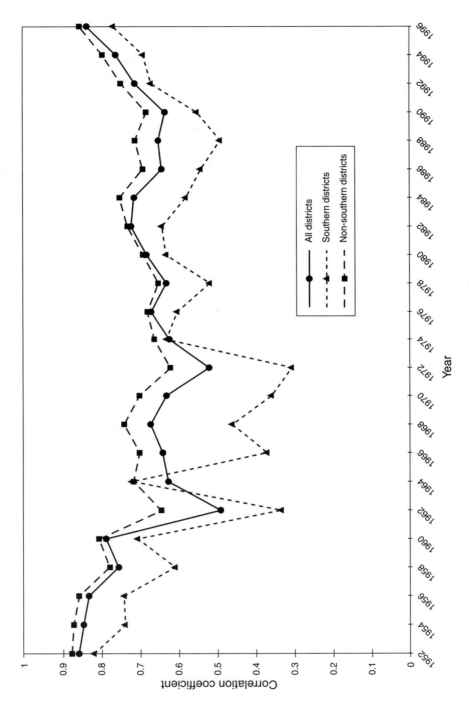

Figure 2.5. Correlations between district presidential vote and House vote, 1952–1996.

not seen since the 1950s. Note that the change was not merely an artifact of congressional Republicans finally running up to potential in the South, for it occurred in districts both within and outside the region.

Beyond the southern realignment working its way down to the House level, the trend toward greater congruity between presidential and House voting in the 1990s has several possible explanations, none mutually exclusive and all traceable to changes in the behavior of political elites. First, the House has become more partisan over the past two decades, with more frequent partisan divisions and higher levels of party unity on roll-call votes (Jacobson 1997b: 210–11). Both congressional parties have become more ideologically homogeneous, with fewer conservative Democrats and fewer moderate Republicans than in past Congresses. Among the consequences have been increasingly polarized congressional responses to presidential initiatives, particularly during the Clinton administration. Thus some convergence in the public's criteria for assessing the two branches is not surprising.

Second, and relatedly, party leaders and other campaign elites have deliberately sought to nationalize recent congressional campaigns. The Republicans took the lead in 1994, tying Democrats to Bill Clinton and his party's tax-and-spend, big-government image, casting them as symbols of the scorned Washington establishment and rallying House candidates around a common set of issues summarized in the Contract with America (Jacobson 1996c). In 1996, it was the Democrats' turn as they sought to identify Republican candidates with the unpopular House speaker, Newt Gingrich, and the "extreme" agenda of the 104th Congress, with its alleged assaults on Medicare, education, and the environment. In both instances, allied political activists reinforced the parties' strategies. In 1994, conservative talk show hosts and militants of the Christian Right helped to sell the Republican campaign message nationally. They were joined in 1996 by the labor, environmental, and women's groups who mounted vigorous independent campaigns using common themes to attack targeted Republican incumbents across the country.

Third, party labels have become more informative to voters as the divisions between the parties have grown sharper and clearer across a range of social and economic issues (Carmines and Layman 1997). At the same time, disgust with politicians as a class and the decline of pork barrel politics under budgetary pressure has apparently diminished the value of incumbency, for which evidence is presented below. Thus in the 1990s, campaign elites have framed the choice in House elections in terms more similar to those of presidential elections than they did in the 1970s and 1980s, and district electorates have responded by making more consistent choices across offices. The prime beneficiaries of this development have, of course, been the Republicans.

Reversal of Fortune

The reversal of party fortunes in the 1990s shows itself in numerous guises. The same electoral patterns that kept the Democrats in the majority for so long now favor the Republicans. For example, in earlier work examining the Republicans' failure to advance in House elections during their long period of presidential hegemony (1968 to 1990), I took pains to show that, despite Republican complaints, neither the enlarged incumbency advantage nor Democratic gerrymandering explained the Republicans' inability to win the House. The incumbency explanation failed because Republicans lost ground even in open seats, where incumbency was not a factor, and because more Republican than Democratic incumbents were defeated during the period (Jacobson 1990a). Table 2.4 shows how dramatically these patterns have changed in the 1990s. Republicans have been far more successful than Democrats in both defeating incumbents and taking open seats from the opposition, inverting the pattern of the previous two decades. The difference is most striking in the South, where Republican success rates in contests for open seats held by Democrats doubled to a remarkable 50 percent. Democrats, in contrast have taken only one open southern Republican seat (vacated by a former Democrat who had switched parties after 1994) so far during the decade.

The gerrymandering explanation failed to account for the Democrats' years of hegemony because redistricting had no net effect on Republican fortunes during the period; Republicans did neither better nor worse, on average, after districts were redrawn. Their problem was not the way House votes were counted, but that they did not win enough House votes (Jacobson 1990a). The difference in 1994 was that they finally won a majority of votes cast in House elections (53.6 percent of the two-party vote) for the first time since 1952, and so they finally won a majority of the seats for the first time since 1952. In 1996, they again won a (bare) majority of the two-party vote and held on to a narrow majority of the seats.

Two other factors contributed to the Democrats' success in the earlier period: superior challengers (Jacobson 1990a; D. W. Brady et al. 1994), and fewer incumbents leaving voluntarily (Gilmour and Rothstein 1993; Ansolabehere and Gerber n.d.). Both advantages have disappeared in the 1990s. A simple but effective measure of a challenger's quality is previous public of-

Table 2.4

House Seats Changing Party Control, 1968–1990 and 1992–1994

	1968–1990		1992–1996	
	Won	*Percent*	*Won*	*Percent*
All districts				
Republican challengers	87	3.1	50	8.3
Democratic challengers	104	5.6	24	4.8
Difference	−17		26	
Republicans seeking Democratic open seats	57	21.1	42	42.9
Democrats seeking Republican open seats	64	30.3	17	24.6
Difference	−7		25	
Southern districts				
Republican challengers	18	2.2	11	6.7
Democratic challengers	24	6.7	3	2.1
Difference	−6		8	
Republicans seeking Democratic open seats	21	23.6	20	50.0
Democrats seeking Republican open seats	9	26.5	1	7.1
Difference	12		19	

fice, for challengers who have held elective office consistently do better on election day than those who have not (Jacobson 1989). From 1968 through 1990, 25.1 percent of Republican incumbents faced experienced challengers, compared with only 15.7 percent of Democratic incumbents ($p < .001$). In the 1990s, the equivalent figures are 19.6 percent and 17.5 percent, respectively, so the Democrats no longer have a significant advantage on this dimension ($p = .37$).

The dearth of strong challengers clearly hurt the Democrats' efforts to retake the House in 1996. Only 22.1 percent of Democratic challengers had previously held elective public office, a figure below their postwar average of 25.3 percent and not at all typical of the party in a good Democratic year. The Democrats needed to pick up at least nineteen seats to win control of the House. In each of the five postwar elections in which they have added nineteen or more seats to their total, at least 31.2 percent of their challengers have held elective office; the average for these elections was 35.7 percent.[12]

Just as a shortage of strong Republican challengers hurt the party during favorable Republican years of 1984 and 1988 (Jacobson 1997b), Democrats were unable to cash in fully on the pro-Democratic trend in 1996 because they fielded too few high-quality challengers (Jacobson 1997a).

The incidence of voluntary retirements now also favors Republicans. In the earlier period, a larger proportion of Republican members left the House voluntarily (9.7 percent compared with 7.0 percent); in the 1990s, Democrats have been more likely to bail out (13.4 percent compared with 11.2 percent). Since 1992, thirty-two more Democrats than Republicans have chosen to leave, magnifying the effect of the Republicans' superior performance in contests for open seats. In both 1994 and 1996, a disproportionate share of Democratic retirees abandoned districts that had been voting Republican for president and that were therefore ripe for Republican picking (Jacobson 1996c, 1997a).

To a remarkable degree, then, the parties have exchanged electoral advantages and disadvantages in the 1990s. Patterns of behavior that helped Democrats preserve their majority for so many years now help Republicans. The only solace for Democrats is that, although the altered partisan balance has left Republicans in the majority, it is a much narrower majority than the one typically enjoyed by Democrats during their forty-year reign.[13] It would not take a very strong partisan tide to put the Democrats back in power—at least temporarily.

Incumbency, Competition, and Turnover

The Republican ascendancy and the growing consistency of presidential and House voting at the district level are certainly the most striking changes in House elections during the 1990s, but several other trends deserve attention as well. By several measures, the notorious incumbency advantage has fallen to its lowest level since the 1960s. Figure 2.6 displays one familiar measure of the incumbency advantage, the "slurge" (the average of the sophomore surge and retirement slumps)[14] for elections since 1946. By this measure, the value of incumbency, in vote shares, has declined markedly from its peak in the mid-1980s. Its 1996 value of 4.6 percentage points is the lowest since 1964 and barely half of its value a decade earlier. The more volatile Gelman-King index (Gelman and King 1990) also hit its lowest level in more than twenty years in 1996 (6.9 percentage points). More generally, the mean share of the two-party vote for House incumbents facing major party opposition has also been lower in the 1990s than in any decade since the 1960s.[15]

Another measure of the incumbency advantage is the frequency with

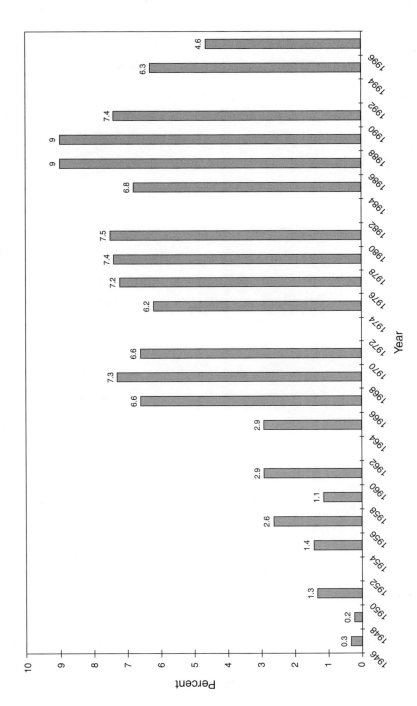

Figure 2.6. Incumbency advantage in House elections, 1946–1996.

NOTE: Incumbency advantage cannot be calculated for census years.

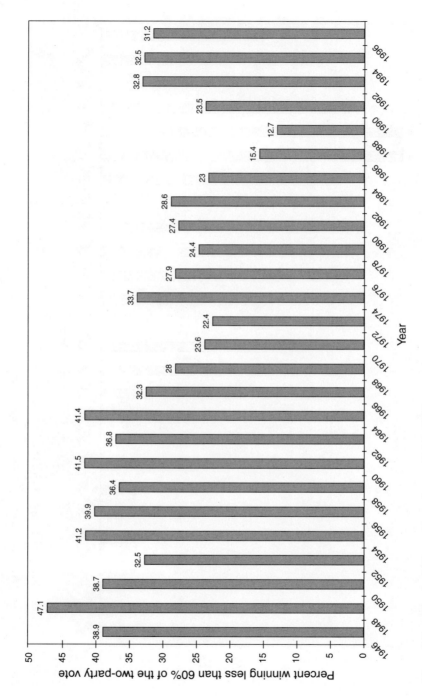

Figure 2.7. Marginal House incumbents, 1946–1996.

which incumbents pursuing reelection succeed. Incumbents have been less successful, on average, at winning reelection in the first three elections of the 1990s than in any decade since the 1940s. The average success rate for House incumbents so far in the 1990s is 91.1 percent; for the previous four decades, the rate ranged from a low of 93.9 percent (in the 1950s) to a high of 96.6 percent (in the 1980s). And finally, the proportion of marginal in-cumbents—those who received less than 60 percent of the two-party vote—has risen to its highest level since the early 1960s (see Figure 2.7).[16]

Incumbency status still gives representatives a head start at election time, but it is a shorter head start than at any time since the 1960s. The shrinking value of incumbency is a predictable consequence of voting patterns increas-ingly shaped by national partisan considerations. The earlier growth in the vote value of incumbency had been accompanied by the increasing hetero-geneity of vote swings from one election to the next across districts (Jacob-son 1990a); hence it is not surprising to find this trend reversed during the 1990s, with interelection vote swings becoming more uniform across House districts. The evidence is in Figure 2.8, which displays the standard devia-tion of the swing from 1946 through 1996 for all candidates and for incum-bents separately. The lower variance in the 1990s is another sign that the na-tional component of House elections has been growing in the 1990s. To be sure, incumbents still win with great frequency, but success rests to a greater degree than in the recent past on their party's underlying strength in the dis-trict. It is, of course, impossible to predict with confidence that this observed reduction in the electoral value of incumbency will continue through the rest of the decade, but its association with the other changes noted here sug-gests that it may well turn out to be more than a temporary dip.

Two additional developments deserve comment. As Figure 2.9 shows, the number of members voluntarily retiring from the House has been unusually high during the 1990s (the average for 1992 through 1996, 54.3, is higher than the average for any other three-year period since 1946). The growth in voluntary departures, combined with the higher-than-usual number of in-cumbent defeats, has produced abnormally high levels of turnover in the House. The average of 90 new members entering the House in the past three elections is higher than for any other three-year period since the 1940s. So much for the notion of an ossified Congress desperately in need of term limits for an infusion of new blood.

Finally, the number of House seats uncontested by one of the major par-ties has fallen dramatically in the 1990s, as the data in Figure 2.10 indicate. In 1996, only nineteen seats were conceded by one party to the other, the lowest number by far for the entire postwar period. Note also that in 1994

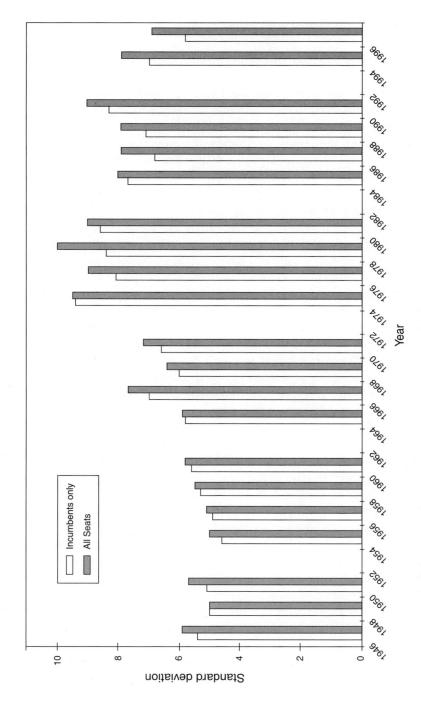

Figure 2.8. Standard deviation of mean district vote swing in House elections, 1946–1996.

NOTE: Because so many districts are re-drawn, the swing vote cannot be calculated for reapportionment years, which are thus omitted.

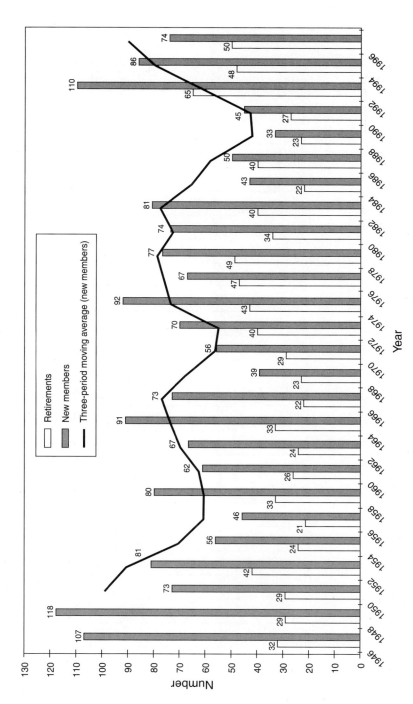

Figure 2.9. House retirements and newcomers, 1946–1996.

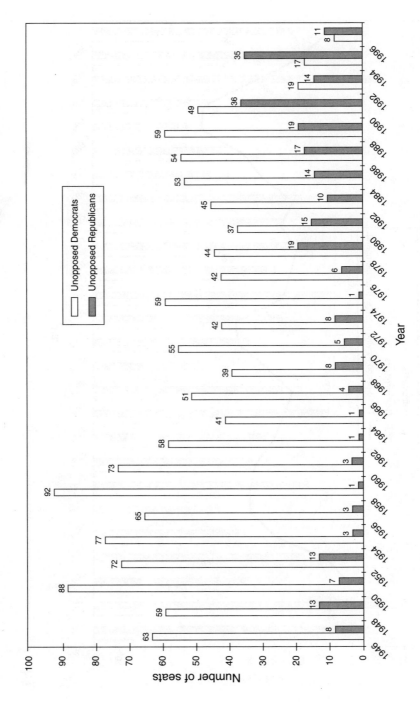

Figure 2.10. House seats without major party competition in general elections, 1946–1996.

and 1996, more Republicans than Democrats enjoyed a free ride in the general election for the first time. This change is a direct consequence of Republican advances in the South, where Republicans now benefit from the remnants of the region's one-party habits; ten of the eleven Republicans [unopposed in 1996 were from southern districts. Of course, Republicans gained some of their southern seats only because they finally began to field candidates against Democrats who earlier had waltzed in unopposed (Frymer 1996). The fall-off in uncontested seats probably has several sources, among them the shake-up brought about by redistricting after 1990, the ferment sparked by the House bank scandal and other events in 1992 (Jacobson 1993), and the increased nationalization of electoral politics in 1994 and 1996. The most important factor, however, is the growing financial and organizational strength of the national party committees, which now invest heavily in recruiting and sustaining House candidates and make it a matter of pride to field candidates in as many districts as possible.

Divided Government in the 1990s

House elections in the 1990s are more partisan, more nationally focused, and more issue oriented than they have been in decades. Incumbency is no longer as potent an electoral advantage as it was in the 1970s and 1980s; all politics is no longer local; district electorates are voting more consistently across offices. House members are more loyal to their parties and less attached to the institution; fewer envision lifetime careers in Congress. Coinciding with these mostly modest and incremental changes is one decisive historical departure: the Republicans' rise to a durable majority in the House (and, most likely, the Senate), with the party finally approaching the level of success in congressional elections that it has displayed for years in presidential elections.

Yet despite these changes, divided government—Democrats controlling one branch of the federal government, Republicans the other—persists. To be sure, divided government reemerged, transposed, after a two-year hiatus only because Bill Clinton was not on the ticket in 1994 (Jacobson 1996a), but in 1996 voters chose a Democratic president and a Republican Congress on the same ticket. And because the historical performance of the president's party at midterm elections offered Democrats little hope of regaining majorities in either house in 1998,[17] divided government is virtually guaranteed for the rest of the century. (The results of the midterm elections in 1998 were consistent with this observation.)

Does divided government in the 1990s have the same electoral basis it had in the 1970s and 1980s? In some important respects, yes. But there are major differences as well. Insofar as divided government reflects the public's own divided and self-contradictory preferences, nothing fundamental has changed. Most voters continue to desire a balanced budget, low tax rates, low inflation, a less intrusive government, greater economic efficiency, and a strong national defense. At the same time, they continue to dislike paying the necessary price: cuts in middle-class entitlements and other popular domestic spending programs, greater exposure to market forces, and greater environmental risk.

In the 1980s, voters expressed both sets of preferences at the polls by electing Republican presidents committed to low taxes, economic efficiency, and a strong national defense, and for congressional Democrats who promised to minimize the price they had to pay for these goods in forgone benefits and greater exposure to market or environmental harm (Jacobson 1990a). George Bush's failure to deliver on the economy or hold the line on taxes (supposedly Republican strong suits) put a Democrat in the White House in 1993. When Clinton's deficit reduction program included a large tax increase and his proposed restructuring of the health care system looked like big government run amok, Republican congressional candidates were able to use (among other things) their presidential themes of low taxes and smaller government to win control of Congress. In this transposed version of divided government, partisan roles remained the same, but institutional bases were exchanged. After 1994, it was the Republican Congress that sought lower spending, lower taxes, and a less intrusive government, and it was the Democratic president who championed the ordinary people targeted to pay the costs of the Republican "revolution."

Indeed, the chance to redefine himself as defender of popular domestic programs threatened by the Republican Congress saved Bill Clinton's presidency. When the House Republicans' plan to balance the budget by 2002 paired a $270 billion reduction in the future growth of Medicare funding with a $240 billion tax cut plan that promised the largest benefits to the wealthiest taxpayers, Clinton seized the opportunity to cast himself as the protector of middle-class benefits against cutbacks to finance tax breaks for the rich. Equally clumsy Republican attempts to roll back environmental regulations let him portray himself as defender of all things green as well. Republicans had mistakenly assumed that public support for their goals— smaller, cheaper government—also meant public support for the means— cutbacks in specific programs, protections, and regulations. Clinton leapt on the mistake, and his vow to protect "Medicare, Medicaid, education, and the environment" became the mantra of his victorious reelection campaign (Jacobson 1997a).

Despite Clinton's comeback, voters continued to endorse the Republican goal of a smaller, cheaper government, and they refused, albeit narrowly, to hand the Congress back to the tax-and-spend Democrats. In this sense, 1996 looks like the 1980s all over again, only with the branches of government switched. This outcome is of course entirely consistent with rational balancing (of parties, policies, or ideologies) explanations for divided government (Fiorina 1996), which at this level of analysis are observationally equivalent to the contradictory preferences explanation. The idea that some voters might want to offset a Democratic president with a Republican Congress, or vice versa, actually became grist for the 1996 campaigns. Despite the implied affront to Dole, Republican leaders did not hesitate to make the near certainty of Clinton's reelection an argument for voting Republican for Congress. On his side, Clinton campaigned for individual Democrats but was conspicuously reticent about asking voters to give him a Democratic Congress.

Still, it is by no means certain that government remains divided only because some voters wanted to keep the Congress Republican to restrain the president on the usual issues of taxes, spending, and big government (or, indeed, that he needed much restraining after the lessons of 1994). A more immediate consideration may well have been the administration's odor of scandal and widespread doubts about Clinton's personal character, which gave suspicious voters sufficient reason to want Republicans to remain in a position to keep an eye on him. Indeed, there is some evidence that revelations late in the campaign of foreign contributions to the Democratic National Committee moved many late-deciding voters into the Republican column, reducing Clinton's margin of victory and thereby killing the Democrats' chances of retaking the House.[18]

Moreover, Clinton won reelection not only by what he resisted, but also by what he conceded to the Republican Congress. While defending programs popular with the middle class, he signed a bill to end welfare entitlements that had been part of the social safety net since the New Deal, agreed to balance the budget by 2002, and conceded that "the era of big government is over." He also opposed gay marriages, supported prayer in school, and advocated the V-chip, school uniforms, and curfews for young people. Clinton sought and won reelection by mutating, effectively, into a moderate Republican. Congressional Republicans saved their House majority by beating a tactical retreat back toward the center as well: giving into Clinton on the budget, supporting modest health insurance reforms, even providing enough votes to raise the minimum wage, that bête noire of free-market purists. Certainly this outcome reads as a triumph of rational balancing—just what the median voter ordered. But it left the policy-based trade-offs remaining to be balanced in 1996 a far cry from those in the heady days of Ronald Reagan v. Tip O'Neill and Ted Kennedy.

Indeed, considering that the Democrats kept the White House only because Clinton moved so far toward the center that he practically became the median voter himself, and that the Republicans retained the House only by moderating their revolutionary fervor, deliberate balancing was not necessary to the outcome at all. Voters could have chosen divided government in 1996 on strictly spatial grounds, for it is more than likely that both Clinton and the House Republicans were closer than their respective opponents to the median voter on a common set of issues. From this perspective, the underlying basis of divided government after 1996 seems far more reminiscent of the Eisenhower era than of the Reagan-Bush years. Eisenhower won election as a "modern Republican" who was willing to concede that the New Deal was here to stay and was, as president, content merely to curb its excesses. His stance invited congressional Democrats to adopt a strategy of cooperation rather than confrontation, and they accepted. Clinton won reelection by conceding that "the era of big government is over" and moderating, but not resisting, the conservative thrust of Republican policies. Both Eisenhower and Clinton were far more popular than their opponents and ran well ahead of their party's congressional candidates in total votes, partly because both could claim credit for peace and prosperity. Yet in both cases, congressional and presidential voting was highly correlated at the district level (recall Figure 2.5), suggesting that the vote for both offices lined up on a common dimension.

Regardless of whether the pivotal voters deliberately balanced their vote for Clinton with one for a Republican congressional candidate or merely voted for the candidates closest to them on the issues, the public was pleased with the final equilibrium. A majority (53 percent) of respondents to a poll conducted for Pew Research immediately after the election said they were happy with Clinton's reelection, but an even larger majority (65 percent) said they were happy that the Republicans had retained control of Congress.[19]

Some of the factors that contributed to divided government in the Reagan and Bush years are clearly absent in the 1990s. Unlike the Democrats in their heyday (Jacobson 1990a), Republicans did not hold on to Congress in 1996 by fielding candidates whose superior skills at retail politics had enabled them to carve out the kind of personal political franchises that are immune to contrary national tides. Although many vulnerable Republican incumbents distanced themselves from Newt Gingrich, declaring independence from party and pledging allegiance to local interests, 1996 was not a year in which House elections were framed in terms of individual accomplishments and district services. Republicans had, after all, shown remarkable unity during the first crucial year of the 104th Congress, explicitly rejecting the particularistic pork barrel politics of the past (if not always disdaining pork when it was available). If nothing else, the independent campaigns mounted by the AFL-CIO and other groups made sure that the performance of the 104th Congress was front and center.

The reversal of institutional roles undercuts another component of the explanation for divided government during the Reagan-Bush years. I had argued that voters, to borrow Fiorina's concise summary of the point, "matched party strengths with institutional responsibilities," viewing Congress as better suited to the distributive politics relished by Democrats, and regarding the president as having primary responsibility for the macro economy and the nation's defense (Fiorina 1996: 65). Plainly such institutional expectations, if they have any force at all, turn out to be of decidedly secondary importance. Of course, voters had no opportunity to put a Republican back in the White House in 1994; those who wanted government to pursue the good things commonly associated with Republicans had no option but to elect Republicans to the House and Senate.

The reversal of institutional roles leaves congressional Republicans in something of a bind. Insofar as they stick to their goals of balancing the budget, reducing taxes, and dismantling the regulatory state, they threaten popular local programs, Medicare recipients, college students, school children, and environmental safeguards. Placing an ideologically driven concept of the national interest above the particular needs and concerns of constituents is inherently risky. The key question Republicans faced in 1996 was, in the words of John Boehner, an Ohio Republican, "how far can we push the revolution and bring back a majority of our members?" [20] It is a question House Republicans will continue to face as long as they pursue their traditional "presidential" agenda. Insofar as they back off (as many vulnerable Republicans did in 1996), they undermine what makes their party distinctive, a problem compounded by a centrist Democrat in the White House already bent on blurring the differences between the parties.

If the idea that voters match institutional roles to partisan strengths has any lingering validity, the kind of divided government we now have is inherently less stable than its predecessor. It is also less stable because neither congressional Republicans nor presidential Democrats have as firm an electoral grip on their respective institutions as had their counterparts prior to the 1990s. Republican majorities in the House after 1994 and 1996 were smaller than any of those won by the Democrats between 1954 and 1992. And despite two victories in the 1990s, Democrats have not won more than 50 percent of the total presidential vote since Jimmy Carter's 50.1 percent in 1976. It is easy to imagine the Democrats winning the House—indeed, they came very close in 1996 even with relatively weak challengers and with only a modest boost from national forces (Jacobson 1997a). It is even easier to imagine a Republican winning the White House (no doubt many ambitious Republican politicians are imagining victory right now).

Yet the Republicans' ascendancy to majority status in Congress could help the Democrats hold on to the presidency. The strong base of support Republicans now enjoy in the South will make it harder for Democrats to retake Congress, but a Republican party that speaks with a heavy southern accent, ideologically as well as literally, may run into trouble in presidential elections. The social and economic conservatism espoused by congressional leaders such as Trent Lott (Miss., Senate majority leader), Dick Armey (Tex., House majority leader), Tom DeLay (Tex., House majority whip), and Jesse Helms (N.C., chair of Senate Foreign Relations) is of limited appeal to moderates, especially among educated and single women. Republicans may find themselves in the same plight the Democrats suffered in the 1970s and 1980s, when control of the party's image and nominating machinery by its more fervent ideologues continually handicapped its presidential candidates. The reversal of partisan fortunes in the 1990s may yet apply to the presidency as well as the Congress; the present configuration of national electoral politics may turn out to have more staying power than we expect.

Chapter 3

Partisan Changes in the Southern Congressional Delegation and the Consequences

CHARLES S. BULLOCK III

When it came to winning congressional seats, the Republican party in the South spent frustrating years, much like the Chicago Cubs, always looking to next year as the time for ultimate success. The Cubs continue to play out the schedule each September, but for Republicans covetously eyeing southern congressional seats, "next year" arrived in the mid-1990s.

Key to Republican success in the South has been attracting sufficient white support since the black vote has been reliably Democratic. In their study of southern voting in presidential elections, Black and Black (1992) divide the white electorate into core Republicans, core Democrats, and a swing group. The core Republican group augmented with swing whites regularly enables the GOP to carry the bulk of the region's electoral college vote. The 1996 elections saw the GOP consolidate its hold on southern Senate and House seats by securing the overwhelming white support that has allowed it to dominate the region's presidential elections for a generation. Republicans have finally overcome the message of successful Democrats who urged white southerners to distinguish between the national Democratic party, as manifest in the presidential contest, and state or local (read as more conservative) Democratic nominees. So long as sufficient numbers of white voters embraced that distinction, Democrats remained the majority party in congressional elections and lower offices even as they lost presidential contests by landslide proportions (Brownstein 1986; Hadley 1985). If the GOP

retains the share of the white electorate that voted for Republican congressional candidates in 1996, the party will continue to dominate the region's
congressional delegation.

Expansion of white support for GOP congressional candidates in the
South has implications both for the region and nationally. The broader base
of support has allowed the GOP to win larger shares of the seats in a greater
range of districts in the region. One concern has been whether the rising tide
of Republican House successes threatens some of the newly reconfigured,
whiter districts currently held by African Americans.

Gains made by Republicans in the South have been critical to achieving what many Democrats thought would never come to pass: a Republican
congressional majority. The solid southern foundation on which Democratic congressional majorities rested are gone with the wind. Today's Republican congressional majorities place the South at center stage, crucial
both numerically and as a source of leadership.[1] If Republicans can maintain
the share of the southern congressional seats they now hold, Democrats will
have to perform much better in the remainder of the country if they are to
reemerge as the majority party in the Senate. This paper explores the bases
for the Republican gains in the South and the consequences for partisan
control of Congress.

Greater Consistency in the White Electorate

Key to GOP success in the South has been the attainment of white support
for down ticket nominees comparable to the vote shares won by presidential candidates. In 1964, in the South as in the rest of the nation, the GOP
ceased to compete seriously for African-American votes. The South's limited black electorate split between John Kennedy and Richard Nixon in
1960 (Bartley and Graham 1975; Sundquist 1983), but in 1964 growing
numbers of enfranchised African Americans went massively for President
Lyndon B. Johnson, producer of that year's Civil Rights Act, over the opposition of the Republican standard bearer, Barry Goldwater. That same
election also witnessed the first congressional success of the GOP in the
Deep South as it won seven seats.[2] The black vote has remained overwhelmingly Democratic; thus, GOP congressional victories require, at a minimum,
majority support from the white electorate. In areas having sizable concentrations of African Americans, Republicans must do exceptionally well
among white voters. The consistency with which Mississippi, the state with
the highest concentration of African Americans, has voted for GOP presi-

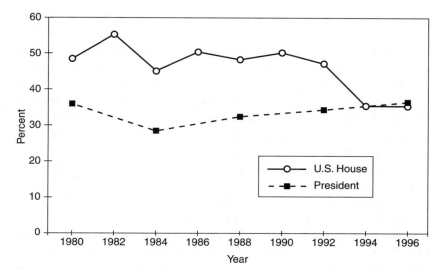

Figure 3.1. Southern white Democratic vote for president and House, 1980–1996.

SOURCE: Data provided by David Bositis.

dential and Senate nominees shows that extraordinary white majorities are not impossible.

Across the South, Republicans have regularly achieved the requisite levels of white support for their presidential nominees. Since 1964, the Democratic presidential nominee has won the bulk of the southern electoral vote only once, and that was in 1976, when the region united behind Jimmy Carter to overcome its disqualification from the presidency stemming from an unreconstructed approach to race relations. Even Carter's win rested on solid black support augmented by a white minority. Figure 3.1 shows that since 1980, Democratic presidential candidates have never managed even 40 percent of the white vote in the South.

Neither Goldwater's nor Nixon's southern strategies (Aistrup 1996) could dislodge enough white support for Republicans to dominate the region's congressional elections. Racial themes that breathed life into the moribund shell of the GOP in the Deep South (Carmines and Stimson 1989) set off a secular top-down or trickle-down realignment (Bullock 1988; Aistrup 1996). For years, Democrats held Republicans at bay and secured congressional majorities by convincing sufficient numbers of whites to treat voting Republican for president as an exception rather than the first item of a straight-ticket decision (on split-level realignment, see Hadley 1985). The key to Democratic success required the party to maintain a tenuous balance that produced a biracial coalition sufficient to win most statewide contests and the vast bulk of congressional and state legislative seats.

After African-American votes became numerous following enactment of the 1965 Voting Rights Act (VRA), a brief period followed during which southern Democrats and Republicans fought to see which could be the more conservative on racial issues. By about 1970, however, southern Democrats began to see the futility of trying to pass the GOP on the right, adopted the strategy northern Democrats had followed since the New Deal, and incorporated black voters into their coalition. While the Herman Talmadges, Orville Faubuses, and George Wallaces had little appeal to black voters, new leaders of the 1970s such as Georgia's Jimmy Carter, South Carolina's John West, and Florida's Reubin Askew abandoned racial appeals and embraced policies that gave both symbolic and substantive rewards to African Americans (cf. Black 1976). The new Democratic leaders and their successors retained power by convincing enough white voters that in-state Democrats were ideologically distinct from Democratic candidates for the White House. Despite erosion, Democrats retained majorities among southern officialdom until the 1990s.

Figure 3.1 shows that from 1980 through 1992, Democratic congressional candidates got approximately half the white vote, more than enough when bolstered by strong black support to remain dominant in the region's congressional contests. From Figure 3.1 we also get an indication of the share of whites who voted Republican for president but retained Democratic loyalties in congressional voting. From 1980 to 1992, the difference in support for Republican presidential and congressional candidates fluctuated between 13 and 17 percentage points. The relatively greater popularity of Democratic congressional candidates evaporated in the mid-1990s, with their vote share among whites dropping by a dozen points between 1992 and 1994. In the last two elections, southern Democratic House candidates have done no better than Democratic presidential candidates.

By 1996, the trickle-down pattern of whites shifting allegiances to GOP House candidates had shown up in Senate voting. No Democratic senatorial candidate managed a majority of the white vote. Seven of ten Democratic nominees polled between 31 and 37 percent of the white vote in exit polls, according to Table 3.1, while in Mississippi the Democrats did much worse. Even the two Democrats who managed more than 40 percent of the white vote lost.

Table 3.1

Racial Voting Patterns in 1996 Southern Senate Elections

State	Candidate	Party	Percent African American	Percent White
Alabama	Bedford	D	84	34
	Sessions	R	12	65
Arkansas	Bryant	D	—	43
	Hutchinson	R	—	56
Georgia	Cleland	D	83	37
	Millner	R	12	59
Louisiana	Landrieu	D	91	32
	Jenkins	R	9	68
Mississippi	Hunt	D	67	13
	Cochran	R	31	86
North Carolina	Gantt	D	89	36
	Helms	R	10	63
South Carolina	Close	D	78	32
	Thurmond	R	20	65
Tennessee	Gordon	D	77	31
	Thompson	R	21	68
Texas	Morales	D	79	31
	Gramm	R	19	68
Virginia	Warner, M.	D	77	42
	Warner, J.	R	19	58

SOURCE: Exit polls reported on *All Politics*, http://CNN.com/ELECTION/

Unless otherwise indicated, all tables in Chapter 3 ar\e based on data compiled by the author.

Figure 3.1 and Table 3.1 display remarkable consistency among white southerners in voting for federal offices in 1996. For all three offices, Democrats managed only about one-third of the white vote—a level of success sufficient for victory only when black participation is high, as in Louisiana, or when a third-party candidate siphons off white votes, as in Georgia's Senate race. After more than a generation, white voter realignment has seeped down at least to U.S. House contests and in some states—most likely Florida—the realignment may have worked its way down to state legislative elections.[3]

Race and Partisan Control

With Republicans attracting the bulk of the white vote, they should do particularly well in heavily white congressional districts. Republicans who could take more than 55 percent of the white vote would be unbeatable in heavily white districts. This awareness undergirded the formation of the Republican-black Democratic coalition present during redistricting in some states in the 1980s and even more active in the early 1990s (Holmes 1982; Bullock 1983, 1995). Republican expectations of doing well in heavily white districts proved accurate in the 103d Congress, for the party captured 62 percent of the districts in which the African Americans constituted less than 10 percent of the population (similar results are achieved in the modeling efforts of Cameron et al. 1996). Republicans from these heavily white districts accounted for almost two-thirds of the southern members of that party in Congress. Republicans won about 30 percent of the seats in districts between 10 and 29 percent black but were shut out of districts more than 30 percent black, suggesting a ceiling on GOP prospects and a safe haven for Democrats.

Republicans had sixteen more southern House seats in the 104th than the 103d Congress, but districts with over a 30 percent black population remained Democratic. Twelve of the seats gained by Republicans came in districts 10 to 29 percent black. Table 3.2 shows that the GOP held 70 percent of the seats in districts at least 90 percent white, broke even in districts 10 to 19.9 percent black, and won three-fifths of the seats in districts in the 20 to 29.9 percent black range, a pattern unlike the negative relationship between black percent and likelihood of GOP seats observed by Cameron et al. (1996: 805).

In the 105th Congress, Republicans have broken the 30 percent black threshold. Following redistricting and party switching Republicans had eight seats in districts more than 30 percent black in the 105th Congress. Although their numbers remained concentrated in the whitest districts, Republican seats spread across a greater range in terms of racial composition than at any time since the 102d Congress. The Republican share of seats in the whitest districts rose above 75 percent but Republicans also filled 64 percent of seats for districts that were 30 to 39 percent black. Democrats control a majority of the seats only in districts more than 40 percent black.

Republican gains reported in Table 3.3 in districts at least 30 percent African American are of three types. The bulk of these districts have Republican incumbents whose districts became blacker as a result of redistricting. Georgia's First, Eighth, and Tenth Districts and the Fourth and Sixth of

Table 3.2

District Racial Composition and Party Control, 104th Congress

Percent black	Percent Republican	Percent Democrat	N
0–9.9	70.0	30.0	50
10–19.9	48.3	51.7	29
20–29.9	60.0	40.0	25
30–39.9	0	100	3
40–49.9	0	100	17

Louisiana received additional black voters during reconfigurations necessitated by court decisions finding the existing districts unconstitutional. For example, when 50,000 Savannah African Americans who had been in Cynthia McKinney's "Sherman District" (so-called because it, like the Union general, went from Atlanta to the sea) were reunited with the rest of Chatham County, Jack Kingston's (R) First District became 31 percent black. Charlie Norwood (R) saw the black percentage in his Tenth District double to 38 percent as he got African Americans from Augusta and several Black Belt counties that had also been in McKinney's Eleventh District.

A second type of district involved new legislators. In Mississippi's Third District, Charles Pickering (R) took 61 percent of the vote to succeed former Veterans' Affairs Committee chair Sonny Montgomery (D), who retired after 30 years in the House. The other district more than 30 percent black with a freshman Republican, Louisiana's Fifth, was created without an incumbent. Republican gains in open seats more than 30 percent black should be the most troubling straw in the wind for Democrats. One implication is that without a Democratic incumbent even districts with substantial black minorities are winnable by Republicans. It may take an especially talented Democrat or a maladroit Republican for Democrats to retain seats in southern white districts through an incumbent retirement transition.

The third type of district with Republican representation underwent partisan transformation following the incumbent's conversion. Mike Parker of Mississippi's Fourth District was one of five southern House members to switch parties in the 104th Congress. Parker's district is the most heavily black district represented by a Republican with its population as of the 1990 census being 41 percent African American.

Table 3.3

District Racial Composition and Party Control, 105th Congress

Percent black	Percent Republican	Percent Democrat	N
0–9.9	73.6	23.4	47
10–19.9	53.6	46.4	28
20–29.9	50.0	50.0	24
30–39.9	63.6	36.4	11
40–49.9	25.0	75.0	4
More than 50	0	100	11

The greater range in racial composition marks a return to the dispersion witnessed during the 1980s. For example, as Table 3.4 shows, in the 102d Congress, 8 of 39 Republicans represented districts at least 30 percent black. Seven of these districts continue to have Republican legislators, with several having the same incumbent in 1997 as six years earlier.[4] The other district, Louisiana's Eighth, ceased to exist when reapportionment reduced the state's delegation to seven members. The elimination of Republican representatives from districts at least 30 percent black in the 103d and 104th Congresses stemmed not from their inability to win but from the bleaching of their districts to create nearby majority-minority districts. Alabama's First and Second Districts gave up black residents to the Seventh; South Carolina's First and Second lost black residents to fashion the Sixth; Virginia's First and Third and two other districts ceded black population to create the 64 percent black district that elected Robert Scott (D) (Weber 1996). The Fourth District, drawn in Louisiana in 1992 to be 67 percent black, took African Americans from the Fifth, Sixth, and Eighth Districts.

Race-based districting of the early 1990s artificially reduced black concentrations in some GOP-held districts. Once the courts invalidated racial gerrymandering and the districts returned to shapes and racial compositions approximating what existed in the 1980s, they retained their GOP representatives.[5] Comparison of figures in Tables 3.3 and 3.4 reveal the breadth of recent GOP successes. In the whitest districts, the Republican share of the seats increased by 28 percentage points from roughly half to three-fourths. Gains of similar magnitude have come in districts 20 to 39.9 percent black. GOP advances have been least frequent in districts 10 to 19.9 percent black,

Table 3.4

District Racial Composition and Party Control, 102nd Congress

Percent black	Percent Republican	Percent Democrat	N
0–9.9	48.4	51.6	31
10–19.9	34.5	65.5	29
20–29.9	21.4	78.6	28
30–39.9	36.4	63.6	22
40–49.9	0	100	2
More than 50	0	100	4

where a 19 point increase has occurred. The level of successes in districts 30 to 39.9 percent black is not predicted by research finding a negative relationship between black concentrations and Republican victories (Cameron et al. 1996). Moreover the incidence of Republicans in these districts is greater than Cameron and his colleagues estimated for such concentrations of blacks in other regions.

Republican wins in House districts more than 30 percent black are further evidence that voting patterns long evident in presidential elections now appear down ticket. Republicans have consistently carried Mississippi and South Carolina (two of the three states at least 30 percent black) in presidential elections and have often won contests for senator, governor, and, in South Carolina, statewide executive offices. In states roughly one-third black, Democrats have had their greatest success in Louisiana, which voted for Bill Clinton in 1992 and 1996 but has yet to elect a Republican senator and has chosen a Republican gubernatorial candidate only twice. Louisiana's unique open primary system has created additional obstacles to GOP advancement, just as its creator, former Democratic governor Edwin Edwards, had hoped.

GOP successes in states and congressional districts that have sizable African-American electorates require commanding majorities among white voters. Growing numbers of GOP wins in districts with 20 to 40 percent black voters conform to findings that whites are more likely to vote Republican as the black percentage in the population increases (Black and Black 1973; Aistrup 1996). Giles and Buckner (1995) have explained this phenomenon in terms of a white threat hypothesis. As Key (1949) observed, whites living in the most heavily black areas most adamantly opposed black political or economic gains, fearing that black power would come at the expense of white influence.

Despite GOP gains in congressional districts more than 20 percent black, Republicans' greatest success has come in the whitest districts. Based on gains during the 1990s, heavily white southern districts held by Democrats would seem to be likely prospects for future GOP advances. The potential for additional GOP gains in districts with the fewest African Americans are limited by the paucity of such districts that are heavily white. Five of the eleven Democratic districts in the 105th Congress—all in Texas and heavily Hispanic—have an electorate comprised of fewer than 10 percent black voters. Currently, Republicans fill only one predominantly Hispanic Texas district, though their fortunes there were lifted by corruption charges surrounding the Democratic incumbent, Albert Bustamante.[6]

If southern whites continue to bring their congressional voting into line with their presidential preferences, districts that voted for Robert Dole while sending Democrats to Congress may be Republicans' best prospects. Of fourteen southern districts fitting this profile (R. Cook 1997), three are less than 10 percent black while another five are between 10 and 19.9 percent black. Four districts are from 20 to 29.9 percent black, whereas South Carolina's Sixth and Virginia's Fifth are about one-third African American. Four of these split-ticket districts sent freshman Democrats to Congress in 1996 (North Carolina's Second and Seventh, Texas's First, and Virginia's Fifth) and therefore may not be prime GOP targets. The other ten will likely become the scenes of vigorous partisan competition when the incumbents retire, if not before.

GOP Congressional Success in the South

In less than two generations, Democrats, who had dominated southern congressional delegations since the end of Reconstruction, have become the region's minority party. Starting from ground zero in the 1950s in most states, GOP gains came slowly in the 1960s and 1970s. By the 1980s, Republicans could, on occasion, capture 40 percent of the region's senatorial and gubernatorial seats, exceed one-third of the House seats, and flirt with one-fourth to one-fifth of the state legislative slots (Bullock 1988). Results through the 1980s showed the South's distribution of public offices to be increasingly like that of the rest of the nation, although always less Republican than in the non-South (Bullock 1988).

GOP disappointments in southern legislative elections contrasted sharply with the party's regional success in presidential elections. Beginning in 1964 Republican presidential nominees fared better in the South than in the rest of the nation, except in 1976. The inability to convert enthusiastic support for presidential candidates into victories in most southern congressional districts frustrated southern Republicans. Even after sweeping all the southern electoral votes in 1972, 1984, and 1988, and winning ten of eleven states in 1980, Republicans never acquired even 40 percent of the southern House seats. Four upsets in 1980 enabled Republicans to secure more than 40 percent of southern Senate seats for three congresses, but otherwise the GOP never attained even one-third of the region's seats in the upper chamber. Enough southern voters continued true to their traditional Democratic loyalties below the presidential level to thwart what Republicans expected to be a sweeping realignment in the region.

Although Republicans failed to secure majorities of southern congressional seats, they had made impressive gains in light of their traditional baseline, as shown in Figure 3.2. Not until 1966 did Republicans secure as many as 10 percent of the Senate seats in the eleven states that joined the Confederacy. Following the 1970 election, the GOP held the bulk of the nonsouthern Senate seats (up from 38 percent six years earlier) and exceeded 20 percent for the first time in the South. With Ronald Reagan's first election to the White House in 1980, the GOP share of southern Senate seats (45 percent) came close to the 55 percent share elsewhere. After successes in Dixie that approximated the GOP performance in the rest of the county during Reagan's first six years, southern Republicans' 1980 gains vanished in 1986. Figure 3.2 shows that this southern deficit was not overcome for six years.

Once they supplanted the dominant Democrats, Republicans came to fill a larger share of southern congressional seats than of nonsouthern seats. In 1992, the GOP share of southern Senate seats (45 percent) outpaced the Republican proportion in the remainder of the nation (42 percent). Figure 3.2 shows the southern advantage increasing in each of the next two elections so that after the 1996 election, Republicans held 68 percent of southern Senate seats, seventeen points better than in the North. From 1990 to 1996, the relative position of the two parties in the South flipped as Democrats slipped from fifteen of the region's twenty-two seats to only seven.

Following the 1996 elections, Republicans held both U.S. Senate seats in Alabama, Mississippi, North Carolina, Tennessee, and Texas, while only in Louisiana did Democrats retain both seats—and there Mary Landrieu's mar-

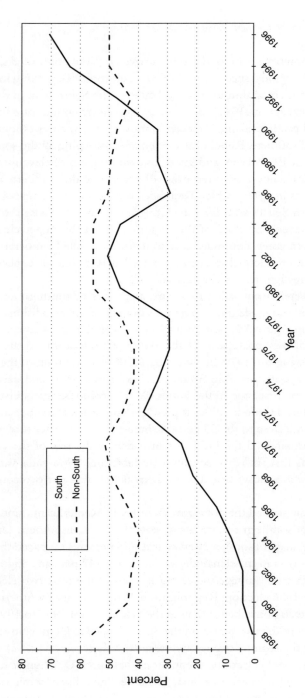

Figure 3.2. Percent Republicans in Senate, South and non–South, 1958–1996.

gin of victory was less than six thousand votes. The parties split the seats in Arkansas (where Clinton's coattails could not prevent the first popularly elected GOP senator), Florida, Georgia, South Carolina, and Virginia.

Regional patterns in the House show similarities to the Senate trends. Republicans, who for years maintained a two-seat enclave in the Tennessee Smokies, began colonizing Rim South urban areas during Dwight Eisenhower's presidency.[7] Even in 1960, Republicans carried most of the Rim South for Richard Nixon but constituted less than one-tenth of the South's House delegation at a time that their party held most of the seats in other parts of the country. From 1962 through 1976, the regional disparity narrowed, although thereafter the GOP share of House seats in the South continued to trail the rest of the country by about ten points, as reported in Figure 3.3. While the GOP trajectory in the South has been upward during the 1990s, even in taking control of the House, Newt Gingrich's fellow southerners lagged behind their northern cousins. Only after four Democrats followed Nathan Deal's (Ga.) lead and shifted partisan allegiance did Republicans secure a larger share of the southern House seats (55 percent) than the nonsouthern (54 percent). In the 105th Congress, Republican House control rests almost entirely on the advantage in the South, where the party filled 57 percent of the seats, while in the remainder of the nation the GOP has a one-seat majority. (The 1998 election results reaffirmed the conclusion that the Republicans would not hold the House without the South.)

While Democratic strength has slipped throughout the region, the party suffered more in the Deep South than in the Rim South. Across the Deep South, Democrats clung to eleven of thirty-five seats (31 percent), of which only four were held by whites—one each in Alabama, Louisiana, Mississippi, and South Carolina. In Georgia, all three Democrats were African Americans, while the eight white legislators were Republicans. Of the four whites, only Louisiana's Chris John, elected in 1996, had less than three terms of seniority. The Deep South, which produced House Democratic giants like Carl Vinson (Ga., chair of Armed Services), Jamie Whitten (Miss., chair of Appropriations), Hale Boggs (La., majority leader), Joe Waggoner (La., leader of the Conservative Coalition), and Bill Colmer (Miss., chair of Rules), finds white Democrats closer to extinction than most animals on the endangered species list. It will be a test to see whether Democrats can hold these four seats when the incumbents retire or whether they will fall prey to Republicans as happened with four of five Deep South open seats in 1996.[8] All but the Louisiana district favored Bob Dole over Bill Clinton.

In House and presidential elections, voters from the Deep South have

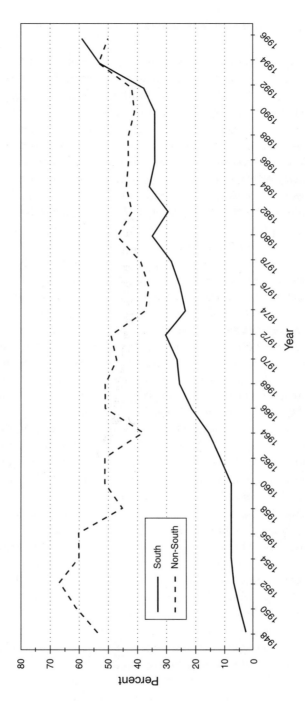

Figure 3.3. Percent Republicans in House, South and non-South, 1948–1996.

become the Republicans' strongest supporters. The Deep South gives the GOP a fourteen-seat edge in the House and, with only Louisiana support-ing the Clinton-Gore reelection bid, the GOP secured 80 percent of the subregion's electoral votes. In comparison, Republicans have a three-seat ad-vantage in the Peripheral South, which allowed Dole to carry 58 percent of that subregions' electoral votes. The emergence of a Deep South more Re-publican than the Rim South marks a significant change in the region's par-tisan proclivities. Initial GOP gains in presidential and down ticket elections came earlier in the Rim than the Deep South (Sundquist 1983: 370–73). The early GOP advances in the Rim South have now been overtaken by victories in the Deep South.

Consequences of the GOP'S Southern Gains for Partisan Control of Congress

Richard Cohen (1994: 910) has warned that "Losing the 'Solid South' to Republicans could be the jolt that finally loosens the Democrats' grip on a chamber that they have controlled for four decades." As Figures 3.2 and 3.3 show, during the years that Republicans languished as a minority in Con-gress, they rarely fell below a 40 percent share of the seats outside the South. In all but two elections from 1948 to 1970, Republicans won most non-southern House seats. Had their performance in the South matched that in other parts of the county, the GOP would not have been exiled from power in the House for 40 years. A larger southern base would also have more fre-quently made Republicans the majority of the upper chamber. While con-tinued Republican success in the South, currently at historic highs, cannot be assumed, neither is it likely that Democrats will reestablish dominance in the region in the near future. The next sections use the past to suggest what Congress might look like if the GOP can solidify its position in Dixie.

SENATE

To provide a retrospective assessment of the impact of Republican gains in the South, we begin by reviewing the partisan makeup of the Senate since just before the first modern southern Republican won a seat. The third col-umn of Table 3.5 shows the actual number of Democrats in each Congress beginning with the 86th, the last Congress before John Tower (Tex.) be-came the South's first popularly elected Republican. In the fourth column are the number of southern Democrats, whereas the fifth column reports the numbers of northern Democrats. In column six is the number of Democrats

Table 3.5

Numbers of Senate Democrats if Southern Democrats
Were at 1996 or 1994 Levels

Year	Congress	Democrats	Southern Democrats	Northern Democrats	ND+ SD 1996	ND+ SD 1994
1958	86	64	22	42	49	51
1960	87	64	21	43	50	52
1962	88	67	21	46	53	55
1964	89	68	20	48	55	57
1966	90	64	19	45	52	54
1968	91	58	18	40	47	49
1970	92	55	17	38	45	47
1972	93	57	15	42	49	51
1974	94	61	16	45	52	54
1976	95	62	17	45	52	54
1978	96	59	16	43	50	52
1980	97	47	12	35	42	44
1982	98	46	11	35	42	44
1984	99	47	12	35	42	44
1986	100	55	16	39	46	48
1988	101	55	15	40	47	49
1990	102	56	15	41	48	50
1992	103	57	12	45	52	54
1994	104	47	9	38	45	47
1996	105	45	7	38	45	47

(seven) who would have served *if the southern contingent had been at the level for the 105th Congress.*

Figures in this column show that had the realignment at the senatorial level occurred earlier, say coincident with Ronald Reagan's defeat of Jimmy Carter, Democrats would have controlled the Senate only once since 1980. Republicans would have had 58 senators during the first six years of the Reagan presidency, which would have given them the largest majority enjoyed by either party since the Eisenhower era if each election had produced seven southern Democrats and other area's Democratic numbers remained unchanged. The one recent Democratic majority would have come in President Clinton's first biennium—albeit a smaller majority than the one that actually existed—which might have given the president even greater problems than he encountered.

Faced with only seven southern Democrats in the Senate, Richard Nixon would not have had to try to create an ideological majority; he would have had 51 to 55 Republicans with whom to work throughout his tenure. Presidents Kennedy, Johnson, and Carter would have operated with the Senate in the hands of their fellow partisans; however, they would not have coasted along with the cushion provided by majorities of 60 or more. Narrower majorities might have curtailed the scope of the reforms Democratic presidents introduced. Rather than President Johnson's Great Society there might have been the Modestly Improved Society or the Somewhat Enhanced Society. Democrats in 1979 would have needed the tie-breaking vote of Vice President Walter Mondale to organize the Senate. Column seven reports the number of Democrats in Congress if the southern Democratic contingent had been at the level of the 104th Congress, in which they held nine seats. Adding two more southern Democrats, of course, would have shrunk GOP majorities or enhanced Democratic ones. Democrats would have been a majority in the 93d Congress and Republicans would have had to rely on Vice President Dan Quayle's vote to organize the 102d Congress.

The important point to take from Table 3.5 is the infrequency in the last two decades of Democratic majorities *if* Republican strength had been at the levels attained in the two most recent elections. If Republicans maintain their mid-1990s successes in the South, Democrats will have to do better in the rest of the nation than they have done in most recent elections. If the southern wing provides Democrats with only seven senators, Democrats in the remainder of the country will need to achieve levels that they have reached only six times in the last 40 years in order to organize the Senate. Only in the post-Kennedy reaction did the North provide enough Democrats to give the party a comfortable majority when augmented with seven southerners.

HOUSE

Table 3.6 presents data similar to that in Table 3.5 but focuses on the House. Given the heritage of at least two southern Republicans in the House, Table 3.6 does not go back to the election of the first southerner but begins with the national Democratic recovery in 1948. The picture of what might have been in the House is much less frightening for Democrats than the hypothetical figures in Table 3.5. Even if southern Democrats had held the same share of seats in the past as they do today (43.2 percent), the Democratic

Table 3.6
Numbers of House Democrats if Southern Democrats
Were at 1996 Levels

Year	Congress	Democrats	Southern Democrats	Northern Democrats	ND+ SD 1996
1948	81	263	103	160	205
1950	82	234	103	131	176
1952	83	213	100	113	159
1954	84	232	99	133	179
1956	85	234	99	135	181
1958	86	283	99	184	230
1960	87	263	99	164	210
1962	88	258	95	163	209
1964	89	295	90	205	251
1966	90	248	85	163	209
1968	91	243	80	163	209
1970	92	255	79	176	222
1972	93	243	75	168	215
1974	94	291	82	209	256
1976	95	292	81	211	258
1978	96	277	77	200	247
1980	97	243	69	174	221
1982	98	269	82	187	237
1984	99	253	73	180	230
1986	100	258	77	181	231
1988	101	260	77	183	233
1990	102	267	77	190	240
1992	103	258	77	181	235
1994	104	204	61	143	197
1996	105	207	54	153	207

party would have chosen the speaker in every Congress from the 94th through the 103d if nonsouthern partisan divisions remained at the size that actually existed. Had the GOP capitalized on southern conservatism earlier, additional Republican House control would have come during the first half of the period covered in Table 3.6. If 43.2 percent of the southern legislators had been Democrats, Republicans would have been the House majority in all but three Congresses from the 81st through the 93d.

If Democrats regain the strength they had outside the South during the 1980s and suffer few additional losses in the South, then the GOP will be relegated to minority status once again. Under the post-1980 apportionment, Democrats averaged 184 of the 319 northern seats. The 1990 census shifted a net of nine seats to the South, and with Democrats averaging 57.7 percent of the northern seats, that would be approximately five Democratic and four Republican seats reassigned to the South. Subtracting five from 184 would leave an average Democratic strength of 179 seats retained by the North in the 1990s. If Democrats can reach that number, then they need only 39 southern seats for a majority. If Republicans keep 71 southern seats, as they hold now, northern Democrats will need a minimum of 164 seats, a threshold that Table 3.6 shows they fell below only three times between 1958 and 1992. In each of the three times northern Democrats failed to achieve 164 during those 18 elections (1962, 1966, and 1968), they came up one seat short.[9] From 1974 until the Gingrich-led revolution, northern Democrats never fell below 174. Unlike in the Senate, Democrats' exile from the speakership is due to losses in both the South and North.

Redisticting and Black Members of Congress

GOP House gains during the 1990s notwithstanding, majority black districts have remained consistently Democratic. In 1992, majority black southern congressional districts increased from four to seventeen. A series of court decisions has invalidated majority-black districts drawn predominantly on the basis of race in Florida, Georgia, Louisiana, North Carolina, Texas, and Virginia.[10] The challenged districts frequently split counties and assumed bizarre shapes as they struggled to link concentrations of African Americans while avoiding intervening whites. Redrawing majority-black districts to give greater weight to traditional districting considerations such as compactness and adherence to political boundaries invariably produces whiter districts. Is redrawing likely to endanger the African-American incumbents and make these districts susceptible to GOP challengers? Table 3.3 suggests that lowering black concentrations might create opportunities for Republicans in these districts.

African-American incumbents who sought reelection in redrawn districts, much like Republicans whose districts were reconfigured prior to the 1996 elections, survived.[11] These wins in two Georgia and Texas districts and one in Florida were not "gimmes" since each victory came over a white

Table 3.7

Racial Voting Patterns in 1996 Georgia Congressional Elections

			WHITES		BLACKS	
	Race	Party	Regression	Homo-geneous Precinct	Regression	Homo-geneous Precinct
District 2						
Bishop	B	D	36.2	36.5	>100	98.2
Ealum	W	R	63.8	63.5	<0	1.8
District 4						
McKinney	B	D	29.1	29.7	>100	94.9
Mitnick	W	R	70.9	70.3	<0	5.1
District 8						
Wiggins	W	D	33.8	34.7	97.3	91.3
Chambless	W	R	66.2	65.3	2.7	8.7
District 10						
Bell	W	D	30.1	30.4	>100	95.2
Norwood	W	R	69.9	69.6	<0	4.8

NOTE: The techniques used here are standard in litigation in which racial voting patterns are part of the evidence. In the ecological regression equations, the racial makeup of the precinct is the independent variable, whereas the vote for the candidate as a percentage of the registered voters is the dependent variable. Homogeneous precincts are defined as ones in which at least 90 percent of the registrants are of the same race.

challenger. Georgia's black incumbents had to first dispose of at least one white primary challenger. Moreover, Georgia Republicans believed that their prospects in these districts were good enough that in each district the GOP primary was contested. When the trial court threw out the results of the Texas May primary, the African-American incumbents had to withstand new challenges that saw three Republicans take on Houston's Sheila Jackson-Lee in the all-comers November vote, while in Dallas, Eddie Bernice Johnson faced two fellow Democrats, a brace of Republicans, and an independent. The survival of all African Americans running in new, whiter districts suggests that, at a minimum, black incumbents can retain their seats in the face of credible opposition so long as the percent black hovers around 40 percent. Florida's Corrine Brown and Texas's Jackson-Lee actually captured larger shares of the vote than they had won in the past when they represented more African Americans.

Black incumbents won on the strength of biracial coalitions. Evidence of the nature of these successful voting patterns is available from Georgia. Since the other African Americans reelected from whiter districts had larger leads over their opponents than did the Georgians, it is assumed that these results are indicative of patterns elsewhere. Sanford Bishop and Cynthia McKinney, running in the Second and Fourth Districts respectively, took the vast bulk of the black vote and added approximately one-third of the white vote. Bishop, whose district had a smaller black percentage among its registered voters, emerged with 54 percent of the vote whereas McKinney swept to victory with 58 percent.

Table 3.7 provides two sets of estimates of support for Bishop and Mc-Kinney. For comparative purposes, the table also includes the two other contested districts in which Georgia Democrats performed best.[12] Democrats in that state and throughout the nation saw the Eighth and Tenth as the best prospects for Democratic pickups in Georgia because these districts became blacker following the redistricting. David Bell, the Democratic nominee in the Tenth, attracted AFL–CIO funds and raised enough money to be competitive.[13] He took 48 percent of the vote, losing the election in a heavily Republican suburban county, where he slumped to 28 percent of the vote, while the Democrat in the Eighth finished with a respectable 47 percent. White support for the four Democrats was similar, approximately one-third, with McKinney and Bell each held to about 30 percent. McKinney won because of a larger black registration and turnout. Bishop's 36 percent was the strongest performance among these four Democrats.

The white vote shares garnered by the black and white congressional candidates corresponded closely to the performance registered by Georgia's Democratic nominees surveyed in exit polls. Max Cleland, the new U.S. senator, took 37 percent of the white vote, whereas Bill Clinton managed only 29 percent. White Georgians' voting behavior was in line with Democratic performances in Senate elections across the South reported in Table 3.1, the white southern electorates' support for Bill Clinton, and white votes for Democratic congressional candidates in the region.

Some have discounted the 1996 victories by African Americans, claiming that the affirmative action districts were necessary for blacks to become incumbents and, without incumbency, African Americans could not have won in these districts (McKinney 1996). Evidence that prior to 1996 "only six African Americans have ever won election from districts with clear Anglo majorities" (Lublin 1995) supports claims that reducing black concentrations makes districts unwinnable by blacks (also see, generally, C. David-son and Grofman 1994). Cameron et al. (1996), using data from the 103d Congress, dispute the necessity of a black majority to elect African Ameri-cans in the South. They estimate that in districts 40.3 percent black in vot-ing age population, African Americans are more likely than whites to win.

Nonetheless, there is the well-documented tendency for incumbents to perform better than open-seat candidates (Erikson, 1971a; Alford and Hib-bing 1981; Levitt and Wolfram 1997). Moreover, incumbency is color-blind, so that black incumbents tend to run better among white voters than do nonincumbent African Americans (Bullock 1984). The true test of whether the redrawn majority-white districts will vote for a black seeking an open seat must await the retirement of the current holders. Given the ages of these legislators, it may be years before an open seat materializes and it is highly likely that after the 2002 reapportionment, McKinney will have a majority-black district in the twelve- or thirteen-seat Georgia configuration.

In the absence of open-seat contests, one source of insight into what might happen comes from reviewing the elections that initially sent African Americans to Congress in 1992. Table 3.8 presents estimates of voting pref-erences by black and white voters for six of the newly created, majority-black seats that had black-white contests in 1992.[14] When available, estimates derived from ecological regression and homogeneous precinct analyses are provided. The homogeneous precinct analyses present results from precincts in which at least 90 percent of the voters (Louisiana), registrants (Florida, Georgia, and North Carolina), or voting age population (Virginia) are of the same race.

The implication of claims that majority-black districts are essential for the initial election of African Americans—although not for retention by incumbents—is that white support increases after the initial election, as Bul-lock found in a variety of Atlanta-area elections (1984). The most appropri-ate comparisons are between the shares of the white votes won by Bishop and McKinney in 1992 and 1996. Comparing results in Tables 3.7 and 3.8, the ecological regression shows that Bishop's white vote share increased by about nine points, although the homogeneous precinct analysis puts the gain at one point. McKinney shows no increase stemming from incumbency and the homogeneous precinct analysis suggests a nine point loss. The magnitude of the redistricting may explain why we do not find consistent evidence of gains in white support when the African Americans ran as incumbents be-cause in much of both districts the incumbent lacked the advantages often conferred by incumbency. While not refuting the proposition, these results

Table 3.8

Racial Voting Patterns in Open-Seat Congressional Elections
Involving African-American and White Candidates, 1992

	Race	Party	WHITES		BLACKS	
			Regression	Homo-geneous Precinct	Regression	Homo-geneous Precinct
Fla., District 3						
Brown	B	D	20	28 (29)	92	95 (95)
Weidner	W	R	80	72 (71)	8	5 (5)
Ga., District 2						
Bishop	B	D	27.4	35.1	97.1	96.4
Dudley	W	R	72.6	64.9	2.9	3.6
Ga., District 11						
McKinney	B	D	30.3	38.2	96.7	95.7
Lovett	W	R	69.7	61.8	3.3	4.3
La., District 4						
Fields	B	D	22.5	—	60.8	—
Hall	B	D	4.3	—	0.9	—
Jones	B	D	4.4	—	18.5	—
Ross	B	D	3.1	—	1.7	—
Shyne	B	D	15.9	—	8.3	—
Williams	B	D	8.1	—	8.8	—
Myres	W	R	23.1	—	0.0	—
Ventre	W	R	18.6	—	1.1	—
N.C., District 1						
Clayton	B	D	33.9	34.6	95.2	97.9
Tyler	W	R	63.6	63.1	4.0	1.9
Williams	B	I	2.5	2.4	0.9	0.2
Va., District 3						
Scott	B	D	49.3	60.1	99.3	95.2
Jenkins	W	R	50.7	39.9	0.7	4.8

SOURCES: Florida—Lichtman (1996), figures in parentheses from Maggiotto (1996);
Georgia—calculated by author; Louisiana and North Carolina—Weber (1993); Virginia—
Handley (1996).

raise questions about the contention that blacks cannot win in districts like Georgia's Second and Fourth, districts that, according to the 1990 census, have a black voting age population less than 40 percent, the figure that has been cited as giving black Democrats an equal chance of winning the South (Cameron et al. 1996).[15]

Also of interest is the share of the white vote initially polled by black legislators for whom 1996 estimates of white support are not yet available. Eva Clayton's one-third of the white vote in North Carolina is in line with the performance of Democrats in Georgia in 1996, whereas Corrine Brown's percentage in north Florida is a bit lower. Robert Scott won his seat in Virginia with about half of the white vote—a performance that would have secured election in a district with a small black electorate. The picture in Louisiana is clouded because of the multitude of candidates in the open primary and a runoff that had no white candidate. Cleo Fields took more than one-fifth of the white vote and another black candidate got one-sixth of the white vote. The set of six African Americans shared almost 60 percent of the white vote. Estimates of white support for black members of Congress in their initial elections do not indicate that winning in whiter districts would have been impossible.

Conclusion

Upon signing the VRA, President Lyndon Johnson warned his aide Bill Moyers that he had just delivered the South to the GOP for the next generation. Except for presidential voting, Johnson's forecast proved premature. For years, southern Democratic politicians showed they could sing "We Shall Overcome" at the same time they were whistling "Dixie." They won over legions of black voters while retaining the allegiance of large numbers of whites. For a generation after enactment of the VRA, Democrats rarely failed to control two-thirds of the South's House and Senate seats and their performance in lower offices was even stronger.

While the GOP remained in the minority, over time its ranks swelled in prosperous suburbs as northern Republicans moved to places where they could play tennis and golf year-round (Black and Black 1987: 241; Stanley 1988). These in-migrants were augmented by younger southerners who lacked their elders' attachment to Franklin D. Roosevelt and hatred of the party of Abraham Lincoln (Beck 1977; Wolfinger and Hagen 1985; Black and Black 1987: 232–56). Following years of gradual gains, the GOP stagnated during the 1980s with about one-third of the southern House seats while losing ground in the Senate as the decade progressed. Figures on white voters' preferences in congressional elections provide further evidence that GOP growth had stalled out in the 1980s. The constancy of the 1980s argues against attributing the change of the 1990s to in-migration or generational replacement because there is no reason to believe that these phenomena accelerated between 1992 and 1994. The dramatic drop in the white vote for Democratic congressional candidates in 1994 must have been triggered by a special event. Conversion of a sizable component of the electorate could account for the shift toward the GOP reported in Figure 3.1. Two factors that might have produced the change were redistricting and reaction to the Clinton presidency.

Aistrup (1996: 245–46) charges that the Department of Justice–mandated affirmative action gerrymandering that affected most southern states undercut the base for electing moderate Democrats. The prolonged debate that preceded adoption of redistricting plans fanned the flames of racial conflict, awakening tensions that Democrats had sought to mute. Angry rhetoric from both races over what steps must be taken to increase the number of majority-minority districts, often accompanied by demands from the Department of Justice to boost black percentages in certain districts, transformed redistricting into another facet of affirmative action. Whites who paid little heed to the jousting over where to draw district lines either had firsthand experience with affirmative action at work or their child's school or knew someone who had. Ironically, while white Democrats typically fought against the black Democrat–GOP coalition championing the bizarre districts, affirmative action was so solidly identified with the national Democratic party that local members of the party often paid the price. White voters angered by affirmative action often found higher quality GOP nominees in heavily white districts and turned against local Democrats in record numbers in 1994.

If white reaction to affirmative action redistricting does not account for the shift in voting behavior, rejection of Bill Clinton as a symbol of southern Democracy may be an alternative explanation. Republicans led by Newt Gingrich sought to nationalize the 1994 election by making it a referendum on the administration's tax plan and bureaucracy-expanding health care plan. To the extent that white southerners accepted GOP criticisms and claims that the Democratic party was out of step with southern values, those charges were underscored by the presence of a southern Democrat in the White House. The drawling exemplar of big government and alleged tax increases whose economic program had been supported by a number of southern Democrats in Congress made more difficult the Democrats' efforts to divorce public images of the national Democratic party and the representatives of the party in southern states. The similarity in the percentages of the white vote won by Democratic candidates for federal offices in 1996 indicates that white southerners were no more attracted to Democratic candidates with roots in southern states or even in their own congressional districts than to the presidential nominee. Moreover, Clinton performed little better with this segment of the electorate than had Democratic standard bearers with no southern heritage, such as Walter Mondale and Michael Dukakis.

More than a decade ago, Wolfinger and Hagen observed that, "support for Republican candidates in the South reflects party-line voting by Republicans, not defection by Democrats. Growing party strength and greater party loyalty go hand in hand" (1985: 9). By the mid-1990s, evidence of party-line voting among whites for Republican nominees suggested that loyalty to the GOP has now spread to about two-thirds of the electorate.

Chapter 4

Money and Office: The Sources of the Incumbency Advantage in Congressional Campaign Finance

STEPHEN ANSOLABEHERE AND JAMES M. SNYDER JR.

One of the most striking features of congressional elections is the advantage that the typical incumbent enjoys in financing campaigns. Over the last two decades the average House incumbent has spent roughly $470,000 (in 1992 dollars) per election. The average House challenger, however, has spent only $180,000. The advantage in the Senate is even more staggering. From 1980 to 1994, the average Senate incumbent spent $3.8 million, while the average Senate challenger spent only $2.4 million.

Incumbents' dominance of campaign finance is widely taken as symptomatic of the irresponsibility of the modern Congress. Money poses twin problems. First, it may increase the political pull of organized interests at the public expense. Money is thought to come with strings attached. Donors may buy access to legislators or influence on important bills that the ordinary citizen just can't afford. Second, it may short-circuit electoral accountability. Money is speech, and very few challengers evidently can amass the resources necessary to run campaigns on the same scale as incumbents. In the end, voters might have a tough time choosing between the devil they know and a complete unknown.

Remove the influence of moneyed interests. Make elections fairer. Those, of course, were the goals of the Federal Elections Campaign Act (FECA) of 1971. This law set up a web of contribution limits that were designed to lessen the influence of specific donors by forcing candidates to raise money from a much larger number of contributors. By most accounts the FECA has failed. Since the 1970s, campaign spending has apparently become more important in congressional elections, and the disparity between those who have it—incumbents—and those who don't—challengers—has ballooned. Americans have reputedly lost faith in the private system of campaign finance in the United States and in the politicians who have learned how to win in that system.

There is a strong impulse to reform the system. Several states have reacted by imposing draconian limits on donations from organizations as ways to stem the influence of "interested money," but these reforms sometimes have perverse consequences (Gais and Malbin 1998). What reforms, if any, make sense depend ultimately on why disparities and apparent excesses in fund-raising exist. The popular wisdom, or at least the one that gets the most air-time, holds that the legislative process is basically for sale to the highest bid-ders (Edsall 1984; Jackson 1990). Scholarly research, however, paints a much different picture. There is relatively little evidence, for example, that con-tributions buy roll-call votes in the House. Those steeped in the details and data more often point to the inexperience and limited personal resources of the typical challenger, and not to the legislative process, as explanations for incumbents' advantages in money and votes.[1]

Our aim in this paper is to examine the importance of office as a source of the incumbency advantage. We accomplish this through careful examina-tion of variation in individual legislators' campaign finance portfolios over time. We address three main questions: What is the incumbency advantage in campaign finance? How important is holding office to establishing this advantage? How does the legislative process within the House contribute to this advantage?

Our findings show that the incumbency advantage in congressional cam-paign finance derives substantially from legislative politics. The positions of power held by particular individuals and the office itself endow members of Congress with a significant financial and, ultimately, electoral advantage. Perhaps the most compelling evidence of the importance of office comes from the transformation that victorious challengers undergo once they reach the House. Challengers and open-seat candidates who win see their cam-paign receipts grow nearly $200,000 by their next elections, the first time that they run as incumbents.

Who gives is as important as *how much*. PACs on the whole are thought to be most attuned to Washington politics and most "interested" in the out-comes of the policy process. The extent to which the incumbency advan-tage derives from PAC money provides further evidence of the extent to which the incumbency advantage in campaign finance derives from the office itself. Ascending to office or positions of power dramatically expands the portfolio of contributors that a candidate can draw on. Most of the increase in freshman fund-raising comes from PAC donations. Moreover, those in positions of power within the House raise even more money from organized interests than the typical incumbent does. We do not interpret this to mean that there is widespread corruption or favor selling. Something more innocent may be at work, such as donors expressing the intensity of their preferences about the direction of public policy. However, we do take this as a further indicator of the significant and often insurmountable power that the office itself grants in campaign finance.

Against this view, we weigh an equally plausible account holding that politics involves the selection of the fittest. Incumbents raise more money and win more votes because they are inherently better politicians. The skills that make someone a good campaigner or a good fund-raiser are highly related to the skills that make for a good representative. Viewed in this light, incumbents' advantages in campaign finance and at the polls are symptomatic of their inherent abilities rather than caused by the act or accident of holding office.[2]

We do not deny the importance of candidates' abilities in determining the dynamics of campaign finance. There is great variability in the sorts of people who run for Congress, ranging from seasoned state legislators to accomplished businesspersons to laborers and artists. And there is a strong hint of social Darwinism in congressional elections. Only experienced, wealthy, and well-known challengers seem to have much hope of gaining a seat. However, the transformation that occurs in office is as large as these differences among challengers. Even the best-funded challengers rarely overcome the advantages derived from office.[3]

What is the Incumbency Advantage in Campaign Finance?

Two metrics are frequently used to gauge incumbents' edge in campaign resources: the absolute difference in spending and the relative difference (or ratio of incumbent to challenger spending). By either standard, legislators' growing dominance of campaign finance is impressive.

Table 4.1 displays the average expenditures of House incumbents and challengers involved in contested races from 1978 to 1996. These figures are translated into real 1992 dollars using the Gross Domestic Product (GDP) deflator. Two measures of relative spending are presented: the ratio of average incumbent spending to average challenger spending and the median of the ratios for each contest.[4]

Table 4.1

Measures of Incumbency Advantage in Campaign Finance
(in constant 1992 dollars)

Year	Average Incumbent Spending ($)	Average Challenger Spending ($)	Number of Races	Ratio of I to C Spending	Median Ratio
1978	284,577	202,863	235[a]	1.40	1.93
1980	298,510	174,031	338	1.72	3.82
1982	400,630	202,689	315	1.98	3.24
1984	417,815	192,433	338	2.17	4.47
1986	488,447	175,418	319	2.78	5.39
1988	496,894	148,723	328	3.34	7.08
1990	479,969	124,899	321	3.84	10.02
1992	609,060	172,802	307	3.52	5.35
1994	573,374	223,664	328	2.56	4.68
1996	630,852	254,964	357	2.47	5.11
All Years	473,421	187,587	3,186	2.52	4.66

SOURCES: The authors have derived data for all tables and figures in Chapter 4 from various years of the Federal Election Commission's *Report on Financial Activity*.

[a]Number of cases is small because of nonfilers.

Real spending by incumbents has doubled over the last two decades. In 1978 and 1980, incumbents averaged just under $300,000 a contest. By the 1990s, that figure had doubled. Over the same period, challenger spending remained largely flat at just under $200,000 per contest, bottoming out in the 1988 and 1990 elections and surging slightly in the 1994 and 1996 elections. One curious pattern is the apparent ratcheting upward of incumbent money in redistricting years. In the 1982 election and again in the 1992 election, incumbent spending jumped (in real terms) $100,000, and continued to trend upward slightly over the subsequent years.

Relative spending shows equally dramatic growth, with some attrition in the 1990s. At the beginning of the 1980s, the average incumbent expenditure was slightly less than twice the average challenger expenditure. By the end of the 1980s, the average incumbent spent about $3.50 for every dollar spent by the average challenger. This reflected both steady growth in incumbent fund-raising and sagging challenger resources, with the field of

challengers in 1990 being the weakest in the entire period. Competition increased in the 1990s. Incumbents continue to spend relatively more than
they did during the first half of the 1980s, but their relative advantage has
shrunk due to a surge in challenger spending. The average incumbent expenditure is now two and one-half times the average challenger expenditure.
Even with this recent uptick in challenger spending, though, incumbents'
relative advantage today is one and one-half times what it was at the beginning of the 1980s.

Even more dramatic is the relative advantage that an incumbent in the
median race possesses. A handful of million dollar candidacies pushes up the
averages well beyond what the typical race looks like. This is especially true
for challengers, indicating that the typical challenger is actually much less
capable of matching the incumbent's resources than the averages indicate.
The median of the ratio of incumbent spending to challenger spending is
5:1. In only 10 percent of the contested races from 1980 to 1996 did the
challenger spend as much as the incumbent. The challengers won one-third
of all races where incumbents spent less than the challenger. In the large majority of cases, though, incumbents spent more than their opponents, and
won 95 percent of the time.

Not surprisingly, the edge in money translates readily into an advantage
at the polls, albeit a much more modest advantage than raw dollar figures
suggest. In a separate paper, we have estimated the effect of incumbent and
challenger spending on the House vote (Ansolabehere and Snyder 1996; see
also Gerber 1995). The statistical results are available upon request. We estimate that incumbents' and challengers' expenditures have approximately
the same effect on electoral competition and that a 100 percent increase in
relative spending produces a very modest percentage change in the vote of
eight points.

This is certainly a very small number, but it is magnified by the enormous
advantage that the incumbent holds in campaign spending. In 1996, for example, the average incumbent outspent the average challenger $630,000 to
$255,000. This amounts to an estimated advantage in the vote of approx-
imately 7 percentage points.[5] Such an edge seems small compared to the
hyperbole infused in popular discussions of money politics. However, we
should not undervalue the significance of this edge. In 1996, the overall incumbency advantage was approximately eleven points.[6] Money, then, represents about half of the overall incumbency advantage today.

These estimates also reveal the extent to which money has added to
the electoral security of incumbents over the last two decades. Incumbent
spending has more than doubled, in real terms, since 1980, while challenger

spending has increased by only 40 percent. Independent of all other factors, the increase in the difference between incumbent spending and challenger spending has added approximately 5 percentage points to the average incumbent's electoral margin.

The Endowment of Office

Fund-raising is a necessity of political life in contemporary America. The cost of a successful House campaign—whether waged by an incumbent, a challenger, or a candidate in an open seat race—easily exceeds $500,000. By business standards, this is a small investment, but by political standards the cost is enormous. To amass a half million dollar fund, House candidates must raise $1,500 a day. The demands of a Senate race are an order of magnitude greater. The most extreme case is California. A U.S. Senate hopeful in California must now set a target of at least $20 million, which amounts to raising $55,000 a day.[7]

To raise money at this pace, candidates must tap their families and friends and business associates and, then, reach out to strangers. Direct mail solicitation and fund-raising events, such as $500- or $1,000-a-plate dinners, have become commonplace. In 1992, for example, House incumbents spent $31 million on such activities. Naturally, people who understand and enjoy this sort of fund-raising, who have extensive social and business connections, or who have something that attracts donors possess considerable advantages. Such talents and resources are not limited to incumbents, but incumbents as a class seem to be uniquely advantaged. Is it that incumbents are people of unusually high talents and resources or that the office adds to their capital? Surely there is some of each factor; our aim is to assess the value of being a sitting member of Congress.

Office may add to politicians' capital in three ways. First, it may add to their *human capital*, their understanding of how they can raise money and compete electorally. In labor economics, human capital theory is premised on the fact that workers learn important skills either in school or on the job, and that such learning spurs wage growth. On-the-job learning happens in politics, too. With each campaign, a candidate figures out new ways to approach people for money and ways to raise money more effectively.

Second, office may add to a politician's *social capital*, the political connections and celebrity status that individuals can draw on to raise money. Being in Washington and being the most prominent politician in a congressional district widens the set of personal contacts that one can draw on to raise money. In addition, a House member becomes something of local celebrity.

Such prominence may provide the member greater exposure to individuals for whom contributing is a civic act or who wish to express their approval of a politician.

Third, office creates *political capital*, power and resources that members of Congress can use to raise funds. One of the main concerns with the private system of campaign finance in the United States is that interested donors, especially the PACs of corporations, unions, and trade associations, get some sort of quid pro quo. Their donations, it is feared, are given in exchange for access to lobbyists, help with the bureaucracy, or even influence on legislation. While challengers and incumbents can promise donors the same political returns, incumbents are in a unique position to make good on their promises.

The significance of office, as opposed to talent, should manifest itself in two ways. First, individuals in office should raise much more money than similar individuals who happen not to be in office. Second, individuals in office should rely much more heavily on PACs than similar individuals who happen not to be in office. PACs are the most heavily concentrated donors in Washington, D.C., so they are most likely to constitute the new fundraising connections that the legislator makes. Also, PACs are thought to be the donors most interested in the outcomes of the legislative process, and thus most likely to invest in incumbents. PAC money, then, should constitute the bulk of the difference in receipts between those in and out of office.

The contrast between all incumbents and all challengers provides a rough measure of the overall advantage that those in office hold in terms of campaign money. It does not, however, reveal the extent to which that advantage derives from the office itself or from individuals' personal resources and talents. More focused comparisons are required. Specifically, we need to hold the individuals in both categories equal to the highest extent possible.

To accomplish this, we examine the campaign finance portfolios of candidates who run for office more than once. Specifically, our measures of the extent to which the incumbency advantage derives from office is the difference between the total receipts that an individual raises as a nonincumbent and the total receipts that that same individual raises as an incumbent. This calculation is akin to the sophomore surge commonly used to compute the size of the incumbency advantage in the vote. The sharpest comparisons can be drawn when two candidates face each other repeatedly. We will also examine races where incumbents faced different opponents in their freshmen elections than the candidates they defeated to win their seats.

The rocky House races of the California First District demonstrate these comparisons nicely. The First snakes along the northern coast of California from the Oregon border to Marin County, ducking inland to include Napa as well. The district is deeply divided into two camps: environmentalists and agricultural interests, especially logging companies. Doug Bosco, who represented the district from 1984 to 1990, said of his constituents that "everyone [in the First] loves trees. Half of them like them standing up. The other half like them lying down." This divide makes the First one of the most hotly contested House districts in the United States. Since 1988 the district has changed representatives four times. This exceptional amount of turnover makes the California First a perfect case to display the financial value of being in office. The comings and goings in the California First are summarized in Table 4.2.

In 1990, four-term incumbent Doug Bosco lost his seat by the narrowest of margins to Republican Frank Riggs. Riggs, a police officer turned businessman, raised a total of $272,100, of which less than $8,000, or 3 percent, came from PACs. Bosco, on the other hand, had accumulated nearly $440,000 for the race, nearly half of which came from PACs.

Two years later, the tables were turned: it was Riggs who found himself fighting to stay in place. Facing a strong Democratic national tide and a new and telegenic opponent, Dan Hamburg, the new incumbent Riggs nearly tripled his campaign receipts to $729,800. One-third of this fund, half of all the new money that Riggs raised, came from PACs. The freshman Republican, however, was unable to stem a strong national Democratic tide. Though he outspent Hamburg, Riggs lost this battle.

But not the war. In 1994, the two met again. This time Hamburg held the seat, and Riggs had to wage the campaign as the challenger. In 1992, Hamburg raised $653,000 as a challenger, of which PAC receipts amounted to $176,000, or 27 percent of all Hamburg's 1992 receipts. As an incumbent, two years later, Hamburg amassed an $807,000 war chest, 25 percent more than he had raised as a challenger. And $374,000, or 46 percent, of the new incumbent's funds came from PACs. What is particularly striking about the freshman Hamburg's fund-raising is that the growth in his PAC receipts actually exceeded the growth in his total receipts. In other words, Hamburg substituted PAC money for money that he raised from other sources as a challenger.

Riggs had also lost much of the financial support that he received when he ran as an incumbent in 1992. In 1994, he raised $575,578, $150,000 less than he had when he was in office two years earlier. And his PAC receipts were off by nearly $100,000. But the vanquished incumbent Riggs was clearly a better fund-raiser in 1994 than he was when he first ran as a challenger in 1990. In his first challenger race, Riggs's receipts were just half

Table 4.2

Campaign Finance and Electoral Competition in California's First District (in constant 1992 dollars)

	REPUBLICAN CANDIDATE			DEMOCRATIC CANDIDATE			
Year	*Name*	*Total Receipts* ($)	*PAC Receipts* ($)	*Name*	*Total Receipts* ($)	*PAC Receipts* ($)	*Democratic Percent of Vote*
1988	Sam Vanderbilt	9,244	0	Doug Bosco	303,997	142,257	68.9
1990	Frank Riggs	272,099	7,952	Doug Bosco	439,449	202,179	48.8
1992	*Frank Riggs*	729,819	221,886	Dan Hamburg	652,592	176,285	51.1
1994	Frank Riggs	575,578	137,783	*Dan Hamburg*	807,407	374,408	46.4
1996	*Frank Riggs*	1,292,733	473,511	Michela Alioto	1,182,053	237,585	47.8

NOTE: Names of incumbents are italicized.

of the fund that he put together in 1994. His PAC receipts in 1990 were not quite $8,000, while his PAC receipts in 1994 were $138,000. With the boost of the Republican tide of 1994, Riggs was returned to the House with 53 percent of the vote.

In 1996, again an incumbent, Congressman Riggs held all of the advantages in fund-raising that office brings. And he needed them. Riggs's opponent was Michela Alioto, daughter of famed San Francisco mayor Joseph Alioto. She raised a whopping $1.2 million for the House race, $237,000 (or 20 percent) of which came from PACs. Riggs topped that. He raised $1.3 million, better than double what he had raised as a challenger two years earlier. Interest groups helped him out enormously in the effort. Riggs pulled in $474,000 from PACs in 1996, fully 37 percent of his total receipts and triple what he had raised from PACs as a challenger two years earlier.

The California First is clearly an exceptional district, but the experiences of the candidates that have battled for this seat since 1990 prove a more general rule. Being in the House provides candidates a considerable edge in campaign money. Those who won the seat saw their resources nearly double, and most of that increase came in PAC receipts. The ups and downs of Frank Riggs's receipts are perhaps most telling of all. Riggs's capital grew in all three ways described above. Upon entering the House Riggs learned how to raise money the D.C. way. He was far superior at raising funds the second time that he was a challenger than he was in his first race. When Riggs lost his seat and ran again as a challenger, he was clearly better at raising money than he had been four years earlier, especially in soliciting money from PACs. He had learned how to raise money and he had established connections that he could bank on. Riggs's story also suggests that there is no small amount of political capital behind incumbents' fund-raising success. Riggs lost much, though not all, of his financial support once he was turned out of office and had to run as a challenger. That support returned once Riggs could again campaign from D.C.

Evidence of the generality of this pattern is found in Table 4.3, which displays the average vote shares, total receipts, and PAC receipts of the candidates involved in four different types of races. The sample in Table 4.3 consists of pairs of elections in which at the first election a new legislator was chosen, and at the second election that individual ran as an incumbent. The four types are defined by two dimensions. The first dimension is the type of race that the new legislator won in the first race. The legislator either ran as a challenger and beat an incumbent or ran in an open seat and beat another nonincumbent. The second dimension is defined by the decision of the new legislator's opponent to run again or step aside. The second race was either a rematch or the new incumbent faced a new challenger. Rematches provide the greatest degree of control, since they keep both candidates constant, but they are rare. Races involving new challengers are also very informative about the value of office, but the comparisons across years are less crisp.

The first case shown in Table 4.3 consists of challenger-incumbent rematches. These thirteen contests were some of the most hard-fought races in the House, and the victors won by the narrowest margins. None of the challengers in the first round won with more than 52 percent of the two-candidate vote, and the freshmen in round two averaged only 50.7 percent of the two-candidate vote. The battle in money resembled an arms race, with the office granting the new incumbents a huge advantage and the incumbents in both elections capturing a disproportionate share of the interested money.

In the first election of each pair, the incumbents, who were defeated, received on average $543,000, compared with the victorious challengers, who averaged $627,000. Even though they were outspent overall, the incumbents managed to raise considerably more from PACs. The average incumbent in the first round brought in $211,000 from organized interests, or 39 percent of his or her total fund, while the challenger brought in $142,000 from groups, just 23 percent of his or her total fund.

Two years later, in the rematch, spending by both candidates scaled upward. The vanquished incumbents, who were now running as challengers, increased their receipts by one-third, from $543,000 to $696,000. The new incumbents, who had won as challengers the last time around, expanded their receipts by 60 percent, from $627,000 to $972,000.

In terms of PAC contributions, the new incumbents in the second round looked much more like the old incumbents, and the old incumbents looked much more like challengers. The new incumbents brought in $341,000 from PACs, fully one-third of their total receipts, compared with $142,000 two years earlier. This increase accounted for a little more than half of the growth in receipts for these freshmen between their first and second elections. By contrast, the old incumbents, now running as challengers, saw almost no change in their PAC receipts. The additional money they raised for the rematches came almost entirely from individuals, the parties, and their personal funds. The second type of race also involved rematches, but in these 31 cases the new incumbents won open seats in the first election. Again, these races exhibit the huge fund-raising endowment that comes with office and reveal that most of these resources came from interest groups. In the first election, the winners outspent the opponents on average by over $250,000: $536,000 to $277,000. Like the first type of race, both candidates increased

Table 4.3

Sophomore Surge in Campaign Finance: Average Vote Shares, Total Receipts, and PAC Receipts, 1978–1994

	Year 1	Year 2
Rematches		
Type 1 [a]		
Chall. 1; inc. 2		
Percent vote	50.7	50.7
Total receipts ($)	626,748	971,848
PAC receipts ($)	142,161	340,848
Inc. 1; chall. 2		
Total receipts ($)	542,800	695,933
PAC receipts ($)	210,805	235,532
Type 2 [b]		
Open winner 1; inc. 2		
Percent vote	58.5	59.9
Total receipts ($)	535,867	680,521
PAC receipts ($)	163,123	277,071
Open loser 1; chall. 2		
Total receipts ($)	277,329	343,404
PAC receipts ($)	66,580	98,815
New opponents		
Type 3 [c]		
Chall. 1; inc. 2		
Percent vote	53.7	58.9
Total receipts ($)	546,874	749,115
PAC receipts ($)	143,178	275,695
Inc. 1; new chall. 2		
Total receipts ($)	688,643	416,588
PAC receipts ($)	295,816	100,751
Type 4 [d]		
Open winner 1; inc. 2		
Percent vote	60.5	64.8
Total receipts ($)	595.669	595,856
PAC receipts ($)	167,845	242,537
Open loser 1; new chall. 2		
Total receipts ($)	382,443	237,550
PAC receipts ($)	96,855	51,903

[a] Challenger beats incumbent in year 1 ($n = 13$).

[b] Open seat in year 1; incumbent contested in year 2 ($n = 31$).

[c] Challenger winner in year 1; faces new challenger in year 2 ($n = 138$).

[d] Open seat winner in year 1; faces new opponent in year 2 ($n = 283$).

their spending between the two elections, but the new incumbents increased their receipts much more than their challengers. The new incumbents raised $145,000 more in the second election; the challengers raised $66,000 more. PACs tilted heavily toward the new incumbents. Seventy-nine percent of the growth in the new incumbents' total receipts came from increased PAC donations; only 47 percent of the increase in the challengers' receipts came from increased PAC funds.

The third and fourth types of races involved new incumbents who faced new challengers. Such races are more common, but also more varied. The overall patterns, though, bear out the same patterns as the rematches. Upon reaching office incumbents expanded their receipts and most of the growth came from interest groups. Those who won as challengers in the first round raised $202,000 more in their second election. Two-thirds of that money came from PACs. The open-seat winners, who were on the whole the safest of the three types, increased their receipts only slightly. However, they quickly substituted PAC money for other sources, especially personal funds.

The new challengers paled in contrast to the candidates they replaced. Opponents' total receipts dropped dramatically from the first election to the next and much of that drop came in PAC receipts. In both types of races, the new challengers spent only about two-thirds as much as the candidates who had run in the previous races. And PACs steered clear of these new candidates, giving them less than half of what they had given the candidate who had contested the seat two years earlier.

These changes in campaign resources point to significant gains that individuals make upon entering the House. Estimation of the effect of holding office requires us to make the contrasts between these groups more carefully. Our approach is to treat the pool of all candidates who ran in two successive elections as a quasi experiment. The control groups in this quasi experiment are candidates whose incumbency status did not change between elections; namely, (1) all candidates who were nonincumbents in two successive elections (denoted N-N), and (2) all candidates who ran as incumbents in two successive elections (denoted I-I). The quasi-experimental treatment groups consist of three types of candidates whose incumbency status did change from the first election to the second: challengers who became incumbents (C-I), open-seat candidates who became incumbents (O-I), and incumbents who lost and became challengers (I-C), which is very rare.

We focus this comparison on the marginal elections, seats won by 55 percent of the vote or less. This restriction narrows the sample to 508 races, but it allows us to hold constant demand for money. As further controls for demand, we include measures of primary competition and seat safety. These

Table 4.4

Effects of Holding Office on Total and PAC Receipts: Change in
Receipts Relative to Non-Incumbent—Non-Incumbent Group

Type of race	Change in total receipts ($)	Change in PAC receipts ($)
C ⇒ I	300,000*	138,000*
O ⇒ I	155,000*	103,000*
I ⇒ I	50,000	−6,000
I ⇒ C	40,000	−46,000
(C, O) ⇒ I	191,000*	112,000*

*t-ratio > 3.0

NOTE: C = challenger; I = incumbent; O = open-seat contestant. The arrow signifies
change from one condition to another.

are the highest demand races: incumbents, on average, spend $722,000 and
challengers spend $476,000. Although the relative campaign finance advan-
tage of incumbents is somewhat below average in these races, the absolute
advantage resembles all races. Incumbents spend about $250,000 more than
their opponents in these close races.[8]

Table 4.4 displays the effects of being in each of four groups of office-
holders relative to the group of candidates who held no office in successive
elections. There is no significant change in the receipts of the I-I group, and
the I-C group registers a slight drop in receipts. As above, challengers and
open-seat candidates who win office receive substantial boosts in their campaign resources overall and from PACs. Combining these two groups reveals
that ascending to office adds $191,000 to a new incumbent's campaign chest.
This is fully 70 percent of the total advantage enjoyed by incumbents in these
races. What is more, PACs are the main source of the increased funds. Of the
$191,000 sophomore surge in receipts, $112,000 (or 60 percent) comes from
interest groups.

Money and Power

Simply winning a seat gives a politician a considerable advantage over even
the best challengers within a congressional district. But there is more to

office than just being there. Power in the House is not shared equally, and the power that comes with committee appointments, leadership positions, and seniority enables those who have it to accumulate still greater campaign war chests. The prominence that comes with power may make legislators more visible in their districts or nationally, give them more contacts with donors, and make their time and political decisions more valuable to interested parties.

Ray McGrath, a Republican who represented the Fifth District of New York from 1981 to 1990, is a case in point. In his first two campaigns as an incumbent (1982 and 1984) McGrath spent $315,000 and $325,000, respectively, and raised approximately 40 percent of this money from political action committees. He won both elections with solid margins, capturing 58 percent of the vote in 1982 and 62 percent in 1984. Following the 1984 election, however, McGrath was appointed to one of the most powerful and coveted positions in the House, the Ways and Means Committee. McGrath's receipts nearly doubled, with almost all of the growth coming from PACs. In his next three elections, McGrath raised $562,000, $596,000, and $576,000, respectively. Eighty percent of the increase in his receipts came from expanded PAC donations. In his first two reelection bids, McGrath brought in $142,000 and $108,000 from PACs. Over the next three election cycles, he brought in $301,000, $333,000, and $356,000. The safety of his seat increased, slightly. Figure 4.1 graphs McGrath's campaign finance history.

The Ways and Means Committee is just one of many powerful positions within the House. We distinguish three systems within the House that provide opportunities for fund-raising: the committee system, the party system, and the floor.

First, the committee system gives those on the relevant committees control over the content of legislation through markups, and it creates opportunities to kill a bill before it reaches the floor. Interested donors might target their contributions to members of key committees to push their own pet project or express their intense opposition to specific bills. Committees that deal with economic regulation, taxation, and budgeting—as well as specific policies—will naturally attract intense interest from groups. In this respect two committees stand out: Ways and Means and Energy and Commerce. There are, of course, poor committees to serve on, from the perspective of campaign finance, just as there are lucrative ones. In general, donors will tend to avoid committees that oversee government administration or deal with symbolic policy areas.[9] In addition, power within the committees is

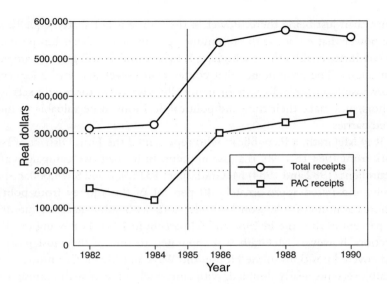

Figure 4.1.   Congressman Ray McGrath's receipts, 1982–1990.

structured along seniority lines, and the most senior members have considerable authority over the conduct of the committees.

Second, the organization of the House grants the majority party, especially the majority leadership, considerable authority over legislation. The party leaders determine committee appointments and even the organization of the committees. The majority party, by convention, dominates the Rules Committee and the budget process, and the speaker structures debate and directs bills to particular committees. These varied and sometimes subtle rules make members of the majority party, on average, more powerful and, thus, more attractive to contributors interested in the policy process. In addition, party leaders, who are not determined by seniority but by the caucus, have considerable power within the party over the political agenda. These individuals also bear much of the responsibility for party fund-raising.

Finally, the extent to which an individual politician is pivotal may increase his or her capacity to raise money. If a legislator is certain to cast the deciding vote on a piece of legislation, then interested donors will certainly want to make their preferences known, either by "voting" with their money or by buying access for their lobbyists. Of course, it is not known who, if anyone, is pivotal, so those wishing to influence the decisive legislators must hedge their bets.[10] Contributors interested in influencing a policy decision, then, will invest disproportionate sums in those closer to the ideological middle of the legislature.

In addition, members of Congress with more seniority might assert leadership on the floor or in the House as a whole. With experience inside the legislature comes knowledge about the legislative process and in-depth understanding of particular policy areas. These resources might make more senior legislators natural people around which to build support for particular programs. It is nearly impossible to distinguish these intangible powers that come with seniority from a pure human capital story, or from any changes that come with age. We do not examine this effect here.

We have estimated the absolute and percentage changes in total receipts and in PAC and non-PAC receipts that come with each of these four sorts of power within the House. As with estimating the extent to which money comes with holding office as opposed to other individual assets, the difficulty here is how to isolate the effects due solely to these factors from other factors that differ from person to person. Our approach has been to consider how individuals' receipts change when they receive a new committee assignment, when they ascend to a position of power within a committee or the party leadership, when they climb in rank within the House, when their status as a minority or majority member changes, or when their proximity to the median of the House floor changes.

Two separate analyses were used. First, we looked at the sample of all incumbents and estimated a regression that contained fixed effects for each individual legislator as well as indicators of the variables of interest and of other factors that gauge the demand for money. The fixed effects remove differences across individual legislators, for example, due to individual fund-raising skills or resources, and for specific years, but they make it impossible to estimate the effects of factors that change very infrequently for individuals. For example, to estimate the effects of majority party status in this model requires more than a handful to switch parties. Second, we considered how these various factors explain variability in the sophomore surge in money. This analysis focuses on the fund-raising of freshmen incumbents in the pair of elections in which they ran as nonincumbents and as first-term incumbents. We regressed change in receipts on variables that describe the individuals' positions within the House, such as committee assignments, and variables that identify features of the individual, such as wealth. This approach allows us to estimate the effects of factors that do not vary or vary little for incumbents. For example, we can estimate the value of being in the majority, since all of these candidates move from being out of the House to being either in the majority party or the minority party in the House.

Table 4.5 displays the estimated effects of different positions within the House on total and PAC receipts (in 1992 constant dollars). The estimated effects are from fixed effects regressions, so the effects represent the average change in individual legislator's receipts when that individual's position within the House changes. Complete results of these regressions are presented in Appendix A.[11] Except for the variable measuring the proximity to the House median all of the independent variables reported in Table 4.5 are dummy variables, so the effects reflect the difference in receipts between those for whom the condition held and for whom it did not. Specifically, legislators with good committee assignments are those on Ways and Means or Energy and Commerce. Those with bad committee assignments are on Standards of Official Conduct (ethics), House Administration, Government Operations, District of Columbia, Small Business, Foreign Affairs, and Education and Labor. Committee leaders consist of the chairs and ranking minority members of each committee. Party leaders include the speaker, the majority and minority leaders, the chief whips of each party, the chairs of each party's caucus, and the chairs of the fund-raising committees. Pivotal is the only complicated variable in the table. For each year we measure the deviation of each member's Americans for Democratic Action (ADA) score from the median. We then rescale this measure so that it runs from -1 to $+1$. The mean ADA score over the entire sample is approximately 0, so we cannot measure the overall drift in the ADA score. We can measure change in the median relative to any individual because the median ADA score of members running for reelection does vary considerably, ranging from $+.29$ (on our -1 to $+1$ scale) in 1994 to $-.34$ in 1996.

Two general lessons emerge from Table 4.5: (1) positions of power correspond to greater fund-raising capacity and (2) increased fund-raising due to position stems mainly from PAC donations. Evidently, legislators in positions of power bank on their political capital.

First consider the committee system. For established legislators, moving onto Ways and Means or Energy and Commerce adds about $43,000 to total receipts. PAC receipts grow by even more and serve as a substitute for fund-raising from other sources. For new legislators, an appointment to one of these committees is an even greater bonanza. Though comparatively rare, freshmen appointed to either of these committees see their PAC receipts increase, on average by $108,000, and their total receipts increase by $100,000. Freshmen experience a much larger boost from these assignments than sitting members do because as nonincumbents their fund-raising lags behind. A good committee assignment makes freshmen as good at raising cash as experienced legislators on those committees. Appointment to one of the

Table 4.5
Effects of Holding Positions of Power in House
on Incumbents' Campaign Fund-raising

	Change in total receipts ($)	Change in PAC receipts ($)
Good committee assignment	42,689***	75,634***
Bad committee assignment	28,891**	−1,296
Committee leader (chair or minority)	55,755**	39,904**
Party leader	637,814***	287,844***
Minority party (from sophomore surge)	132,790***	68,304***
Pivotal	58,722*	49,124**

* t-ratio is between 1.5 and 2.0

** t-ratio is between 2.0 and 3.0

*** t-ratio > 3.0

bad committees costs sitting legislators about $29,000, though very little of this loss comes from PACs. New legislators lose only an insignificant edge in fund-raising when appointed to one of the least lucrative committees, in part because they have little to lose. Committee leadership, either a chairmanship or a ranking minority member, is more valuable still, adding nearly $56,000 on average to the member who ascends to one of those posts. About 70 percent of this increase comes from expanded PAC donations.

Important as the committee system is, party seems to have much bigger effects on individual members' fund-raising. Becoming a party leader boosts fund-raising enormously. While very few individuals ascend to these posts, leaders' fund-raising totals grow by an astounding $637,000. Most of this comes from non-PAC sources, but PACs give an additional $288,000 to these individuals. These figures do not include the resources accumulated through the legislators' "leadership" PACs. Part of this growth surely reflects the demands of holding one of these jobs, but much of it also stems from the enormous power that these individuals have over the public agenda.

The value of being in the majority provides further evidence of the power of party in fund-raising. We can only reliably estimate this effect from the fund-raising portfolios of freshmen. Legislators who enter the majority party see their campaign funds grow by $133,000 more than legislators who enter the minority party, with half of this sum coming from expanded PAC donations.

Lastly, ideological positioning in the House as a whole strongly influences fund-raising. A unit change in our measure of pivotalness increases total receipts by $53,000, with nearly all of this change coming from PACs. Unlike the other measures of position within the House, the measure of pivotalness is much harder to interpret.

There are two ways to think of ideological positions being important for fund-raising. First, candidates might change their voting records to accord with the interests of donors. As the contributor pool changes—as it certainly has since the late 1970s—then politicians should move in pursuit of money. In fact, there is very little variance in the ideological ratings of *individual* members of Congress, which suggests very little movement in search of money (Poole and Rosenthal 1997: 73–77). The ideological rating of the median member of Congress has, however, changed considerably over time, suggesting a second way that ideology affects individual's fund-raising. The ideological composition of Congress may change through turnover, and with those changes come shifts in power. The median voters in the Congresses of 1986 and 1996 are far apart. Even though the Richard Gephardts and Newt Gingriches continue to push agendas similar to the agendas they forwarded a decade ago, those agendas are received very differently by the rank-and-file legislators. This shift in the preferences of the median member have dramatically altered power and fund-raising ability within the Congress.

At the beginning of the 1980s, the median member of Congress, on our scale of -1.00 to $+1.00$, had a rating of around $+.1$. By the late 1980s, the median hovered around $+.25$. This leftward shift meant that those to the right of this new median lost about $8,000 each, while those to the left made equivalent gains. The first Clinton Congress was the most liberal in this era, with a rating of $+.29$ for the median. The Democratic crash of 1994 not only demoralized the party, but also shifted the modest gains in fund-raising dramatically in the opposite direction. The median incumbent running for reelection in 1996 scored $-.34$, a swing of $.63$! Those to the left of this new median saw their fortunes drop, on average, by $33,000 each; those on the new right rose by approximately that amount.

These changes may seem small, especially compared to massive advantages that come with party leadership and certain committee posts. However, unlike leadership positions, which very few ever get to hold, changes in the composition of Congress affect the fund-raising of all. As interest groups pursue the influence of pivotal legislators, accidental shifts in the median caused, say, by the popularity or unpopularity of the president, can elevate one ideological wing of Congress at the expense of the other. The average loss of $33,000 on the left made it that much more difficult for every Democrat in 1996 and that much easier for the typical Republican incumbent.

Conclusions

Members of Congress rely heavily on money as the means to win reelection. Over the last two decades, incumbents have cultivated significant fundraising advantages over their opponents. This has translated into greater electoral security, at least as much as can be bought through campaigns.

We have established a pair of simple results that help explain how this has come about. The first is that most of the incumbency advantage in campaign finance can be attributed to the office itself, as opposed to the talents of those who win. The sophomore surge in campaign money accounts for two-thirds of the difference between the typical incumbent's and the typical challenger's receipts. Second, interest group money is the main source of this advantage. Most of the sophomore surge stems from increased PAC donations.

To put the matter somewhat differently, our results speak to a simple conclusion: PACs pursue power. They invest in those in office, not those hoping to win. They give to those legislators on key committees, especially the committees dealing with economic regulation and taxation. They give considerably more to those in the majority, and to those who lead the majority. And they give disproportionately to those whose votes are likely to be decisive on legislation that comes before the House as a whole. As a result, incumbents have a much easier time raising money than their opponents.

A number of implications can be drawn from these results. We emphasize two. First, the private and decentralized system of campaign finance in the United States insulates the majority party. This happens through both the advantage that each incumbent possesses and the advantage that incumbents in the majority receive. The incumbency advantage in money adds to the electoral security of each legislator. This, in turn, lessens the frequency of marginal incumbents and dampens the effects of national party tides. In addition, interest group contribution strategies give the majority party an added boost. PACs seem to be especially drawn to the majority. They target their donations at the pivotal votes in the legislature, a disproportionate share of which are necessarily in the majority party. In addition, interest groups seek to influence those in the majority party, since the majority organizes the legislature. These factors give majority party members in close races an added capacity to raise funds.

Second, interest group politics drive campaign finance in the United States. Perhaps the most important feature of American campaign finance under the FECA is the enormous and continued *growth* in incumbents' resources. Throughout the 1980s and 1990s the typical challenger's total PAC receipts hovered between $35,000 and $45,000. The average incumbent's PAC receipts rose from $111,000 in 1980 to $270,000 in 1996. The growth in PAC contributions and its skew toward incumbents accounts for 60 percent of the increase in incumbents' receipts since 1980.

This observation raises a more fundamental question. Why has interest group involvement in campaign finance increased? Our analysis suggests two forces. First, legislators may use the office to raise more today than they did two decades ago. A recent, provocative paper by John Lott (1995) suggests that the growth of campaign spending stems from the growth in government spending. Lott shows a strong correlation between the size of government and campaign spending at the state and federal levels. One problem with this explanation is that in the 1990s discretionary spending has shrunk at the federal level, while PAC contributions continue to increase.

A second force that may have caused the growth in campaign spending and, specifically, incumbents' expenditures is the expansion in interest group activity that has occurred over the last two decades. The 1980s witnessed an increase in interest group activity of all sorts—lobbying, grassroots organizing, and campaign contributing. Our results suggest that as more groups get involved in politics and as groups' resources increase, those resources will be directed toward those in power. In American politics this has provided incumbents greater resources to draw on. This is certainly an unintended effect of the system of limits imposed by FECA and, possibly, an unfortunate one.

It is tempting to conclude from this that campaign finance reforms should come down hard on PACs. If interest group money is indeed what ails the American campaign finance system, then lower contribution limits or even a ban on PACs would level the differences between incumbents and challengers and lessen the influence of organized interests in the legislative process. We take a more cautionary conclusion about reform from our results. The incumbency advantage in campaign finance has grown, it seems, because interest group activity has grown. The relevant issue for those interested in political reform, then, is why so many groups are organized and involved in national politics today.

Chapter 5

Majority-Minority Districts and the New Politics of Congressional Elections

DAVID EPSTEIN AND SHARYN O'HALLORAN

The elections of 1994 saw the Republicans win an unprecedented number of seats in the House of Representatives, returning to the majority after 40 years in the wilderness. Whodunit? Was it national electoral tides, changing demographics, President Bill Clinton's unpopularity, campaign finance laws that disproportionately favored the Republicans, or any of the number of other variables that are discussed in the present volume?

Any or all of these factors may have contributed to the Republicans' victory, but in this paper we argue that the creation of so-called majority-minority districts also had a large impact on congressional elections. While it is undoubtedly true that concentrated minority districts have served to increase the number of minorities holding public office, it is equally true that they have changed the complexion of electoral competition, particularly in the South, and that these changes have ultimately undermined some of the substantive policy advances obtained by minority constituents during the past three decades.

The logic of the argument is as follows: The concentration of minorities into a few districts has created safe seats for minority candidates, where incumbents win by large majorities. But the aggregate effect of these districting schemes has been to dilute the influence of minorities in surrounding areas, leading to the election of representatives with few ties to the minority community and its interests. The result has been an increasingly polarized national legislature and a hollowing out of the moderate bipartisan coalition

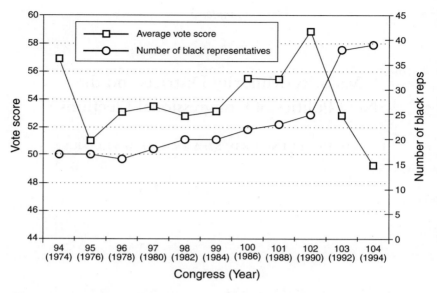

Figure 5.1. Number of black legislators and substantive representation, 1974–1994.

that formed the basis for the advancement of minority concerns in the 1960s and 1970s.

Consider, for example, Figure 5.1. The x-axis identifies the Congress, beginning with the 94th (1975–76) and continuing to the 104th (1995–96). The right-hand axis represents the number of African Americans holding office in the House of Representatives, and the left-hand axis represents the average number of times that all members voted with the majority of the black caucus on *Congressional Quarterly* key votes.[1] What is most apparent from the picture is that after the 1990s reapportionment, the number of minority representatives jumped 62 percent, from 24 in the 101st Congress to 39 in the 104th. At the same time, however, the average vote score supporting minority concerns plummeted nearly 20 percent, from a peak of close to 59 in the 101st Congress to a low of 49 in the 104th, following the 1990s reapportionment. These data suggest that there may now be a tradeoff between the number of minorities elected to office and the substantive representation of minority interests. Of course, minority districting is not the only factor contributing to these trends. But given current voting patterns, these districts may hinder rather than promote the substantive representation of minority interests.

To make our argument, we will first briefly review the logic behind the creation of concentrated minority voting districts. We will then analyze the impact of these districts on elections, focusing on partisan trends, the safeness of seats for incumbents, and the number of contested elections. We then focus on a crucial but oft-neglected aspect of majority-minority districts: their impact on the substantive representation of minority interests, which is affected both by who is now being elected to office and the voting patterns of these representatives once in office. We conclude with a summary of our findings.

Constituency and Representation

In plurality winner elections, what influence will politically cohesive minorities have over the actions of their representative and what types of electoral systems or districting schemes will assure minorities the greatest possible degree of substantive representation? In general, the answers to these questions depend on the overall distribution of preferences in the given polity. Consider the situation depicted in the top half of Figure 5.2, for instance, where the darkened circles represent voters from the majority group, the triangles represent the minority, and there are two salient issues to be decided, A and B.

Here we assume (1) that policy is enacted by simple majority rule, (2) that majority and minority voters have different preferences over the direction of public policy, and (3) that the majority and minority vote as a bloc. As shown in Figure 5.2, preferences are polarized with one group commanding a clear majority. Hence the enacting coalition will likely be composed only of members from the majority community, and the resulting policies will lie within the sphere of the majority's preferences. Minorities in this scenario will have only a tenuous relation with their representative and will have little or no impact on policy outcomes.

On the other hand, consider what happens if we relax condition (3) above, so that the majority is itself divided; minorities may then have a good deal of influence over outcomes. This possibility is illustrated in the bottom half of Figure 5.2, where the majority finds itself split over issue B. Some coalition must be formed to create a legislative majority, and if the split within the majority is large enough minority voters will become attractive coalition partners for each of the majority factions, who will bid for the sup-

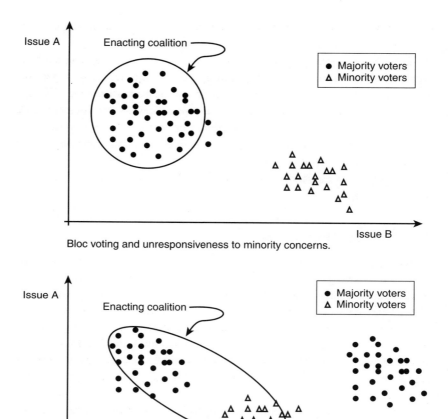

Figure 5.2. Alternative scenarios for the role of minorities in enacting legislation.

port of the minorities. In these circumstances the enacting coalition may look something like the oval indicated in the figure, with one of the majority factions and the minority group trading off policy concerns across the two dimensions.

These two figures depict the position of blacks in American politics at different places and times. The bloc voting scenario in the top half of Figure 5.2 corresponds to the situation of most blacks in local southern politics since Reconstruction, where the white majority consistently opposed blacks on issues of public policy. The bottom half of Figure 5.2 illustrates the position of blacks as key swing voters in national politics from the late 1950s to the mid-1960s, the era in which Democrats and Republicans vied for the black vote and vast strides were made in social issues such as civil rights, housing, and busing that were important to minorities.

Note that each of these two possibilities implies a distinct strategy for minority districting to maximize substantive representation. Under bloc voting, the creation of majority-minority districts is a necessary precursor to minorities having any substantive representation at all. When majorities and minorities vote cohesively, that is, the latter will be unable to influence their representative's behavior if their votes are submerged in a sea of unsympathetic majority voters. Therefore only by concentrating minorities in a few districts so that they can elect some representatives of their choice can these voters hope to have some impact on public policy.[2] Here, descriptive representation—electing members from the minority community to office—and substantive representation—producing policy outcomes favored by minority voters—go hand in hand.

One objection might be raised to this line of argumentation; namely, that if minorities are elected to a legislature but still form a minority within that legislature, then they will be consistently outvoted by the majority's representatives. Thus it is not clear that majority-minority districts alone can assure minorities of favorable outcomes in all cases.[3] Indeed, if majorities and minorities are unalterably opposed to each other on all issues, then no democratic electoral scheme will be able to protect minorities from losing every time, and one must look to the courts to protect minority interests in such circumstances. On the other hand, if the majority itself is divided on some issues, then the majority factions may wish to bargain with minority representatives, thus giving minorities some leverage to trade for substantive policy gains. This is, of course, a restatement of James Madison's argument in *Federalist 10* that large, diverse republics provide the best defense against the tyranny of the majority.

If the majority is divided on many issues, then we arrive at the swing voter situation in the bottom half of Figure 5.2. Here, minorities may be able to wield influence in many districts by assuming the role of kingmakers, playing the majority factions off against each other. Policy gains in this situation are best secured by dividing minority voters equally across districts; in fact, creating concentrated minority districts under these conditions would actually reduce substantive minority representation by removing these voters from surrounding districts, even though it would result in the election of more minorities to the legislature. One would then have a tradeoff between descriptive and substantive representation; past a certain point, increasing one comes at the cost of the other.

The general point to keep in mind from the analysis of these two canonical examples is that the presence of a minority population with cohesive preferences different from the majority does *not* necessarily imply a unique districting strategy to secure substantive minority representation. In some cases concentrated minority districts may best serve the minority's policy goals; other times, they may be second best to a strategy of spreading minority voters more evenly across districts. The correct answer depends on the voting patterns of the majority; consequently, districting patterns should change as majority voting patterns change over time. The remainder of this essay examines these trends across the past three decades.

Majority-Minority Districts and Descriptive Representation

Majority-minority districts have combined with national partisan trends to dramatically change the political landscape, particularly in the South. As noted by Charles Bullock and Gary Jacobson elsewhere in this volume, one of the biggest stories in American politics over the past quarter century has been the conversion of conservative southern Democrats to the Republican party. In 1945, the Democrats comprised 95 percent of the total representatives from the South; by 1994, Democrats represented less than 40 percent of southern House seats. Thus, while Democrats have lost strength in all regions of the country, it is especially noticeable that in the formerly "Solid South" the percent of Democratic representatives is now less than it is in the country as a whole.

At the same time, due mainly to the creation of majority-minority districts, blacks have been getting elected to the House in record numbers. As the number of districts with majority black voting age populations rose from 8 in the 1970s to 15 in the 1980s and 26 after the 1990s redistricting, the number of black representatives in the House soared to a historic high of 39 in the 104th Congress, of whom all except two were Democrats. This phenomenon was not confined to Congress; all over the South, blacks were winning office at the state and local level as well, and these gains have come almost completely from changes in voting systems brought about by vigorous enforcement of the VRA.[4]

Electorally, majority-minority districts are distinguished by having a high

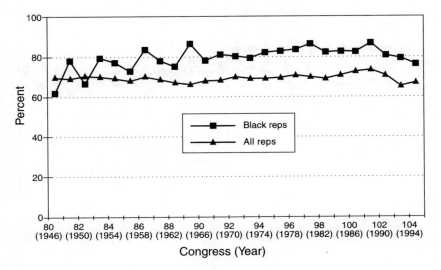

Figure 5.3. Winners' percent of two-party vote, 1946–1994.

proportion of safe seats, or districts where a candidate wins by a large majority. Figure 5.3 shows that, while minority representatives started off about even with all others in earlier Congresses, they now win by a margin of about 10 to 15 percentage points higher than the average margin of victory. In 1994 contested elections, the average candidate from all districts wins with 64.1 percent of the popular vote, while the average candidate from a majority-minority district wins on average with 78.1 percent of the vote. Furthermore, although black representatives have gained seats formerly held by whites, no black representative has lost a seat to a nonminority since the enactment of the VRA.

On the other hand, Figure 5.4 shows that while candidates in majority-minority districts win by large margins (and perhaps because of these margins), they do not run uncontested. In fact, throughout the 1950s and 1960s some of the fiercest electoral competition was for the representation of concentrated minority districts, with minority incumbents facing more contested elections, on average, than other candidates. By the 1990s, however, minorities faced challengers at nearly equal rates as all other candidates. Combining Figures 5.3 and 5.4, it seems that while black candidates face the same percent of contested elections, they win by bigger margins, and overall this has led to safer seats for incumbents from majority-minority districts.

One factor contributing to the rising number of blacks in Congress has

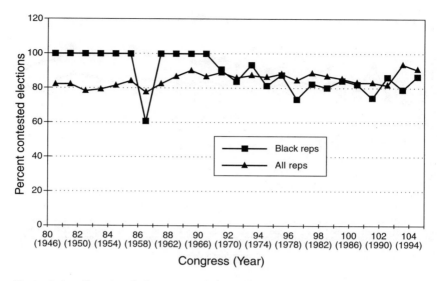

Figure 5.4.   Contested elections, 1946–1994.

been the slow but sure disappearance of majority black districts represented by nonminorities. Whereas at one time liberal white Democrats such as Wyche Fowler in Georgia, Lindy Boggs in Louisiana, and Peter Rodino in New Jersey could still win office from minority black districts, now Tom Foglietta in the Pennsylvania First is the only white elected from such a district.[5] Jumping ahead a bit, Foglietta has also continued to maintain a liberal voting record while in office; he has consistently voted with a majority of black representatives upwards of 90 percent of the time.

The overall result of these trends has been an increase of black strength in the Democratic party, both in numbers and in terms of seniority. Figure 5.5 shows that where blacks once found it impossible to vote at all in the South, black representatives in 1996 comprised close to 30 percent of all southern Democrats and about 16 percent of the total Democratic contingency in the House. At the same time, as shown in Figure 5.6, the average years of seniority of black representatives is virtually identical to that of the chamber overall and the Democratic party despite blacks' relatively recent entrance to the House.[6]

It is clear that the creation of majority-minority districts has been an important factor in dramatically raising the number of black representatives in Congress. And in fact, this phenomenon has been repeated throughout the southern states at all levels of political officeholding; the rise in the number

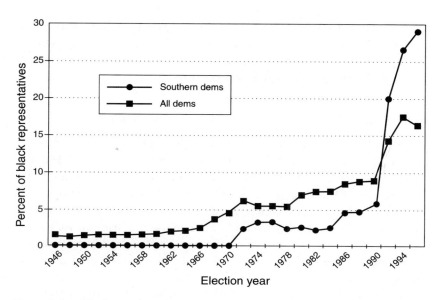

Figure 5.5. Blacks as a percent of all Democrats and southern Democrats, 1946–1996.

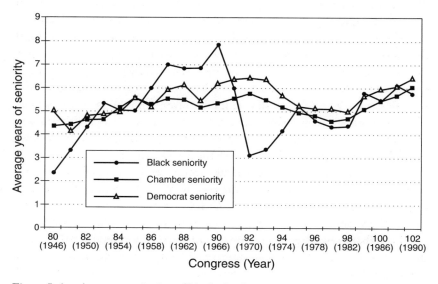

Figure 5.6. Average seniority of blacks in Congress, 1946–1990.

of minorities elected to office is due almost entirely to changes wrought by the VRA. What is less clear is the impact of these districts on the substantive representation of minority interests; this is the other side of the coin to racial gerrymandering, to which we now turn.

Majority-Minority Districts and Substantive Representation

To estimate substantive representation we follow a two-step procedure developed in Cameron et al. (1996) and extended in Epstein and O'Halloran (1999). First, we determine the probability of electing a Republican, Democrat, or black Democrat, given the percent of black voting age population in a district. We call these *electoral equations*. Second, given the type of representative elected, we ask what his or her likely voting patterns are once in Congress; these are the *representation equations*. Finally, combining these two figures, we are able to determine the configuration of districts that leads to the highest chance of enacting legislation favorable to minority concerns. Because we are interested in the evolution of majority-minority districts and their impact on elections and policy outcomes over time, we perform our analysis separately for the elections of 1974, 1984, and 1994; that is, the 94th, 99th, and 104th Congresses.

DATA

Table 5.1 provides a description of the data used in the analysis. Legislators' support for minority issues is measured by the variable vote score, which is the percentage of times that a member voted with the majority of the black caucus on *Congressional Quarterly* key votes for each Congress. In constructing this measure, we identified the position adopted by the majority of black representatives on each key vote and coded whether or not a member voted with this majority.[7] So for instance, if on a given vote the majority of black representatives voted aye, then any member voting aye would receive a vote score of 1 for that roll call, and all those voting nay would get a 0. We then averaged these vote scores by member for each Congress.

As shown in Table 5.1, the average vote score has declined over time, from 56.53 percent in the 94th Congress, to 52.55 percent in the 99th, to 49.10 percent in the 104th. The standard deviation increased from the 94th to the 99th Congresses, but then declined again in the 104th. One might expect both that the average vote score would decline more in the 104th, given that it was the only Republican-controlled Congress of the three, and that the standard deviation, which is a convenient measure of polarization, would increase even further.

Table 5.1
Summary Statistics

| Variable | CONGRESS | | | | | |
| | 94TH | | 99TH | | 104TH | |
	Mean	*Std. Dev.*	*Mean*	*Std. Dev.*	*Mean*	*Std. Dev.*
Vote Score[a] (%)	56.53	29.84	52.55	33.24	49.10	27.92
BVAP[b] (%)	9.20	12.76	10.30	13.87	10.50	15.22
Party[c]	0.67	0.47	0.58	0.49	0.47	0.50
Race[d]	0.04	0.19	0.04	0.20	0.08	0.28
Covered[e]	0.24	0.43	0.21	0.41	0.29	0.45
South[f]	0.28	0.45	0.30	0.46	0.31	0.47
East[g]	0.27	0.44	0.25	0.43	0.23	0.42

SOURCES: Bott (1991) and various years of Barone and Ujifusa and the *Congressional Quarterly Almanac*.

[a] Support for *Congressional Quarterly* key votes in which over 60 percent of black representatives voted alike.

[b] Percent of black voting age population in district.

[c] One for Democrats; 0 for Republicans.

[d] Race of member: 1 for black; 0 otherwise.

[e] One if district covered under section 5 of VRA; 0 otherwise.

[f] Southern states are Alabama, Arkansas, Florida, Georgia, Kentucky, Louisiana, Mississippi, North Carolina, Oklahoma, South Carolina, Tennessee, Texas, and Virginia. Coded 1 for southern states; otherwise 0.

[g] Eastern states are Connecticut, Delaware, Maine, Maryland, Massachusetts, New Hampshire, New Jersey, New York, Pennsylvania, Rhode Island, Vermont, and West Virginia. Coded 1 for eastern states; otherwise 0.

The explanation for both these facts lies in the distribution of the votes used by *Congressional Quarterly* in its key vote index. As it turned out, the 32 key votes for the 104th Congress included 5 votes in which fewer than 50 members voted against the given bill, as compared with 1 in the 94th Congress and 0 in the 99th. These nearly unanimous votes tend both to inflate average vote scores and compress their variance. If one uses another measure of overall support—the median vote score—then the pattern is more pronounced; the median fell precipitously from 64.0 percent in the 94th, to 53.5 percent in the 99th, to 37.0 percent in the 104th.

The distribution of vote scores by Congress is illustrated in Figure 5.7, which shows a noticeable spike in vote scores of around 0.2 in the 104th

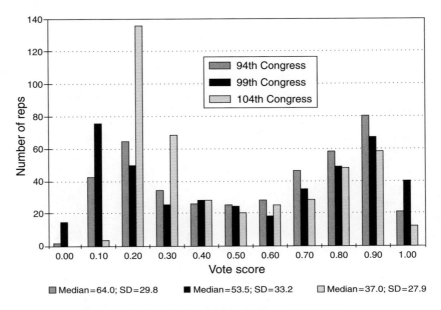

Figure 5.7.   Vote score distribution, 94th, 99th, and 104th Congresses.

Congress; this is again an artifact of the number of nearly unanimous votes included in the key vote index that year. Figure 5.7 also shows the increase in polarization from the 94th to the 99th Congresses quite clearly, especially at the lower end of the scale. Because biracial coalitions are usually necessary to pass legislation important to minority voters, this increase in polarization should be counted as a potential negative by-product of the increase in the number of majority-minority districts.

The key independent variable in the analysis is black voting age population (BVAP) in each district as a proportion of total population. We also record each representative's region: South, East, and other. A number of studies have tried to capture additional subregional distinctions by including a Deep South variable in their analyses. A better proxy for historic discrimination against minorities is to control for coverage under the preclearance procedures of the VRA, as amended.[8] The variable labeled "covered" codes which districts are subject to judicial oversight of any changes to electoral systems or reapportionment plans. In our sample, on average 24.67 percent of all districts are covered, including 65.37 percent of all southern districts. Finally, we have recorded the race and partisan affiliation of each member.

Our overall strategy is to analyze patterns of descriptive and substantive representation according to the formula:

$$E(VS \mid BVAP) = \Sigma_{\Theta} E(VS \mid BVAP, \Theta) \cdot P(\Theta \mid BVAP)$$

Here, VS refers to vote score, so the formula indicates that a representative's expected vote score given the percent of black voting age population in her district is composed of two factors: (1) the expected vote score given BVAP and the representative's type Θ (where this can be Republican, nonblack Democrat, or black Democrat); and (2) the probability that each type is elected to office given the percent BVAP in her district. Thus we must first estimate two classes of relations corresponding to the representation and electoral equations, respectively. The next two subsections perform these estimations, followed by an overall analysis of substantive representation in the three Congresses studied.

WHO DO YOU ELECT?

We began by determining, for any given region and level of BVAP, what type of representative is likely to be elected. For this purpose, we partitioned our sample of representatives into six subgroups:

1. noneastern Republicans
2. eastern Republicans
3. nonblack Democrats from covered southern districts
4. nonblack Democrats from noncovered southern districts
5. nonsouthern nonblack Democrats
6. black Democrats

For each Congress and region, then, we determined the probability of electing a Republican, nonblack Democrat, or black Democrat, which we refer to as a type 1, 2, or 3 representative, respectively. We estimated the electoral equations using a multinomial logit functional form.[9] The resulting equations are shown in Table 5.2. As indicated, type 2 representatives were the baseline category for the 94th and 99th Congresses, while type 1 representatives were the baseline in the estimations for the 104th Congress.

The results reported in Table 5.2 are summarized graphically in Figure 5.8, which shows the estimated probabilities of election by type and region for all three Congresses. The three curves in each diagram show the probability that each type of representative is elected as a function of BVAP in her district. As such, the three curves sum to one at every point, and the slope of the curve indicates the change in the probability that each type is elected as BVAP changes.

Note that for the 94th and 99th Congresses, the slopes are relatively low, implying that the probability of electing any given type did not change

Table 5.2

Electoral Equations: Estimates of the Relation Between District
Characteristics and Type of Representative Elected

	CONGRESS					
	94TH		99TH		104TH	
	Type 1	*Type 3*	*Type 1*	*Type 3*	*Type 2*	*Type 3*
BVAP[a]	−2.569	13.019	−6.7	21.7	8.213	105.163
	(1.643)	(2.453)	(0.017)	(0.048)	(2.065)	(57.608)
BVAP East	−5.832	−2.424	−4.0	−11.0	0.161	−38.086
	(3.702)	(2.462)	(0.035)	(0.040)	(3.367)	(24.414)
South	−0.465	−1.258	0.193	−6.207	−0.699	−11.812
	(0.316)	(0.844)	(0.297)	(2.037)	(0.290)	(9.652)
Constant	−0.270	−5.219	0.258	−5.657	−0.636	−28.559
	(0.137)	(0.792)	(0.143)	(0.945)	(0.149)	(16.173)
$\chi^2(6)$	92.670		146.950		265.510	
Log likelihood	−291.815		−289.683		−263.302	
Pseudo R^2	0.137		0.202		0.335	

NOTE: *T*-statistics in parentheses.

[a]See Table 5.1 for explanation of variables and coding.

precipitously with changes in BVAP. This is partially due to the fact that for
these years some districts with concentrated black populations were still represented by nonblack Democrats, and even Republicans in some cases. But
in the 104th Congress these slopes increased dramatically, given the fact that
almost all concentrated minority districts have minority representatives. At
this point, the lines appear to be almost step functions; they go from zero to
one in a relatively short window of percent black voting age population.

ESTIMATING EQUAL OPPORTUNITY AND PARTISAN EFFECTS

Also shown in the figure are the estimated percentages that would be necessary to have a 50 percent chance of electing a minority to office; this is
known in the legal literature as the "point of equal opportunity." Until the
104th Congress, these percentages generally stood at around 50 percent
BVAP. But by the elections of 1994, the point of equal opportunity had declined significantly, even in the South. This, then, is our first indication of
how general voting patterns have changed over time; it is now easier for minority candidates to win office than it was during the previous two decades.

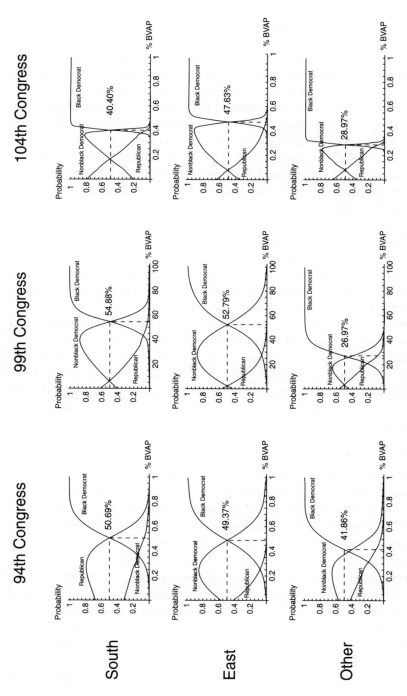

Figure 5.8. Electoral equations and point of equal opportunity, 94th, 99th, and 104th Congresses.

In other words, racially polarized voting among whites has decreased, indicating that policy divisions among majority voters are beginning to weigh more heavily than the previous desire to vote against any minority candidate.

Along similar lines, we can ask what the opportunity cost is of creating majority-minority districts in terms of overall partisan divisions in Congress. To answer this question, we examined the slope of the southern Republican election probability curve at the point of average BVAP for the region in each of the three Congresses. For the 94th Congress, this slope was about 0.5 percent, meaning that every one point increase in BVAP above the regional average also augmented the probability of electing an extra Republican by 0.5 percent. In the 99th Congress, this figure jumped to 1.5 percent, and in the 104th Congress it was just over 2.0 percent.

From this we draw two conclusions. First, as discussed below, the trade-off between descriptive and substantive representation was sharpening over time; increasing the probability of electing a minority representative in one district meant trading off more and more Republicans elected in other districts. Throughout this period the Republican vote scores were significantly lower than any Democrat's, black or nonblack.

Second, the racial gerrymandering of districts has had greater and greater effect on the overall partisan composition of Congress. Removing minority voters from districts represented by Democrats makes it more likely that these representatives will lose office if an anti-Democratic electoral tide arises. Thus the increase in the number of majority-minority districts has left the electoral position of the remaining nonblack Democrats more fragile, more susceptible to shifts in national electoral tides.

HOW DO THEY VOTE?

Our next task is to estimate the expected voting patterns of elected representatives, given their type and BVAP in their districts. Summary statistics for each of the six subgroups by Congress are provided in Table 5.3, which shows two interesting patterns that have developed over time. First, the gap between Republicans and Democrats, represented by the difference between groups 2 and 3, has increased. In the 94th Congress the voting patterns of eastern Republicans and nonblack southern Democrats were nearly identical, but these patterns diverge in subsequent Congresses. Thus the party of the representative elected, always an important factor in minority representation, has become even more important in the last two decades.

Second, the gaps among Democrats—groups 3, 4, and 5—have also narrowed over time. The total gap between the average vote score for groups 3 and 5 has gone from roughly 40 points in the 1970s, to 30 points in

Table 5.3

Mean and Median Vote Score by Group

	CONGRESS								
	94TH			99TH			104TH		
Group	Mean vote score (%)	Average BVAP[a] (%)	N	Mean vote score (%)	Average BVAP (%)	N	Mean vote score (%)	Average BVAP (%)	N
1. Non-Eastern Republicans[b]	20.93	6.15	106	15.55	6.09	139	24.17	5.29	185
2. Eastern Republicans	40.97	3.60	38	36.00	4.16	43	34.98	5.01	45
3. Nonblack Democrats from covered Southern districts	42.76	18.02	62	52.33	20.55	47	53.78	13.55	36
4. Nonblack Democrats from noncovered Southern districts	56.78	11.81	27	60.06	13.94	33	61.09	11.18	11
5. Non-Southern nonblack Democrats	81.30	5.52	186	84.21	6.71	154	77.57	6.41	122
6. Black Democrats	93.69	46.86	16	91.58	52.42	19	90.06	54.72	36
Overall mean	56.53	9.200	435	52.55	10.300	435	49.10	10.500	435
Overall median	64.0	4.0		53.50	5.0		37.00	4.0	

[a] BVAP = black voting age population.

[b] See Table 5.1 for explanation of variables and coding.

Table 5.4

Representation Equations: Estimates of the Relation Between Type of Representative Elected and Voting Scores

| | CONGRESS | | | | | | | | |
| | 94TH | | | 99TH | | | 104TH | | |
Group	Constant	$BVAP^a$	N	Constant	BVAP	N	Constant	BVAP	N
1. Non-Eastern Republicans[b]	0.21 (0.01)	-0.25 (0.11)	105	0.14 (0.01)	-0.03 (0.10)	139	0.24 (0.01)	-0.09 (0.66)	185
2. Eastern Republicans	0.40 (0.05)	0.09 (0.93)	38	0.34 (0.05)	0.30 (0.80)	43	0.31 (0.27)	0.53 (0.41)	45
3. Nonblack Democrats from covered Southern districts	0.44 (0.05)	-0.10 (0.27)	62	0.52 (0.06)	4×10^{-5} (0.24)	46	0.62 (0.06)	-0.58 (0.34)	36
4. Nonblack Democrats from noncovered Southern districts	0.61 (0.78)	-0.32 (0.58)	27	0.57 (0.07)	0.30 (0.40)	33	0.65 (0.10)	-0.31 (0.81)	11
5. Non-Southern nonblack Democrats	0.82 (0.001)	0.19 (0.10)	185	0.84 (0.013)	0.20 (0.12)	154	0.79 (0.01)	0.19 (0.14)	122
6. Black Democrats	0.94 (0.30)	-0.01 (0.06)	16	0.92 (0.03)	-0.01 (0.05)	19	0.89 (0.06)	0.02 (0.11)	36

NOTE: T = statistics in parentheses.

$^a BVAP$ = black voting age population.

^{b} See Table 5.1 for explanation of variables and coding.

the 1980s, to 20 points in 1996. This convergence again indicates that factors previously significant in estimating a representative's expected voting behavior regarding minority-supported issues have faded in importance in recent years.

Given these patterns and trends in the data, we estimated the representation equations using general additive models, thus allowing for the possibility of a nonlinear relation between BVAP and vote score. These models were then tested against more parsimonious linear models to determine whether nonlinear functional forms performed significantly better than linear specifications. In all groups these tests were negative; thus we employed robust ordinary least squares (OLS) estimation for each subgroup in each succeeding Congress. The results of these estimations are provided in Table 5.4.

As indicated, the constants followed the same general pattern as the means in Table 5.3; as one moves from group 1 to 6, baseline representation scores increase. Note also that, as expected, the impact of BVAP on vote scores was positive in most cases; it was negative and significant only in group 1 (noneastern Republicans) in the 94th Congress. On the other hand, given the range of BVAP for each group, the largest impact on substantive representation came not from adding minority voters to a given type of representative's district (most of the slope coefficients in the table are not statistically significant), but from electing a different type of representative in the first place. In short, electoral effects—who you elect—usually dominate representation effects—how they vote.

WHAT IS THE BEST DISTRICTING PLAN?

We now come to the main point of the analysis: the changing impact of majority-minority districts on substantive representation. First, combining the electoral equations estimated in Table 5.2 and the representation equations from Table 5.4 we can estimate the overall expected vote score for a representative in each region as a function of the percent BVAP in her district. Using this information, we can calculate two key statistics: the point of diminishing returns to minority districting and the point of optimal gerrymandering. Together, these statistics allow us to identify the districting strategy in each Congress and region that maximizes average expected vote score.

The expected vote scores by Congress and region are illustrated in Figure 5.9. For the South, the upper and lower lines represent noncovered and covered districts, respectively, in each Congress. Note that for all graphs, the representation function generally rises with the percent BVAP in a district, as would be expected. But the relation sometimes rises more quickly in

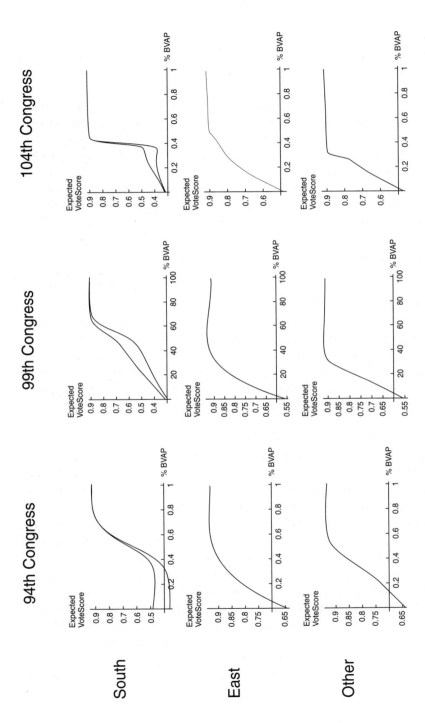

Figure 5.9. Expected vote score by Congress and region, 94th, 99th, and 104th Congresses.

some regions than in others, and it is these features that we will exploit when evaluating the effect of different districting strategies.

A visual inspection of the graphs shows clearly that the patterns in the South differ significantly from other regions. The graphs for the South in general rise slowly at first, then increase rapidly over a relatively small region, then level off again. In other regions we observe a general rise and then a tapering off. When devising a districting strategy for a state, the key point is that concentrating minority voters in a few districts will necessarily remove these voters from surrounding districts. This is the basic tradeoff of districting; assuring minority voters of more responsive legislators in some districts might come at the cost of less responsive legislators elsewhere.

The question then becomes this: What division of minority voters across districts yields the highest average expected vote score? The answer comes from examining the first derivative of the expected vote score equation; that is, the expected gain in substantive representation from adding one more minority voter to a given district. If such a switch could increase total substantive representation, then a given districting scheme would not be optimal. Therefore, optimal strategies have equal marginal returns to adding an additional minority voter to any given district.

These calculations can be summarized by two key quantities: the point of diminishing returns and the point of optimal gerrymandering. The former, represented by the percent BVAP at which the first derivative is maximized, indicates the point at which the impact of adding more minority voters begins to decline. Letting $E(VS \mid BVAP)$ be the expected vote score at any given level of black voting age population, the latter is calculated as the value of BVAP at which $E(VS \mid BVAP)' = E(VS \mid 0)'$. This denotes the point at which adding an additional minority voter to an already concentrated minority district just balances the impact of adding an additional minority voter to a district with no minority voters at all. Past the point of optimal gerrymandering, concentrating minority voters more heavily does more harm than good in terms of overall substantive representation of minority interests.

Three general possibilities exist for the results of this exercise. First, the marginal impact of minority voters may decline throughout the relevant range, implying that the more such voters are concentrated in a district, the lower the marginal impact of the last voter added. This would correspond to the swing voter situation in the second part of Figure 5.2. Here, both the point of diminishing returns and optimal gerrymandering are equal to zero, and the optimal scheme is simply to equalize minority voting populations across districts.

Second, the marginal impact may rise across the entire range, or it may

Table 5.5

Percent of District BVAP Need Optimal Gerrymanders
by Region and Congress

	CONGRESS					
	94TH		99TH		104TH	
Region	*PDR^a*	*POG^b*	*PDR*	*POG*	*PDR*	*POG*
South covered^c	50.73%	100%	54.57%	66.48%	40.42%	45.72%
South uncovered	51.46	100	53.2	61.38	40.40	45.15
East	0	*BVAP^d*	0	*BVAP*	0	*BVAP*
Other	37.14	52.37	21.44	27.61	28.73	31.43

^{a}PDR = point of diminishing returns for vote score by adding additional minorities to a district.

^{b}POG = point of optimal gerrymander.

^{c}See Table 5.1 for explanation of variables and coding.

^{d}BVAP = average black voting age population within a state.

decline but still stop short of the marginal returns to the first voter in the district, as in the bloc voting situation in the first part of Figure 5.2. Here, either the point of diminishing returns or the point of optimal gerrymandering would be 100 percent or greater. Under these circumstances, districting strategies should concentrate minority voters as much as logistically possible given current residential patterns.

Third, an intermediate case may be obtained, where the point of optimal gerrymandering lies somewhere in between 0 and 100 percent. This might occur under a combination of both parts of Figures 5.2, in which the majority votes cohesively on some issues but not on others. Some concentration of minority voters is optimal here, even if it means splitting these voters unequally across districts, but there is still a point past which concentrating minority voters loses more support than it gains.

The results of these calculations, divided by Congress and region, are shown in Table 5.5. Beginning in the eastern states, the patterns of election and representation are such that the marginal impact of adding minority voters declines the higher the level of BVAP. Here, then, equal districting strategies were optimal in all three Congresses. For states outside the East and South, an intermediate strategy was optimal. In the 1970s, optimal gerrymandering implied the creation of districts with a little more than 50 percent BVAP, but this figure fell to about 30 percent in the 1980s and 1990s.

Finally, the South shows the most dramatic change of all three regions. In the 1970s, there were essentially no diminishing returns to concentrating minority voters ever more heavily. The increased responsiveness of minority representatives, combined with the low probability of electing a Republican, spoke heavily in favor of creating majority-minority voting districts. In the 1980s, this picture changed a little, but the point of optimal gerrymandering remained rather high: about 61 percent in uncovered districts and 66 percent in covered jurisdictions. Interestingly enough, then, even though the informal 65 percent rule enforced by the courts was higher than necessary to ensure minorities equal opportunity during this period (Figure 5.8 shows it to be about 55 percent), it was roughly correct as a rule of thumb to maximize substantive minority representation.

During the 1990s the electoral landscape has changed once again to the point that optimal gerrymandering has fallen to about 45 percent. This is clearly due to the increased probability of electing Republicans in southern congressional elections, as well as the increased ability of minorities to gain office outside of strictly majority-minority districts. So the marginal gains in substantive representation that derive from virtually assuring that a minority will win in one district are more than offset by the increased probability of electing a racially conservative representative elsewhere.

Conclusion

The analysis presented in this paper points toward two conclusions regarding the impact of majority-minority districts on modern congressional elections. First, these districts have done much to increase the descriptive representation of minorities in Congress over the past quarter century. Most minority representatives have been elected from concentrated minority districts, and this has helped secure them a significant place within national politics in general, and the Democratic party in particular.

Second, our analysis of trends in substantive representation over the past 30 years implies that the patterns displayed in Figure 5.1 are not accidental. Over time, there has developed a fundamental tradeoff between descriptive and substantive representation, especially in the South. Specifically, the logic of electoral and representation patterns during the 1970s and 1980s was such that concentrated minority districts were the most effective route to both substantive and descriptive representation. But the decrease in polarized voting in the 1990s, coupled with the increased probability of electing Republicans in southern districts, dictate that less concentrated minority districts will be optimal in the next round of decennial redistrictings.

Chapter 6

Public Disapproval of Congress Can Be Dangerous to Majority Party Candidates: The Case of 1994

JOHN R. HIBBING AND ERIC TIRITILLI

Though it may be somewhat more stridently expressed than before, Americans' general level of dissatisfaction with Congress in the 1990s is nothing new. True, we cannot speak with certainty regarding the period prior to 1940 and the advent of modern survey techniques and, true, even since 1940 there have been occasions when people were not totally displeased with "the first branch,"[1] but indications are that Congress has rarely been the object of warm public feelings and, when it has, these feelings have not lasted long. Perhaps because of the persistence of negative feelings, it has been assumed by most analysts that displeasure with Congress has not had overtones for the electoral prospects of individual members or parties. If dissatisfaction has been rampant for most of the postwar period, how could it explain variations in outcome from year to year? And at the individual level, if in any given election year most people do not approve of Congress, this limited variance will reduce the ability of disapproval to generate any kind of relationship with vote choice. Moreover, Fenno's (1975) observation that even though people may view Congress as the "broken" branch they still tend to "love" their own member of Congress has been taken to heart by most students of politics. It is widely assumed that the public is quite skilled at separating its reactions to Congress from its votes on individual members of Congress (but see Born 1990).

Our operating hypothesis in this paper is that there are times and situations in which public disapproval *can* have an important influence on elec-

110

tion outcomes. Further, we believe that 1994, for reasons we will specify, was one of those probably rare instances in which disapproval and election results were related. By detailing the features of 1994 that seem to have set it apart from other election years and by comparing 1994 to other recent congressional elections to see if public disapproval of Congress did act as we predict, we hope to help account for the unique and momentous outcome in 1994 but, more broadly, we also hope to specify the manner in which voters tend to assign blame or credit for the perceived performance of the institution of Congress.

Previous research has not been particularly probing on this point and this is unfortunate in light of the extent to which public disapprobation of Congress and government is such a salient component of the public mood in the 1990s. When scholars *have* looked for a connection between public approval of Congress and congressional vote choice, the most common expectation has been that disapproval would work to the detriment of all incumbent candidates (see Boucher and Cover 1996; and Luttbeg and Gant 1995). After all, if Congress has gone amuck, who better to blame than those people who were in Congress when it was judged to be performing inadequately? But results from tests of the hypothesis that institutional disapproval will harm the electoral prospects of all incumbents have been disappointing (see especially Boucher and Cover 1996) and we believe the reason is that voters do not necessarily blame all incumbents. Rather, there are situations in which only incumbents of the majority party will be held responsible for a poorly performing Congress. After all, if the majority party is perceived to be calling all the shots, why should members of the minority party—even incumbents—be punished at the polls? These minority party members might be as critical of congressional operations as the voters themselves and as eager to change the way Congress has been functioning.

We do not believe that majority party members are always blamed for the perceived institutional shortcomings; but we do believe that in certain circumstances they will be, and in this our hypothesis of party-defined culpability is quite different than that of incumbent-defined culpability. There is no reason to think a lowly member of an oppressed minority party will be held just as accountable for perceived congressional failings as a high-flying member of the majority. On the other hand, there is no reason to think such differentiation across parties will always occur. Rather, certain circumstances need to be present; we believe they were present in 1994 and that this is part of the reason for the astounding and unexpected loss of 52 seats by the erstwhile majority party, the Democrats.

Does the Public Know Which Party Has the Majority in the House?

Is there evidence to support our theory that 1994 was unusual in the degree to which members of the majority party were held responsible for a Congress alleged by most of the citizenry to be doing badly? Our logic makes a number of demands on voters. First, it is necessary for them to be aware of which party controlled Congress. This may seem easy enough but, of course, most people do not follow such matters closely. Many are unaware of which party is the majority in each house of Congress. This is particularly true when the country is experiencing divided partisan control of the executive and legislative branches (as has been common in the postwar period) and it is even more particularly true when there is divided partisan control of the two houses of Congress (as was the case briefly in the 1950s and from 1981 to 1987). People are most likely to know which party controls the houses of Congress when there is unified government; they are less likely to know which party controls the houses of Congress when the president is of one party and the congressional majority is of the other party; and they are even less likely still to know which party controls the houses of Congress when one party controls the House and the other party controls the Senate. This pattern is demonstrated in Figure 6.1, which focuses, as we do throughout this paper, on the House of Representatives and not the Senate.

Whether or not people desire party balancing in government (Fiorina 1996), they are confused by it. In illustrating this point, we first restrict our attention to midterm elections, since the nature and knowledge level of the electorate tends to be somewhat different in midterm and on-year elections (see A. Campbell 1960; J. E. Campbell 1997). In 1982 and 1986, when the Republicans controlled the Senate and the Democrats the House, people had a difficult time correctly identifying the majority party in the House going into the election. Less than one-third of all respondents were able to do this in those two years. Respondents did a little better when the houses of Congress were controlled by the same party *but* that party was not the same as the party of the president. This was the case in 1990 with President George Bush and a Democratic Congress, when the percent correctly identifying the majority party in Congress went up from one-third to nearly one-half.[2] But the public does by far the best when one party controls House, Senate, and presidency, as was the case in 1978 and 1994.

The point we wish to stress, however, is that, even given its status as a unified government election, 1994 stands out. It is far and away the election year in which people were the most aware of the majority party in the House. Practically three out of four adults were able to state in 1994 that the Dem-

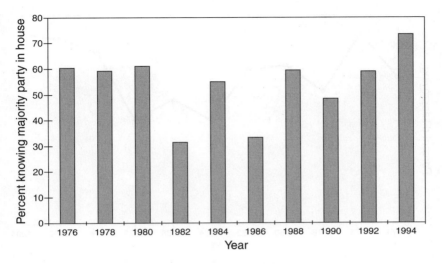

Figure 6.1. Knowledge of majority party in House, 1976–1994.
SOURCE: NES 1976–94.

ocrats had been the majority party in Congress coming into the election, nearly 13 points higher than in any other testable election year (even presidential election years) and 30 points higher than the mean for all other available midterm election years.

Does the Public Disapprove of Congress?

But just because people were unusually aware of Democratic control of Congress in 1994 this did not necessarily spell trouble for Democratic congressional candidates. Perhaps the people felt Congress was performing its job admirably and therefore they were eager to assign credit rather than blame. Those familiar with modern American politics know this not to be the case, but the point is that public recognition of the majority party is not in and of itself detrimental to that party. For it to be detrimental other traits need to be present, and one of these is a high level of disapproval. If our theory is correct, and high levels of public disapproval with Congress in 1994 *were* channeled into votes against majority party (that is, Democratic) candidates, then one precondition must be a relatively high level of congressional disapproval in that year. Figure 6.2 indicates that this was generally the case.

The standard NES question on congressional approval has been asked since 1974 and we used this item to determine public approval of Congress in

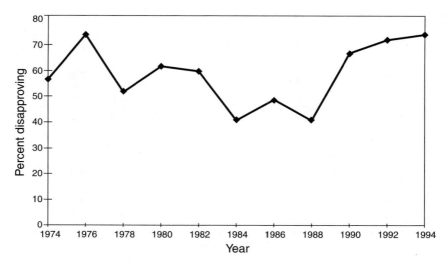

Figure 6.2.   Disapproval of Congress, 1974–1994.

SOURCE: NES, 1974–94.

NOTE: Disapproval is calculated as a dichotomous variable; zero represents disapproval and one represents approval.

recent election years. We plot disapproval instead of approval in Figure 6.2.[3] The mean response in the available eleven election years is 59.5 percent disapproval. As implied at the beginning of this paper, during the past couple of decades there has been only modest variation in people's approval of Congress. The public was most favorable in the mid- to late-1980s and the least favorable in the 1970s and 1990s. Nineteen ninety-four saw a disapproval level that was actually slightly lower than 1976 and only a little higher than 1992. This is roughly in line with our expectations: disapproval of Congress in 1994 was higher than usual but not vastly out of line with disapproval at the time of some other modern elections.

Does the Public Connect Its Displeasure with Congress to Its Votes For or Against Majority Party Candidates?

Others have noted that public disapproval of Congress was not grossly elevated in 1994 (see, for example, Jacobson and Kim 1996). Perhaps this is why disapproval levels have not played much of a role in the explanations of 1994 that have been proffered (see, for example, the essays in Klinkner 1996). We believe this is a mistake. What was unusual about 1994 was not that disap-

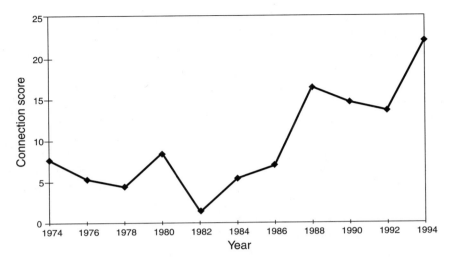

Figure 6.3. Connection between Democrats and congressional approval, 1974–1994.

SOURCE: NES, 1974–94.

NOTE: The connection score is calculated by subtracting the percentage of respondents who approved of Congress and voted for a Democrat from those who disapproved of Congress and voted for a Democrat.

proval with Congress was inordinately high. We have just seen that was not entirely the case. Rather, what was unusual about 1994 was the public's willingness to attribute responsibility for the problems of Congress to the majority party and, then, to vote on the basis of that attribution. Of course, it is impossible to prove that voters made this connection, but we can provide circumstantial evidence. This we do in Figure 6.3.

One such piece of evidence involves comparing the voting behavior of those who approved and those who disapproved of Congress. If we are correct that voters in 1994 were more likely than voters in other years to make their vote choice on the basis of whether or not they approved of the job Congress had been doing, then we should see a bigger than usual difference in vote choice between people who approved and people who disapproved of Congress. Put differently, if congressional approval were totally irrelevant to vote choice, there would be no reason to expect those who approved of Congress to vote any more or less Democratic than those who disapproved of Congress. But if approval of Congress were tied to the majority party, then disapprovers should have been less likely to vote Democratic than approvers. Consequently, we subtracted the percent who disapproved of Congress but voted for a Democratic congressional candidate from the percent who approved of Congress but voted for a Democratic congressional candidate. The results are presented in Figure 6.3.

Our expectation was that 1994 would be unusual in the degree to which disapproval with the overall performance of Congress led to a vote against Democratic candidates, and Figure 6.3 is totally consistent with this interpretation. For as long as the question has been asked in the biennial NES surveys, those disapproving of Congress have been less likely to vote Democratic than those approving of Congress. Although the difference was minuscule in 1982 and only slightly larger in the other early years of the period we cover, it is safe to conclude that Democrats (the majority party in all these elections) have fared worse among disapprovers of Congress than among approvers. This is not surprising. What interests us, however, is whether this gap in Democratic voting among disapprovers and approvers was bigger in 1994 than in other years.

On this score, Figure 6.3 provides reasonably compelling evidence that, as expected, in 1994 approval of Congress made more difference to vote choice than in any other modern election. The "gap" was fairly modest until 1988, when it increased markedly to 16.3 points. But after dropping slightly in 1990 and 1992, the gap moved to an even higher level in 1994: 21.9 points. In the past twenty years, disapprovers of Congress have always tended to vote more Republican than approvers of Congress, but the difference between the two groups was unprecedented in 1994. Just as we expected, disapproval of Congress seemed to have more partisan implications in 1994 than in typical election years. In 1994, 62.4 percent of those approving of Congress voted Democratic. Though somewhat lower than comparable figures for 1990 and 1992, the 1994 level was consistent with that found in most years since 1974. What was not typical in 1994, however, was the percent of disapprovers voting Democratic. Barely 40 percent did so; this was more than eight points lower than the second lowest total since 1974 (1988) and fifteen points lower than the comparable figure for 1992.

These procedures are far from perfect, of course. No doubt many other variables are influencing vote choice, and they were all left uncontrolled in this formulation. It could be, for example, that Democrats were held more accountable for everything in 1994 because they had control of the House, Senate, and presidency, a rarity in modern American politics. It is possible, then, that the actual motivation for a specific vote choice was not in fact disapproval of the job being done by Congress. Nonetheless, the pattern is consistent with our preferred interpretation and we will leave it at that until we present multivariate results later in this chapter. Democrats, more and more, may have come to be seen as the party responsible for the problems of Congress—and 1994 serves as an exclamation point for this trend.

What Happens When Levels of Disapproval and Degree of Democratic Culpability Are Combined?

The distinctiveness of 1994 is best seen when these last two components are combined; that is, when we interact the overall level of congressional disapproval with the degree to which voters tended to connect the disapproval to Democratic candidates. To do this, we simply multiply (after standardizing each) the mean level of disapproval (presented in Figure 6.2) times the degree to which the Democrats were held accountable for Congress (presented in Figure 6.3).[4] We call the resultant variable the "danger index" since it provides a composite indication of the extent to which Democrats are at risk as a result of public disapproval of Congress. Danger to Democrats is present when high levels of disapproval combine with an inclination on the part of the public to trace problems to the majority party in Congress. This danger index is presented graphically in Figure 6.4.

We see that 1994 was definitely the outlier. The combination of the second highest disapproval score in the data set and by far the highest *Democratic accountability for the condition of Congress* score created a lethal combination for Democrats in 1994. Only in 1978, 1990, 1992, and 1994 did this index achieve notable size, but it was clearly much higher in 1994 than even 1992 (8.68 compared to 5.32). We submit that part of the reason for the surprising election results in 1994 (remember that economic conditions were quite strong and the Democratic president's popularity was not all that low) was that the congressional disapproval danger index for Democrats was higher than it had ever been.

Why Did the Democrats' Majority Party Status Make Them Especially Vulnerable to Public Disapproval of Congress in 1994?

What explains the fact that Democrats were apparently blamed in 1994—more than in any other year—for the perceived poor performance of Congress? Why did we expect the figures to indicate precisely what they have to this point? Certainly the Democrats' status as the majority party for 40 years could be suspected of playing a major role. If ever a party were going to be held responsible for the nature of Congress it would be a party that has been the majority party for an extended period. The long-running Democratic

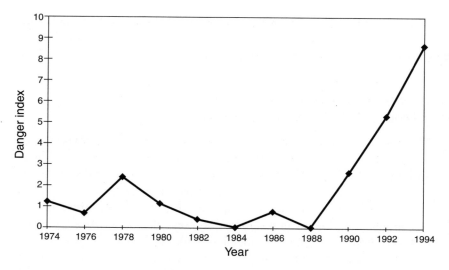

Figure 6.4.   Danger confronting Democratic members as a result of
congressional disapproval, 1974–1994.

SOURCE: NES, 1974–94.

NOTE: The danger index is calculated by multiplying the standardized disapproval
of Congress (Figure 6.2) by the standardized connection score (Figure 6.3) for
each year.

majority offered an inviting target for those eager to assign blame for a mal-
functioning Congress.

Relatedly, 1994's status as a midterm election made it easier for Republicans to make an issue out of Congress and its perceived problems. Without the distractions of a presidential election, it is more likely that people
will be open to a message stressing, in this case, Democratic responsibility
for the mess Congress was believed by a significant majority of the American population to be in. In a midterm election those voters wishing to voice
some displeasure are left only the option of using their votes for Congress.
Moreover, given the fact that people, contrary to much conventional political science wisdom, actually believe Congress to be much more powerful than the president (see Hibbing and Theiss-Morse 1995), dissatisfaction
with government generally, in addition to Congress specifically, might very
well be channeled into midterm congressional voting behavior. Under the
right circumstances dissatisfaction with Congress and even all of government
could be laid at the doorstep of the majority party in Congress. If that party

also controls the White House, as was the case in 1994, blame is even easier for voters to apportion.

Also relevant is the fact the Democratic party is traditionally seen as the party of big government. This concept means not only that the Democratic party generally supports a more active governmental role in certain areas of society, but also that it is the party "of government," and not just any government but rather a government seen as unnecessarily large, with many staffers, many committees, many bureaucracies, many perquisites, and many support structures. A major aspect of what the public feels is wrong with Congress is its institutionalized and professionalized nature (see Hibbing and Theiss-Morse 1995). Though the public wants a populist, citizen legislature, it is instead presented with an institutionist, professional legislature—a legislature with lots of bells and whistles that can only serve to obstruct the voices of ordinary people. Democrats' general orientation toward government and governing, we would argue, makes it easier to pin them with responsibility for the way Congress is perceived to be conducting itself (see also Jacobson 1990b).

But the most distinguishing and important element of the 1994 campaign was the success of Newt Gingrich and others in the Republican leadership at getting ordinary people to make the connection between the candidates of the Democratic party and people's view of the job Congress was doing. This was how the *Congressional Quarterly Weekly Report* described the plans of the minority party in 1994: "The Republican strategy has been to place a national template over this year's House elections, stressing that longtime Democratic control of the House has stifled a number of popular legislative proposals" (Kaplan 1994: 3005). Then, after noting that the 103d Congress "disintegrated into dilatory partisan squabbling" and an "incapacity to act," *CQWR* reported that "Gingrich and Texan Dick Armey . . . are leading the Republican charge to 'nationalize' this year's [1994's] contests" (Kaplan 1994: 3005). And, of course, Ross Perot was also active in 1994, beseeching "his supporters to vote Republican in most districts to give the GOP a chance at running things" in Congress (Kaplan 1994: 3005). If voters in 1994 sought to send a message that Congress was not working (the argument went), they should have cast a vote against the Democrats. This was a message the Republican leadership never tired of promoting.

What was different about 1994 was not that people were so much more dissatisfied with either Congress or government than they had been in previous elections, but rather the ability of Republicans to capitalize on the opportunity they were given to brand Democrats as the party of government and the party of Congress. It is possible to imagine a midterm election campaign in which Congress is unpopular and government is unified under a long-dominant "party of big government" but in which public displeasure with Congress is still unrelated to decisions to vote Democrat or Republican in House races. In fact, we would argue that this description fits 1978 reasonably well. But Gingrich was determined that this would *not* occur in 1994. Our hypothesis is based on the belief that he was successful in getting people to hold majority party candidates culpable for Congress's failings. This situation helps to explain the unusually poor performance of Democratic congressional candidates in 1994.

So 1994 was not the first election in which Democrats were the long-standing majority party; it was not the first election held under unified government; it was not the first midterm election; and it was not the first time that Democrats had to answer for being the party "of government"; but it was the first time that all these features were pulled together and rubbed in the public's face by an enthusiastically aggressive minority party leadership. This leadership was able to nationalize the race in 1994, not around typical nationalizing issues like economic conditions or foreign policy crises, but around the issue of how government and, especially, Congress were perceived to be operating. The consequences are well known.

This whole argument hearkens back to the party responsibility model, but with an important modification. What we are discussing is not responsibility for a certain policy but rather responsibility for how government is operating and, of course, the perception in 1994 was that it was operating badly, with much waste, with special interests trumping the people's interests, with out-of-touch professional politicians, with bloated staffs, confusing committees, nitpicking bureaucracies, with lots of talk and no action, with cocktail parties and fund-raisers, and with special privileges for slovenly and undeserving elected officials.

These process concerns are much easier for people to grasp than the intricacies of policies. People recognize that many policy problems today are incredibly difficult to solve and, accordingly, differ greatly on how to solve them. But people feel that problems with the processes of government are easier to solve, and there is amazing public consensus on what needs to be done. Limit terms, cut staff, cut salaries, remove the influence of money from elections, and drastically curtail the influence of political parties and special interests. More than with any other recent election, the outcome of 1994 bore the imprint of this dissatisfaction.

So the potential for people's votes to be influenced by process concerns had been present prior to 1994 but never fully realized. Usually, people see both parties as pretty much equally culpable for the procedural mess that they perceive to surround Washington. A special confluence of circumstances such as that described above is required for people to project dissatisfaction onto members of one political party but not the other. This may be why 1994 was a year of disarray for congressional Democrats.

What Was the Individual-Level Impact of Disapproval, 1974–94?

While taking note of year-to-year shifts in levels of congressional disapproval, Democratic culpability, and Democratic vote totals is helpful, additional information on the relationship between disapproval and voting can be gleaned at the individual level. Thus, in this section we attempt to explain why certain voters behave differently than others, not why certain election years are different than others. This shift will also make it easier to incorporate the kinds of control variables that are noticeably absent from the findings reported thus far.

Specifically, we will attempt to explain congressional vote choice with four independent variables: party identification (Democrat = 2, Independent = 1, Republican = 0); perceptions of the country's economic conditions (better = 2, same = 1, worse = 0); type of race in the district (Democratic incumbent = 2, open seat = 1, Republican incumbent = 0); and approval of Congress (approve = 1, disapprove = 0).[5] Given these codings, we expect each variable, *with one exception*, to have a positive relationship with the dependent variable (vote Democratic = 1, vote Republican = 0). In other words, we expect a Democratic party identification, a favorable perception of the country's economic conditions, a Democratic House incumbent, and approval of Congress all to make it more likely for an individual to vote for the Democratic House candidate.

The exception pertains to economic perceptions in certain years. Countless studies of economic conditions and voting have determined (or at least assumed) that responsibility for economic conditions is accorded the president. The sign for perceived economic conditions, therefore, should be sensitive not to the controlling party in Congress but rather to the controlling party in the White House. Thus, while the signs for the other three independent variables should always be positive, the sign for perceived economic conditions should be positive when there is a Democrat in the White House and negative when a Republican is in the White House. In other words, when a Republican is in the White House favorable economic conditions should actually harm the electoral fortunes of Democratic House candidates. This situation points to an important difference between attribution of responsibility for economic conditions (to the party of the president) and for

Table 6.1

Explaining Congressional Elections, 1974–1994

	1974	1976	1978	1980	1982
Approval of Congress	.02	.21*	.16	.03	.15
Party ID	.94***	.85***	.93***	.71***	1.06***
Race type	.49***	.58***	.85***	.66***	.63***
Economic perceptions	−.29**	−.26***	.00	.19	−.15**
Constant	−1.18***	−1.33***	−1.92***	−1.60***	−1.72***
Pseudo R^2	.50	.50	.50	.49	.49
Chi-square	623.64	943.41	725.47	544.91	534.36
N	619	921	704	552	547

  * $p < .10$
 ** $p < .05$
*** $p < .01$

a poorly rated Congress (to the majority party in Congress). But this is all conjectural. What do the results indicate?

Given the fact that we have a dichotomous dependent variable, we have employed probit analysis, a preferable estimation procedure with a limited dependent variable. We ran the analysis separately for each available election year to get a feel for variations in the coefficients across time. This practice allowed us to test our expectation that the effects on vote choice by the main variable of interest in this analysis, congressional disapproval, were greater in 1994 than in most other years. The results are presented in Table 6.1.

For the most part, the results are quite consistent with the expectations stated above. Coefficients for party identification, type of race, and congressional approval are always positive (except for approval in 1984, which is barely negative), and coefficients for economic conditions follow the anticipated pattern of positive signs under Democratic presidents (1978, 1980, and 1994) and negative signs under Republican presidents (all other years). Of course, obtaining results consistent with expectations is no big trick when expectations are as obvious as "Democratic voters will be more likely to vote for Democrats" and "incumbent candidates will tend to do better than nonincumbent candidates." The strong effects for district type and party identification are totally unsurprising. The effects for economic per-

1984	1986	1988	1990	1992	1994
−.02	.19	.48**	.17	.20*	.33**
.67***	.75***	.84***	.82***	.76***	1.09***
.73***	.80***	.91***	.74***	.55***	.58***
−.27***	−.24***	−.40***	−.17	−.39***	.14**
−1.28***	−1.41***	−1.66***	−1.53***	−1.18***	−2.19***
.50	.49	.50	.51	.50	.51
967.13	640.60	761.09	595.54	1241.16	849.50*
955	653	733	568	1230	786

ceptions are weaker, often not achieving traditionally accepted levels of statistical significance. But these control variables are not of much interest to us here given their previously well-known effects.

In this chapter, we focus on the congressional approval variable, since this has not been used much previously in attempts to explain congressional vote choice. But remember, our expectations held that congressional approval would be relevant only in certain election years. To be precise, we felt that 1994 would be a year in which approval was more relevant than usual for vote choice. This prediction was upheld by the data. The effects of congressional approval on a vote for the Democratic House candidate were strong and easily statistically significant in 1994. This statement does not apply to most other years in the analysis, with the exceptions of 1976, 1988, and 1992. The former barely attains significance and both the sizes and the significance levels of the coefficients suggest that congressional approval has exerted a greater impact in more recent years, with the 1994 results indicating that a substantial impact emanated from approval.

But probit coefficients do not lend themselves to straightforward interpretations and, therefore, cross-equation comparisons. A better way to obtain a sense of variation from year to year regarding the influence of congressional approval on vote choice is to convert the probit coefficients into

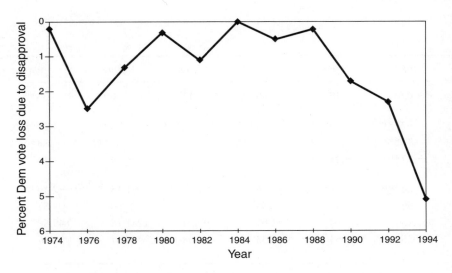

Figure 6.5.   Vote loss attributable to congressional disapproval, 1974–1994.

SOURCE: NES, 1974–94.

NOTE: Vote loss is calculated using probit coefficients to compute the probability of
a Democratic vote when all independent variables are set equal to their means for that
year, then subtracting these from the probability of voting Democratic if approval levels had been as high as they were in 1984 but all other variables remained at actual
mean levels for that year.

probabilities (see, for example, Gujarati 1988: 467–99). To make these probability estimates even more intuitive we have constructed Figure 6.5 in the
following fashion. As noted in Figure 6.2, 1984 was the year in which approval of Congress was the highest of those we are analyzing. For each election year, we used the coefficients and a normal probability table to compute the expected Democratic vote given mean levels of all four independent
variables in that year.[6] We then repeated this procedure for each election
year, except that we substituted the higher 1984 level of congressional approval for the actual level in that year. By comparing the two results we produced an estimate of the degree to which the probability of voting Democratic was lowered as a result of the reduced congressional approval in the
pertinent year relative to 1984. Figure 6.5 thus provides a sense of how much
worse Democrats did in each year than they would have done if the high approval levels of 1984 had applied.

   We expected that the largest disapproval-induced drop would be evident
in 1994 and this was clearly the case. The lower level of approval in 1994 obviously hurt the Democrats. Best estimates are that the Democrats would

have done 5.1 points better than they did in 1994 if the people had been as approving of Congress in 1994 as they had been just ten years earlier. Parallel procedures for the other years indicate that drops were quite a bit smaller. Effects were modest in 1976, 1990, and 1992, and even smaller in the other years. In no year was the consequence of lower congressional approval on the majority party even half as great as in 1994.

In some respects Figure 6.5 can be seen as an individual-level corollary of Figure 6.4, which, it may be recalled, interacted approval and Democratic culpability at a more aggregated level. Disapproval of Congress, too, showed a more marked effect in 1994. In addition to presenting corroboration with totally different computation procedures, Figure 6.5's advantage is that the estimated effects of approval it reports (unlike those reported in Figure 6.4) were produced even though other obvious influences—such as party identification and district type—were controlled. This is even more convincing evidence, then, that low congressional approval levels cost the Democrats many votes in 1994 in a way unmatched in other modern elections.

A shift of 5.1 percent may not seem like much until it is noted that the swing ratio in 1994 was 1.97; thus, we could predict that an increase of 5.1 percent of the vote would have translated into a gain of 10.05 percent of House seats, or 44 seats. Thus, if 1984 approval levels had been operating in 1994 but everything else had remained constant, a rough estimate of the election results would have the Democrats losing only 8 seats instead of 52 and easily retaining majority control. Public disapproval with Congress does not always come back to haunt the majority party in Congress, but it did in 1994.

Do Voters Target the Rascals? A Closer Look at 1994

We may be able to specify further the conditions under which general disapproval of Congress can harm congressional candidates. Although the results above depict quite clearly that certain election year conditions can lead to majority party candidates losing votes because voters disapprove of Congress, they say nothing about the type of majority party candidate most in peril. It is to this task that we now turn, focusing on the 1994 situation because it is of particular interest in light of the surprising results and because we now know that in overall terms disapproval did have an effect in 1994.

Logic suggests that *incumbents* of the majority party should be more electorally damaged by low congressional approval than nonincumbent candidates of the majority party. If voters are greatly displeased with the job done by Congress, and if people have become convinced that the majority party in Congress is responsible, it is easier to blame incumbents of that party. They have been in Congress during the time it was perceived to have done a bad job. Majority party challengers, whether running in an open seat or challenging a Republican incumbent, have not been in Congress during that period and, while their status as Democrats may raise some problems, charges that the poor performance of Congress should be attributed to them are less likely to stick (for similar expectations on another issue, see Hibbing and Alford 1981; Fiorina 1983).

To test these expectations, we divided districts into three groups: those in which a Democratic incumbent was running in 1994; those in which no incumbent was running; and those in which a Republican incumbent was running. We hypothesized that in a properly specified multivariate model, we would find a strong positive relationship between House vote choice and congressional approval in districts with Democratic incumbents (rascals), but no significant relationship between House vote choice and congressional approval in districts with no Democratic incumbent running—either in open seats or seats with Republican incumbents. In Table 6.2, we present separate equations for these three distinct situations as well as the overall baseline results for 1994.

The overall 1994 results merely repeat those listed in the relevant column of Table 6.1, whereas the other three equations parallel the procedures leading to the overall results except that race type has been excluded because we are selecting cases of a single race and therefore eliminating variance on this variable. Congressional approval does not have a significant effect on vote choice *except* if there is a majority party incumbent to anchor that choice. Congressional disapproval, in other words, generally does not matter in open seats when (usually) neither candidate has ever served in Congress and generally does not matter if there is a Republican incumbent, because it is apparently difficult for many people to view either Republican incumbents or Democratic challengers as the individuals responsible for the failings of Congress. This is important confirmation of our expectation: when the analysis is restricted to respondents in Democratic incumbent districts, congressional approval is strongly, positively, and significantly related to House vote choice. However, in districts without Democratic incumbents, the coefficient for approval is small and statistically insignificant.

Too much should not be made of coefficients that fail to achieve statistical significance, but one passing remark is in order. When the analysis is restricted to respondents in districts with Republican incumbents, the coefficient for congressional approval is positive, just as for those respondents in

Table 6.2

Explaining Congressional Elections in Different District Types

	All Voters	Republican Incumbent District Only	Open Districts Only	Democratic Incumbent Districts Only
Approval of Congress	.33**	.18	.24	.45***
Party ID	1.09***	1.08***	1.19***	1.06***
Race type	.58***	—	—	—
Economic perceptions	.14**	.29**	1.19***	.12
Constant	−2.19***	−2.32***	−1.62***	−.99***
Pseudo R^2	.51	.55	.50	.52
Chi-square	849.50*	291.84***	138.07	453.82*
N	786	231	136	568

   * $p < .10$
  ** $p < .05$
 *** $p < .01$

districts with Democratic incumbents. If congressional approval helped *all* incumbents (as the old incumbent-culpability hypothesis claims), then we should see a coefficient for Republican incumbents that is negative and approximately equal in absolute value to that for Democratic incumbents (remember, the dependent variable is a vote for the Democratic candidate). But this is not what happens at all. Although the coefficient for Republican incumbent districts is weak and insignificant, it is positive, which suggests that, if anything, congressional approval actually harms Republican incumbents. Perhaps this concept is more easily understood when stated in the reverse: public disapproval of Congress may help Republican incumbents, but it definitely does not harm them, as erroneously assumed by those expecting all incumbents to be hurt by public disapproval. All incumbents are not alike, but the results in Table 6.2 also reveal that all members of the majority party are not alike. Just as we anticipated, Democrats who have been serving in Congress are much more susceptible to implications that they are responsible for a disappointing congressional performance than Democrats who have not been in Congress.

Conclusion

Going into the election of 1994 most people disapproved of Congress. This fact does not distinguish 1994 from most other modern elections (except 1984–88). Going into the election of 1994 many voters were convinced that the majority party was responsible for Congress's disappointing performance. This fact *does* distinguish 1994 from most other modern elections. The upshot was an unexpectedly bad electoral performance by the majority Democrats, a performance that resulted in a 52-seat swing and the first Republican House majority in 40 years. The politicization of congressional unpopularity in 1994 made election outcomes more sensitive to that unpopularity. This sensitivity, in fact, was such that if congressional approval levels had been at even average levels for the past two decades (40.5) but everything else had remained as it actually was in 1994, it is quite likely the Democrats would have still been the majority party, with a projected loss of only 30 instead of 52 seats and a resultant party split of 228 Democratic to 206 Republican.

But statements such as these should be taken for what they are: counterfactuals that are based on numerous assumptions and will never be tested anyway. As fascinating as the elections of 1994 might have been, a more lasting contribution of our study would be to say something about how people view congressional unpopularity and about how they view responsibility for the condition of Congress itself (not for conditions of the country or for particular policies). Here we can conclude that, most of the time, even when people are quite disapproving of Congress, this disapproval does not have direct electoral repercussions. People usually see the great majority of members of Congress—regardless of party—to be tainted. On occasion, however, situations can cause disapproval with Congress to result in votes against the majority party. The clearest instance of this was 1994.

Even in 1994 not all members of the majority party were equally implicated. Those majority party members who were not incumbents—that is, who had not been in Congress during the period it was alleged to have been performing badly—were not harmed in a statistically significant fashion by public disapproval of Congress. To the extent 1994 is typical, minority party incumbents should not fear public disapproval. If anything, it helped them in 1994 because the public was encouraged to see congressional performance as a partisan issue. Similarly, Republicans running in open seats in 1994 may have been helped a little by congressional disapproval, but the important point is that the relationship between congressional approval and vote choice was strong and significant only in those districts with Democratic incumbents—with rascals.

The people are often assumed to be thinking in policy-oriented ways when they are actually thinking in process-oriented terms. An important part of the public mood in the 1990s has been dissatisfaction with government and with the institution thought to be at the center of that government: the U.S. Congress. This dissatisfaction places important constraints on the government, but this far-reaching issue is the topic of another day. What we have stressed in this paper is that dissatisfaction, when handled with perspicacity and shrewdness, can be turned into a partisan issue. Figures 6.4 and 6.5 both indicate a post-1988 trend toward congressional disapproval playing a bigger role in congressional elections. This is not surprising in light of the drift of the parties toward policy consensus on many issues and in light of ordinary people's (possibly related) focus on process issues at the expense of policy issues.

Popular postmortems of the 1998 midterm elections remind us of the potential relevance of public attitudes toward Congress for explaining election outcomes. The startling fact that the president's party actually gained seats in a midterm election was widely attributed to the public's perception that Congress (read the Republican majority) was fixated on impeaching a political enemy rather than working hard to solve the country's problems— a message reinforced by the Republican leadership's decision right before the election to launch an advertising campaign reminding voters of the Monica Lewinsky–Kenneth Starr–Bill Clinton imbroglio. (Perhaps the success of the Republicans at nationalizing the election of 1994 mistakenly emboldened them to try it again in 1998.) If this explanation is accurate, it suggests that, although 1994 was unusual compared to earlier elections, a connection between public displeasure with Congress and congressional election outcomes may not be that unusual in election years subsequent to 1994, should the right conditions obtain.

Chapter 7

The Nationalization of Electoral Forces Revisited

DAVID W. BRADY, ROBERT D'ONOFRIO,
AND MORRIS P. FIORINA

In the 1994 elections the Republicans surprised the nation (as well as most of the political science profession) by capturing the House of Representatives for the first time in 40 years. In the aftermath of the election political journalists (R. Cook 1994) and political scientists (Jacobson 1996c) attributed the surprising outcome to the fact that the Republicans had succeeded in "nationalizing" the election. This claim raises two questions: (1) did they? (2) if they did, how?

Answering the first question requires us to stipulate what it means to nationalize an election, and indicate how we would identify and calibrate nationalization empirically. Answering the second requires a demonstration that in 1994 Republican elites followed strategies that could plausibly be identified as nationalization strategies, and that voters responded to those strategies in a way measurably different from how they had chosen in the recent past.[1]

This paper addresses the first question, the meaning and measurement of nationalization, which we consider to be logically prior to the second one. In the next section of the paper we discuss the idea of nationalization. In the third section we review an earlier line of work that attempted to measure nationalization. In the fourth section of the paper we present our own approach and discuss the findings. In the fifth section we discuss some possible explanations of nationalization. We conclude with some suggestions about profitable lines of future work.

130

"All Politics is Local—Not!"

Leading up to 1994, two decades of congressional elections research indicated that modern congressional elections, especially those for the House, were local, not national events (Mann 1977). The classic Stokes and Miller (1962) portrayal of House elections as low-information party-line affairs apparently began to fade soon after its publication (Fiorina 1982). The electoral advantage of incumbency soared during the late 1960s (Erikson 1972a; Mayhew 1974a). Interelection vote swings grew more heterogeneous (Mann 1977; Jacobson 1987), and the swing ratio (the rate at which vote gains translate into seat gains) declined (Ansolabehere et al. 1992; cf. Jacobson 1987). Presidential coattails grew weaker (Ferejohn and Calvert 1984), and midterm losses were smaller than predicted based on historical experience (Witt 1983). In short, one specific finding after another contributed to the general conclusion that factors and forces that worked uniformly in House elections across the nation were on the wane, while individual district and candidate factors were growing stronger.

In offering larger interpretations of such developments political scientists argued that congressional elections had become "insulated" from national forces (Burnham 1975) and that the United States had developed a two-tiered electoral system (Ladd and Hadley 1975: 259–66) in which national forces dominated only at the presidential level. Popular commentators suggested that changing national forces had not penetrated very deeply into the electoral order, producing a "split level" realignment (Phillips 1985), or only "half a realignment" (Schneider 1984). Practicing politicians put the matter most succinctly. In his famous aphorism, Speaker Tip O'Neill pronounced that "all politics is local." Presumably he was referring mainly to House elections.

At least temporarily, the 1994 elections called this prevailing wisdom into question. In a 1984 "morning-after" piece William Schneider (1984: 20) could write "It was incumbency that saved the Democratic Party from ruin." Ten years later the morning-after pieces could make no such claim as thirty-five Democratic incumbents fell, while Republican incumbents went completely unscathed. The swing against the Democrats was more uniform than in the recent past, and the midterm loss was considerably in excess of several well-known political science predictive models.[2]

In the aftermath of the election there seemed little doubt that, relatively speaking, the election had been nationalized in the sense that considerations that had been driving the presidential vote in recent decades finally broke through the "split-level" into the "second-tier" and drove the congressional vote as well. Several studies demonstrated that positions on controversial national policies had been electorally significant. Jacobson (1996c) showed that support for Bill Clinton's 1993 budget and North American Free Trade Agreement (NAFTA) had been harmful for Democratic incumbents. Similarly, Ferejohn's (1998) analysis found that specific votes were related to incumbent losses. Seemingly, Democratic incumbents in 1994 were unable to insulate themselves from the harmful effects of their support for Clinton's proposals.

Although analyses like these are extremely suggestive, the difficulty they pose for any systematic study of nationalization is that of temporal comparability. For example, three decades ago Schoenberger (1969) showed that Republican incumbents who signed a preconvention declaration of support for Barry Goldwater suffered electorally in the 1964 elections. How can we compare this finding with Jacobson's and Ferejohn's results, not to mention other results for elections in between? Individual, year-by-year studies like these are extremely suggestive, but they can tell us little about whether nationalization is going up, down, or staying about the same.

One possibility is to use voting indexes that appear to possess cross-temporal validity. *Congressional Quarterly*'s presidential support scores are a good example. This is the approach followed by D. W. Brady et al. (1996), who show that Democratic incumbents who came from districts where Clinton was weak suffered electorally for supporting him. Moreover, in a chapter in this volume, Brady, Canes-Wrone, and Cogan show that losing incumbents have voted either too liberally or too conservatively for their districts. Although a more powerful research design, this approach is not beyond question because the president's agenda is not exogeneous; it is in part a result of strategic calculations about what will pass and what will not, as well as whether the president would prefer to have an accomplishment or an issue. Moreover, presidents differ in their ambitions; one president's agenda may be modest, while another's may be ambitious. For all of these reasons, a given level of support in one year may not truly compare to a numerically identical level in another.

After considering the problem we decided that the best approach to the temporal study of nationalization might be one based solely on election returns. This research strategy is not new, of course; an older literature based on voting returns addresses precisely this question.

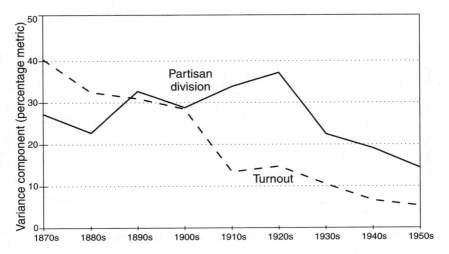

Figure 7.1. Changes in constituency component of House turnout and partisan division, by decade, 1870s–1950s.

SOURCE: Adapted from Stokes 1967. Unless otherwise noted, all tables and figures in Chapter 7 are based on the authors' data.

The Nationalization of Electoral Forces

Ironically, just prior to the "incumbency and insulation" era just described, there was a small flurry of studies arguing that House elections were becoming *more* nationalized. In a classic article Donald Stokes (1967) used a modified analysis of variance technique to decompose the variance of the House vote into a national component, a state component, and a district component.[3] After trending generally upward from the 1890s to the 1920s, the constituency component began a sharp downward drop through the 1950s (Figure 7.1). Stokes considered this a substantively plausible development. Advances in transportation and communications were inevitably eroding regional differences; consequently, politics and elections should become more homogeneous.

Katz (1973a, 1973b) criticized Stokes on conceptual grounds. Probably reflecting his ongoing work with David Butler (Butler and Stokes 1969), Stokes viewed nationalization as a condition analogous to the uniform swing that characterized midcentury British elections: variation was national only if it was of the same magnitude and direction across congressional districts. Contrary to Stokes, Katz argued that in 1960 John F. Kennedy's Catholicism certainly was a national force, even if it cost him votes in Protestant

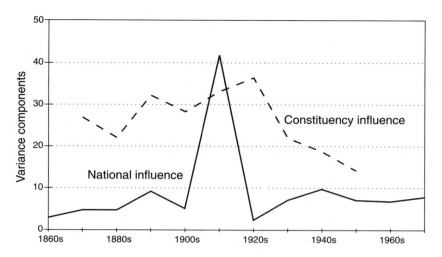

Figure 7.2. Constituency component of House voting versus national component: Stokes method, 1860s–1960s.

SOURCE: Adapted from Claggett et al. 1984.

areas while it gained him votes in Catholic areas (Converse 1966).[4] Rejecting Stokes's analysis of variance approach, Katz regressed the district House vote for the five elections within a decade (1952–60) on the national and state House vote in those elections, thus allowing the coefficients to vary across districts. This alternative method inevitably leads to higher national estimates. Katz concluded that Stokes had *underestimated* the national component of the vote: "The American political system looks considerably more national, and less like a loose federation of unrelated local political systems, than Stokes' analysis would lead one to expect" (Katz 1973a: 825). Ironically, this conclusion appeared between the publications of Erikson (1972a) and Mayhew (1974a), which inaugurated the "all politics is local" era.

Some clarification was offered by Claggett et al. (1984). Reverting to the uniform swing notion of nationalization, they pointed out that the estimates presented by Stokes (Figure 7.1) were not normed. Thus, while the constituency component had declined since the early part of the twentieth century, the national component had not increased, although there is a huge spike in the early twentieth century (Figure 7.2). This conclusion was buttressed by their alternative analysis incorporating a number of data decisions that differ from Stokes (but eliminate the large turn-of-the-century spike in the national component).[5]

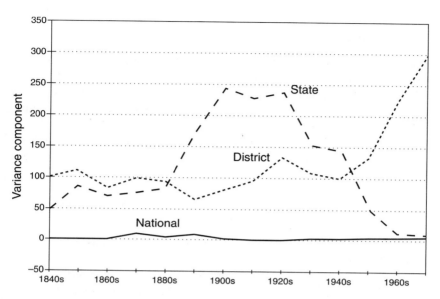

Figure 7.3. Components of House Democratic vote, 1840s–1960s.

SOURCE: Adapted from Kawato 1987.

Finally, Kawato (1987) reported decompositions carried out on voting returns and interelection swings directly rather than on the variances calculated from them. His results finally began to show the picture familiar to a recent generation of congressional elections researchers (Figure 7.3). The district component of the vote begins to increase in the 1950s and shoots sharply upward in the 1960s and 1970s. So, after some back-and-forth, exactly twenty years after the decomposition of the vote literature began, its contributors produced a portrait that fits the cumulated research of the past several decades.

Like Katz, we reject any concept of nationalization analogous to uniform swing. Most contemporary researchers would agree that a vote for the assault weapons ban that helped urban Democrats and hurt rural Democrats in 1994 certainly was a "national" force distinguishable from the casework, local projects, newsletters, social appearances, and so forth that are the stuff of district forces. At the same time Katz's method—regressions based on five observations, with the district component measured by the residual—seems rather crude. The intervening literature suggests a better, if still imperfect, way.

An Alternative Approach

After the 1994 elections, we began to explore the election returns to check the accuracy of some of the claims that were being made. In particular, had the United States entered a "brave Newt world" where incumbency had given way to national forces so that House elections would now resemble the British elections long used as a contrast?

We began by estimating the incumbency advantage in 1994, using the standard Gelman and King (1990) unbiased estimator obtained from the following regression:

$$\text{House Vote(t)} = b_0 + b_1(\text{House vote(t}-1)) + b_2(\text{party of winner}) + b_3(\text{incumbent running})$$

We modified the basic equation in two ways. First, although Gelman and King (1990: 1158 n. 10) found no significant difference between incumbency effects for Democrats and Republicans, in view of the one-sided nature of the 1994 elections, we thought it prudent to divide their $(1, 0, -1)$ party variable into two separate dummies. Second, inasmuch as the 1994 House vote seemed to parallel the 1992 Clinton vote fairly closely, we added previous district presidential vote to the equation. This reduced the sum of squared errors, while not altering other desirable properties of the equation. We then compared the 1994 estimates with those for the closest midterm, 1990. The results are quite striking.

As Table 7.1 shows, the incumbency advantage for Democrats in 1994 was only two-thirds that for Republicans, but as Gelman and King found for earlier elections, this difference was not significant at conventional levels. Contrary to postelection hype, however, the incumbency advantage by no means disappeared in 1994; it is significant at conventional levels for Democrats as well as Republicans, and the coefficients for both parties are indistinguishable from those in 1990. Consistent with popular and professional impressions, there was a tide evident in 1994: over and above the incumbency status of the district and its previous voting history, Democratic winners ran 3 percent worse than Republicans. But contrary to what we might have expected, that tide was marginally lower in 1994 than in 1990, when Democratic winners ran five points worse. Finally, in 1994 the constant was zero, whereas in 1990 the constant shows a significant Democratic edge. To jump ahead for a moment, in every analogous regression from 1954 onward the constant was positive (pro-Democratic), usually significantly so. That Democratic edge disappeared in 1994.

Table 7.1

Modified Gelman–King Equations, 1990 v. 1994

	1990	1994
Democratic incumbent	7.36*	7.45*
	(2.24)	(1.12)
Republican incumbent	−11.1*	−11.1*
	(1.80)	(1.36)
Democratic winner	−5.06*	−3.55
	(1.55)	(.902)
Previous House vote	.521*	.492*
	(.055)	(.043)
Previous presidential vote	.150*	.426*
	(.047)	(.037)
Constant	20.2*	−.555
	(2.77)	(2.11)
N	307	366
Adjusted R^2	.802	.871

NOTE: Standard errors in parentheses.

*$p < .05$

Of particular interest to us are the coefficients of previous House and presidential vote. The presidential and congressional votes have a common partisan component, of course, and this is reflected in the fact that inclusion of the previous presidential vote reduces the coefficient of previous House vote by about one-third from its conventional levels of .6 or greater in such Gelman–King equations. But in the 1994 equation, the coefficient of previous presidential vote is statistically indistinguishable from the coefficient of previous House vote and more than twice as large as the presidential vote coefficient in the 1990 equation. That is, the House vote in 1990 was much more closely related to the 1988 House vote than to the 1988 Michael Dukakis vote, whereas in sharp contrast, the House vote in 1994 was almost as closely related to the Clinton vote in 1992 as to the House vote in 1992.[6] Given that students of congressional elections often have used presidential vote as an indicator of national forces in studies of coattails (Ferejohn and Calvert 1984), midterm effects (Erikson 1988), and surge and decline (J. E. Campbell 1993), comparisons of the kind shown in Table 7.1 might be a very parsimonious way of tracking temporal variation in nationaliza-

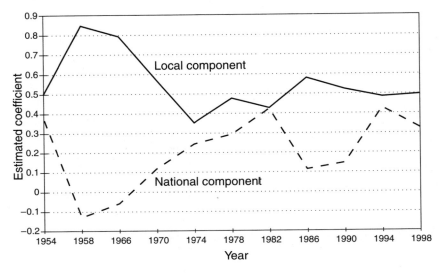

Figure 7.4a.   Decomposition of midterm House elections, contested seats, 1954–1998.

tion. Without implying that the presidential vote is entirely national or the House vote entirely local, in what follows we will adhere to the practice in the literature and refer to the presidential vote coefficients as indicators of nationalization, or the national component of the vote.[7] By no means are we implying that this is a perfect indicator, only that it has some validity and possesses the great advantage of temporal comparability.

The presidential vote by district is available from 1954 onward.[8] As is common in empirical studies using lagged vote data, reapportionment prohibits analyzing the 1962, 1972, and 1992 election years.[9] In analyses of this sort, there is always a question of what to do with uncontested seats.[10] Including them directly will bias our results (Gelman and King 1990), yet excluding them biases the sample because one of the most important effects of incumbency may be the ability to scare off potential challengers (Cox and Katz 1996). Thus, we have carried out two sets of analyses, one omitting the uncontested seats and one imputing values to them via Gary King's JudgeIt procedure.[11] Neither analysis is above question, but if the results are consistent, we can have greater confidence than relying on one or the other.

We have run regressions like those reported in Table 7.1 for all off-year elections since 1954.[12] Figures 7.4a and 7.4b plot the regression coefficients for previous House and previous presidential vote, first for the sample that

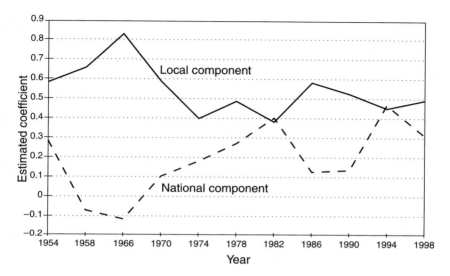

Figure 7.4b. Decomposition of midterm House elections, all seats, 1954–1998.

only includes districts with contested elections, and then for the sample that includes uncontested seats. The qualitative picture is striking and it is the same whether uncontested districts are omitted or included with imputed values for the congressional vote. The national component of the vote plunged in the late 1950s while the district component soared. But the national component had begun a process of recovery by 1970 that peaked in 1982, before plunging once again, then recovering in 1994. Meanwhile, the coefficients for previous House vote basically stabilized in the early 1970s.

Thus, during the heyday of the literature on incumbency, insulation, and so forth, the underlying trend was actually moving, albeit slowly, in the opposite direction! Those movements probably were obscured by the 1986–90 plunge in the national component, when incumbent reelection rates soared to then-historical highs—an average of 97 percent over the three elections (Ornstein et al. 1994: 58). The 1994 estimates of the national component are high points for these series, but they do not look so unusual if viewed as straight-line extensions of the trend from 1970 to 1982.

Midterm elections are only half of the story, of course, but we can not run completely analogous regressions for presidential years. The House vote lagged two years is available, but one must use either contemporaneous presidential vote, or the presidential vote lagged four years. The former seems

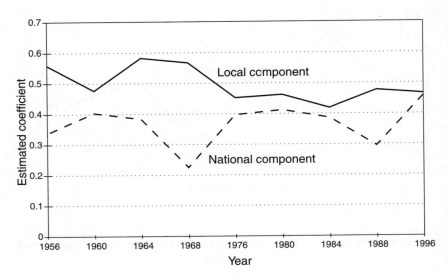

Figure 7.5a. Decomposition of presidential-year House elections, contested seats, 1956–1996.

preferable on a variety of grounds.[13] Figures 7.5a and 7.5b plot the presidential and House coefficients, again first for only contested seats, and then for the larger sample that includes uncontested races.

Interestingly, in every election in the series the coefficient on *previous* House vote is larger than the coefficient on *contemporaneous* presidential vote, a striking indicator of the distinctiveness of the two electoral arenas in modern times. In Figures 7.5a and 7.5b we see a pattern less dramatic than and somewhat different from the pattern for midterms. There is a late-1960s plunge in the national component, but the recovery is quick, and the 1980s decay is less striking. Figure 7.5a (uncontested seats excluded) suggests that aside from the 1968 George Wallace interruption and the particularly vacuous 1988 campaign, the national component has been stable. Figure 7.5b (uncontested seats included) suggests a slight increase in the national component across the period. Meanwhile, the local component has been gradually *declining* over the series, a trend particularly evident with uncontested seats included. The overall pattern is somewhat surprising in that it suggests that the balance between national and local forces shifted to the present equilibrium in the mid-1970s.

Putting the two analyses together, the national component of the House

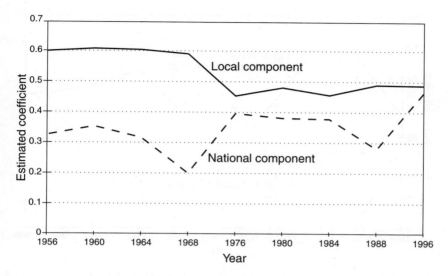

Figure 7.5b. Decomposition of presidential-year House elections, all seats, 1956–1996.

vote dropped in the late 1950s and stayed low through the politically turbulent 1960s. By the 1970s a recovery was taking place, a recovery missed by political scientists who interpreted Richard Nixon's election as a "personal" victory and viewed 1974 as a somewhat unique event. Electoral outcomes in the mid- to late-1980s fit the picture painted by a decade of research, so the "nationalized" elections of 1994 and 1996 came as a complete shock. But although these two elections are the most "nationalized" in the past 40 years by our estimates, they were foreshadowed by the growing nationalization evident in the midterm elections of 1974 to 1984, and the presidential elections from 1976 onward.

An obvious objection to the preceding analyses is that they drastically understate the importance of the local component of the House vote. The coefficient on previous House vote captures the two-year continuity in the vote *after separating out the effect of an incumbent running for reelection.* But given that incumbency encapsulates a host of factors thought to be local in nature (district service, personal contact, and issue positions tailored to the district), it is arguable that a better measure of the local component of the House vote is the *combined* impact of lagged House vote and incumbency.

There is no perfect way to measure this combined impact. One possibil-

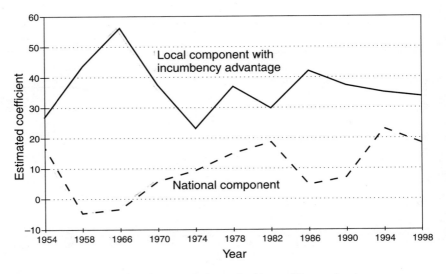

Figure 7.6. Alternative decomposition of midterm House elections, 1954–1998.

ity is to set the lagged House and presidential votes to their means each year, and then multiply the means by their respective regression coefficients. The resulting product is the average House vote controlling for incumbency. The estimate of incumbency advantage (b_3) in a given year could then be added to the average estimated House vote. In these combined estimates the local component explicitly includes the electoral impact of incumbency, while the national component remains exactly the same as before. Figures 7.6 and 7.7 provide an alternative look at nationalization with this expanded conception of the local component of the vote.

For midterm elections, the basic trends noted earlier remain evident: after the late-1950s collapse, elections became more nationalized affairs during the Nixon administration, a trend interrupted in the late 1980s then resumed in 1994. Reflecting the large 1980s incumbency advantage, the local component shows an upward trend after the 1974 dip. For presidential elections, however, the pattern is more one of stability with a sudden convergence of local and national influences in 1996. Looking at the evidence as a whole, it suggests a gradual process of increasing nationalization since the disruptions of the late-Dwight Eisenhower–John F. Kennedy–Lyndon Johnson years, a process that was severely interrupted in the late 1980s, but resumed with a vengeance in the 1990s.

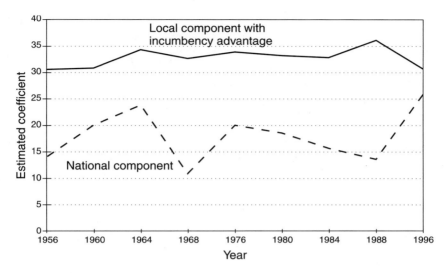

Figure 7.7. Alternative decomposition of presidential-year House elections, 1956–1996.

Sources of Change

In order for the national component of the House vote to have grown in importance over time, either other factors affecting the vote have been declining in importance over the same period or the House vote as a whole has been becoming more predictable. In some of our figures the local component of the vote appears to be waning in magnitude, while the national component generally has been on the rise, yet the figures do not show a neat tradeoff as they would if they had been the only factors influencing the House vote. In general, there is more variation in the national component than in the local component. However, Figures 7.6 and 7.7 show that this is less true when the incumbency advantage is taken into account, suggesting that incumbency might be a good starting point in trying to understand why elections have become more nationalized.

It is possible that the growth in the national component of the vote has come at the expense of the incumbency advantage. If voters today are more likely to make their electoral decisions based on national concerns, incumbency would necessarily decline in importance as a voting cue in House elections. Given that the incumbency advantage is a reflection of district and personal considerations, it is logical to suppose that incumbency should fade as House elections become more nationalized.

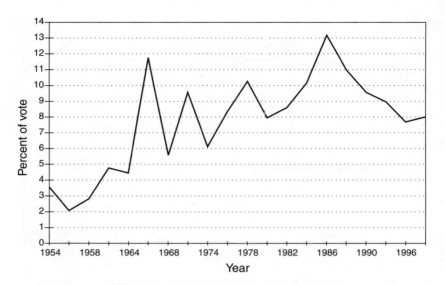

Figure 7.8. House incumbency advantage, 1954–1998 (vote share attributable to incumbency).

Estimates of incumbency advantage (b_3) for the entire time series are presented in Figure 7.8, several features of which are quite interesting. The first observation is that the incumbency advantage in the 1996 House elections was the smallest it has been since 1980. Indeed, the drop in the incumbency advantage since the mid-1980s noisily tracks the increase in the national component of the vote.[14] The years in which the advantage is the largest— 1966 and 1986—are also years in which the gap between the local and national components is quite large. The general trend for all nineteen House elections is that the national component is larger in years when the incumbency advantage is smaller, and vice versa. Thus, there is some preliminary evidence that a decline in the incumbency effect is one of the factors related to the nationalization of modern House elections.

The causal links are ambiguous, however. Have elections become more nationalized because incumbency has become less valuable as a voting cue, or has incumbency weakened as a voting cue because elections have become more nationalized? The relationship is likely to be simultaneous, so that the question of what has produced greater nationalization cannot be answered simply by treating changes in the incumbency advantage as exogenous. Unfortunately, it will no doubt be a difficult task to explain the decline in the incumbency advantage given that there is still scholarly disagreement over what caused the advantage to surge three decades ago!

Some other factors that may have contributed to increased nationalization deserve mention. First, voting trends could reflect changes the South has undergone in the post–civil rights era at both the House and presidential levels. The percentage of southern seats with two-party competition has nearly doubled from 1954 to 1996, and apportionment has increased the size of the southern delegation by twenty seats.[15] The Republican party has succeeded not only in making the congressional races more competitive, but in the last three elections it has managed to capture and sustain a majority of seats in the South for the first time in history. This regional victory was the key to the party's 1994 capture of both chambers of Congress (Bullock in this volume).

Perhaps in the past, House elections outside the South were always fairly nationalized, and now the changes in the South have caused the national component in southern elections to attain levels comparable with the rest of the country. To examine this hypothesis, we repeated our modified Gelman-King regression analysis on districts outside the south.[16] The resulting estimates of the local and national components are plotted in Figures 7.9 and 7.10 for midterm and presidential elections. Perhaps somewhat surprisingly, the trends resemble those in Figures 7.4a and 7.5a, except that in presidential elections the decay in the national component is more gradual and lasts longer before recovering after the 1968 elections. But all in all the figures do not suggest significant regional variation in the process of nationalization. Thus, realignment in the South does not appear to be a major factor underlying the growth in the national component of the House vote (see also Jacobson's essay in this volume).[17]

A second, related possibility concerns the changing ideological faces of the two major political parties. Historically, the Democrats have tended to be a coalition party, more ideologically heterogeneous than the Republicans, a description particularly appropriate for the New Deal period and afterward, when the Democratic party contained a large, conservative southern contingent while the minority Republican party was more internally consistent (Mayer 1996). Since then, however, issues such as civil rights, taxes, and welfare have led to conservative Democrats' defeats, defections, and retirements, leaving the party more liberal and more homogeneous. At the same time, the influence of the religious right has grown in the Republican party, which has become indisputably a conservative party.

Because this ideological shifting has primarily been a regional phenome-

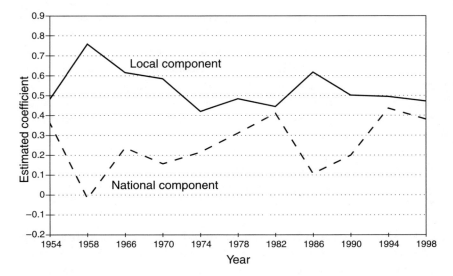

Figure 7.9. Decomposition of midterm House elections, non–southern contested seats, 1954–1998.

non, a major part of the argument is implicitly about the South. But we have shown that the South in and of itself does not account for the growth in the national component; thus, the argument requires further elaboration. If the parties have become both more distinct and more internally homogeneous, then voters in different districts in the South and non–South increasingly are being presented with similar alternatives.[18] Thus, their voting could appear to be more national in its basis although they are simply responding to the more distinctive alternatives the nomination process now generates.

A final possibility concerns the effects of public policy on voting decisions. In particular, since Jimmy Carter's administration high-level budgetary politics has come to dominate the legislative agenda. This placed much of the consequent congressional debate in full view of the public. At the same time, PACs grew in importance both financially and with regard to member visibility, often publicizing members' votes on roll calls of particular interest to the PACs. Today, it is much harder for individual members to hide their votes or fudge their positions than a generation ago. Today's voters in principle have access to considerable policy information in addition to the usual local heuristics.

There is some preliminary evidence for this claim. As mentioned previously, several authors have shown that losing incumbents in 1994 could of-

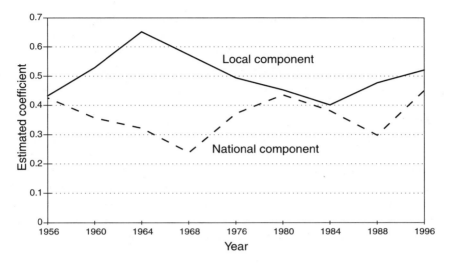

Figure 7.10. Decomposition of presidential-year House elections, non-southern contested seats, 1956–1996.

ten trace their defeat to a particular roll-call vote. Brady, Canes-Wrone, and Cogan (this volume) generalize these findings and empirically demonstrate that there is a direct link between a member's voting record and her probability of reelection. These results lend credibility to a policy-based explanation, and a more systematic examination of the relationship between nationalization and the rise in the importance of budgetary politics might provide further evidence in support of this interpretation.[19]

Conclusion

In this paper, we have sought to empirically test the claim that the 1994 and 1996 House elections were national elections, standing in contrast with the conventional wisdom that modern House elections have been purely local affairs. To do so, we first assessed existing definitions of nationalization—both conceptual and empirical—and suggested a different and improved approach. We proposed an alternative, simple measure of nationalization, the two-party share of the district presidential vote, and analyzed nineteen House elections from 1954 to 1996. We discovered that, since the late 1960s or early 1970s, the national component of the House vote has been increasing, while the local component has been holding steady or gradually declining in importance. This finding is robust; including uncontested seats via imputation yields similar results, and even excluding southern districts from the analysis does not disrupt the trend.

Having shown that House elections do indeed seem to have become more nationalized, we examined some possible explanations. One was a decline in the incumbency advantage, a decline that has very roughly paralleled the growth in the national component of the House vote. Our results showed that when incumbency was high, the national component was smaller relative to the local component, and vice versa. A second explanation was that the recent changes in southern congressional elections and party politics might directly affect nationalization, but our preliminary evidence suggests that this is not the case. We then speculated about other possible causes of nationalization and concluded that there are several avenues of research that may be important in gaining a deeper understanding of nationalization.

Chapter 8

Representation of Constituency Ideology in Congress

ROBERT S. ERIKSON AND GERALD C. WRIGHT

The job description for membership in the House of Representatives contains the important maxim to represent one's district. House members represent their districts in a variety of ways. They intercede on behalf of constituents in interactions with the federal bureaucracy. They protect the economic interests of their districts when at risk in Washington. They promote the flow of federal pork to their districts. The standards of performance for these activities are well understood. The member who ignores constituents is likely to be given the boot by the voters. The fact that over 90 percent of incumbents typically get reelected is testimony to their success at satisfying constituents that they are doing their job well enough to earn reelection.

Of the ways that members represent their districts, the most challenging is *ideological* representation. All districts—whether conservative or liberal—contain a range of ideological voices and policy demands, sometimes shrill and sometimes muted. Members must determine the distribution of district ideological preferences and then calculate an ideological strategy to maximize their reelection chances. Since their personal preferences sometimes conflict with the strategically best ideological response, members must gauge when they must reflect the district ideologically rather than risk defeat, and when they can afford the risk of shirking district preferences by achieving personal ideological satisfaction.

This chapter focuses on the representation of district ideological preferences in the House of Representatives and the mechanisms by which representation is achieved. Members of Congress believe that their ideological positions affect their reelection prospects, and behave accordingly. As we will see, members tend to represent the mean or median ideological position of their districts, and do so in direct proportion to their electoral insecurity. They do so for good reason, as constituencies often will turn incumbents out of office when they are ideologically unresponsive.[1]

Theory: Variations on the Downs Model of Electoral Representation

A useful starting point for discussing the role of ideological positioning in two-candidate elections is the Downs model of ideological voting, so named because Anthony Downs (1957) was the first to articulate the model in great detail. The Downs model assumes a set of voters arrayed on a single-dimensioned ideological continuum ranging from left to right. These ideological voters select candidates based on the relative proximity to the voters' ideological positions. In other words, people vote for the ideologically closest candidate.

The question becomes this: If voters choose in this strictly ideological manner, what strategies should the candidates pursue? Downs assumes that the candidates are driven solely by the pursuit of electoral victory with no concern of their own about achieving ideological satisfaction. Given this assumption, candidates should gravitate to the position of the median voter, or the voter at the 50th percentile on the left–right scale. The reason is that when both candidates are positioned, neither has an incentive to leave (Downs 1957; Calvert 1985).

To see why this is the case, assume candidate D is at the 50th percentile position. Opposing candidate R could claim the same position or a different one. Assume candidate R moves to the right, to the position of the voter at the 60th percentile of conservatism. Everybody from the 55th percentile to the left would vote for D, their closest candidate; everybody from the 55th percentile to the right would vote for R, their closest candidate. The result would be that candidate R would lose with only 45 percent of the vote. This realization would compel candidate R to join candidate D at the 50th percentile where they would split the vote about 50–50.

The Downs model requires two important modifications in order for it to depict electoral reality. First, as many empirical studies of voting have shown, voters do not vote solely on the basis of ideology. They vote their party identifications and take into account the perceived competence of the candidates apart from ideology. Besides, not all voters pay sufficient attention to become aware of the ideological signals sent by candidates. Rather than claiming that voters will *always* vote for the ideologically closest candidate, we can only claim that voters are *somewhat* more likely to vote for the closer candidate, everything else being equal. The upshot is that elections are not always won by the candidate with the greatest ideological proximity to the electorate.

The second source of simplification in the Downs model is that the candidates are motivated not only by winning but also by their personal ideological preferences and those of their strongest supporters. Within the Democratic party, the candidates, political activists, and primary electorates all tend to be more liberal than the median constituent. Within the Republican party, the opposite is true; candidates, activists, and primary electorates tend to be more conservative than the median voter. In each party, candidates are pulled two ways: toward the center by the electoral logic of the Downs model, and toward the ideological periphery by their party's ideological extreme and, perhaps, their own ideological preferences.

With not-so-ideological voters wooed by rather ideological candidates, the situation gets complicated. Candidates are only somewhat motivated to move to the center, and only when they perceive a strong electoral threat. Thus, the Democratic and Republican candidates tend to be somewhat far apart from one another ideologically. With ideologically divergent candidates, the voters are in a position to reward and punish candidates based on their ideological positions. Almost always, the Democratic candidate will be to the left of most constituents and almost always the Republican candidate will be to the right of most constituents.[2]

Given the complications to the Downs model, candidates are only *somewhat* motivated to move to the center. And voters only reward *somewhat* candidates who move toward the center. In our empirical analysis, we will look for incumbents within each party to be *somewhat* more moderate when their district is more typical of the other party. And we will look for constituencies to punish incumbents *somewhat* when they stray from moderation.

Measurement: Scoring Constituency and Member Ideologies

When we try to observe the role of ideology in House elections, we are mildly handicapped because it is usually the case that while the ideological behavior of incumbent candidates is observable from their roll-call votes, we usually lack data on the positions of challengers or for open-seat candidates. Roll-call voting records can be scored on the ideological dimension as relatively conservative or relatively liberal. By the Downsian logic discussed above, Democrats have an incentive to move toward the right from their party tendency. Their electoral incentive is at the center, or even to the right of most constituents if their Republican opponent is fixed in a far right position. By the same logic, Republicans have an incentive to moderate or move even more liberal than the district if the Democratic opponent is fixed at a far left position. Thus, we look for incumbents to moderate when electorally threatened. We also look for evidence that such moderation pays off at the polls.

As a measure of constituency ideological preferences, we use the constituency vote for president. Liberal districts vote more Democratic for president; conservative districts vote more Republican. We expect districts' presidential voting to predict roll-call ideology due to two codependent dynamic processes at work. One process is the responsiveness of House members to their constituencies' ideological preferences. Members cater to constituency preferences from a desire to stay elected. The second process is electoral selection on the part of the voters. When members stray too far from district opinion, constituency electorates are more likely to send them to defeat. The first of these two processes depends on the presence of the second. If electorates were indifferent to the policy stands of their elected representatives, then Congress members would have no strong incentive to follow constituency opinion.

District presidential voting predicts the representative's ideological behavior because it reflects district ideology. Since district presidential voting also reflects district partisanship, it represents the member's level of electoral security as well. The more Democratic the district presidential vote, the safer the seat is for Democrats to hold and the more difficult for Republicans to hold. Thus, we expect Democratic districts to elect Democratic incumbents who are safe enough to not need to moderate, and (more rarely) Republican candidates who can survive only by moderation. Similarly, we expect Republican districts to elect mainly safe Republicans who do not moderate and an occasional Democrat who survives by moderating.

It should be noted that measures of roll-call ideology and district presidential voting are measured on different scales. Fortunately, this lack of common calibration presents no serious difficulty. The reason is that candidates' electoral incentives to move away from their parties' extremes hold true even if candidates move to the opposite side of the district's median voter. The strategically "best" position is not necessarily the median position; if the opponent is firmly planted at one extreme, then a candidate's "best" position is just slightly closer to the center than the opponent. As long as he or she stays more liberal than the Republican, a Democratic candidate always gains by becoming more conservative. Similarly, as long as he or she stays more conservative than the Democrat, a Republican candidate always gains by becoming more liberal.[3]

We observe representation from the relationship between district ideology, on one hand (reflected in district presidential voting) and member ideology, on the other (reflected in roll-call voting). The index of roll-call voting we use is the member's liberalism/conservatism as measured by a composite of the ratings of two ideological groups, the liberal ADA and the conservative American Conservative Union (ACU). Each rates the members based on their votes on what the group perceives to be key roll calls. We take the average of the member's percent liberal as scored by the ADA and 100 minus the percent conservative as scored by the ACU. For a few years, we include only the ADA scores due to data availability. Percent liberal is of course the polar opposite of percent conservative. When discussing Republican members, we generally refer to the correlation between member and district *conservatism*. For Democratic members, we generally refer to the correlation between member and district *liberalism*. Below, we consider group ratings for all Congresses between the 94th (elected in 1974, up for reelection in 1976) and the 104th (elected in 1994, up for reelection in 1996).

Our analysis includes the congressional vote in all election years from 1976 to 1996, except 1992. The reason for the one omission is difficulty in matching members in new and old districts, following the 1990 census. For all Congresses from 1983 through 1996, we have available as a regular measure of constituency ideology the presidential vote from the 1988 presidential election within contemporary districts' boundaries. Even though the districts changed with the 1990 census, we are able to utilize the 1988 George Bush–Michael Dukakis vote in the new districts of members serving in the 1990s. For 1976, 1978, and 1980 election years, we substitute the presidential vote in 1972 (George McGovern–Richard Nixon).

Constituency Ideology, Party Affiliation, and Congressional Roll-Call Voting

Table 8.1 shows regression equations predicting member ideology from district presidential voting (ideology) and member party affiliation for nine of the ten Congresses from 1977 to 1996. We omit 1991–92 due to data diffi-

Table 8.1

Effects of Party and Constituency (Presidential Vote)
on Roll-Call Liberalism, 1976–1996

Year	Presidential vote[a]	Member's party[b]	Adjusted R^2
1976	1.21	35.2	.64
1978	1.22	29.6	.62
1980	1.11	36.8	.69
1982	1.14	31.2	.65
1984	1.07	40.5	.73
1986	1.12	38.8	.75
1988	.96	46.4	.77
1990	1.03	43.9	.78
1994	.97	50.4	.85
1996	.68	59.5	.86

SOURCE: Unless otherwise indicated, all tables and figures in Chapter 8 are based on the author's data.

NOTE: Values in the second and third columns are unstandardized regression coefficients. All coefficients are significant at $p < .01$.

[a]This variable is the McGovern vote (1972) for 1976–80 and the Dukakis vote (1988) 1982–96.

[b]Member's party is score 1 for Democratic incumbents, 0 for Republican incumbents. Open seats are excluded.

culties. The most important point of the coefficients in Table 8.1 is that constituency presidential voting is almost as strong a predictor of congressional ideological positions as is the member's party affiliation. We can see this from the sizable t-statistics for both independent variables. Table 8.1 also shows an appreciable growth in the effect of party affiliation as Congress moved into the mid-1990s. (We discuss the impact of this growth later in this chapter.) The effect of "party" largely reflects the ideological pull of party elites, primary electorates, and personal ideological preference of the member, rather than an imposed party discipline. Thus, the twin effects of party and constituency on roll-call voting reflect the sometimes conflicting influences of constituency general electoral pressures v. the member's partisan coalition.

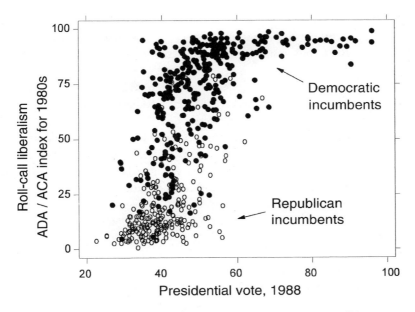

Figure 8.1. Roll-call ideology with presidential vote, by party affiliation.

Figure 8.1 shows this graphically for members elected in the 1980s. It shows constituency position on the horizontal axis, represented by the 1988 presidential vote. It shows average ideological position on the vertical axis. Republican and Democratic members are distinguished by the hollow dots for Republicans and solid dots for Democrats. To observe the twin effects of party and constituency, note first that within each party the most liberal members represent the most liberal (Democratic) districts and the most conservative members represent the most conservative (Republican) districts. Note second that for any particular value of the presidential vote, Republican members are considerably more conservative than Democrats. This pattern reassures us that the voter's choice of electing a Republican or a Democrat almost always makes an ideological difference.

Elections and their anticipation determine the pattern shown in Figure 8.1. Liberal districts are also Democratic districts and therefore usually elect Democrats. Similarly, conservative districts are also Republican districts and therefore usually elect Republicans. Democratic House members representing liberal districts and Republican House members representing conservative districts normally have few electoral worries. It is with constituencies in the middle of the spectrum that election outcomes are often in doubt. It is in competitive or middle-of-the-road districts that candidates are best able to affect their own electoral prospects by manipulating their ideological posture.

Districts in the middle are generally represented by relatively moderate Republicans or relatively moderate Democrats. There are two related reasons. First, via ideological voting, middle districts tend to elect moderates over more extreme candidates. Very conservative Republican candidates and very liberal Democratic candidates are more likely to lose in the first place. Second, candidates anticipate ideological voting and respond accordingly. To help assure their election, candidates from middle districts are less likely to attach themselves to their party's ideological extreme.

Ideological Selection by Congressional Constituencies

To what extent do constituencies select congressional representatives based on ideological proximity? One way to observe evidence of electoral selection based on ideology is from regression equations predicting the congressional district vote from the member's roll-call ideology, while controlling for the district presidential vote. For Republican members, we measure ideology as conservatism. For Democratic members we measure it as liberalism. Table 8.2 shows the relevant regressions for roll-call ideology for elections from the 1970s through the 1990s.

Table 8.2 shows that member ideology is strongly but negatively related to the congressional vote. For Republican members, the more conservative the roll-call record the fewer votes received for Congress. For Democrats, the more liberal the roll-call record, the fewer votes received for Congress. This is electoral selection at work. Shortly we will see the impact on actual outcomes—who wins and who loses.

For a closer look at the two sides of the representation process, we concentrate on the set of House elections from the 1980s, which we define as the elections of 1982–90, following the post–1980 Census redistricting. For each member serving during this period, we identify the mean roll-call position on the ideological scale. For each district, we measure district partisanship/ideology as the district vote for president in 1988. Table 8.3 represents two composite regression equations for the 1980s, one for each party. Each equation accounts for district congressional voting on the basis of constituency partisanship/ideology (the 1988 presidential vote), from member ideology and for a set of "dummy variables" representing the varying short-

Table 8.2

Regression of Incumbent Vote Margin on Ideology, 1976–1996

	Rep. Incumbents			Dem. Incumbents		
Year	Coefficient	(T-value)	N	Coefficient	(T-value)	N
1976	0.12	(2.57)	104	0.10	(2.42)	162
1978	0.07	(1.16)	92	0.13	(2.71)	157
1980	0.15	(2.64)	103	0.18	(4.21)	163
1982	0.17	(3.42)	104	0.20	(3.46)	110
1984	0.14	(3.61)	126	0.17	(4.93)	187
1986	0.16	(3.23)	136	0.10	(2.60)	176
1988	0.25	(5.18)	142	0.15	(3.61)	182
1990	0.28	(6.01)	119	0.13	(3.37)	198
1994	0.08	(1.80)	119	0.19	(5.29)	208
1996	0.17	(4.65)	182	0.15	(3.06)	142

NOTE: Controlling for presidential vote variables for the decade, South, and presidential vote–South interactions. Some districts are excluded due to redistricting. Ideology is mean of ADA and 100 − ACU, except for 1996, when only ACU is used.

term forces represented by the year of the election. The coefficients for district presidential voting and for the member's ideology both achieve high levels of statistical significance. In incumbent races, districts tend to vote for Congress like they vote for president, but they modify their vote according to their members' ideological record.

The sizes of the coefficients for roll-call ideology in Tables 8.2 and 8.3 are revealing. They achieve values sometimes greater (in absolute magnitude) than 0.20. This means that every point on the 100-point ideological roll-call scale is worth roughly 0.20 percentage points at the polls. Put another way, every five points of ideology in roll-call voting is worth about one percentage point at the polls. A shift of 50 percentage points in ideological roll-call voting is worth about 10 percentage points. For instance, a Republican who is expected to win 45 percent of the vote with a 100 percent conservative voting record would expect to win about 55 percent of voters with a 50 percent conservative voting record.

The information contained in Table 8.3 is also known to members of Congress. They know that their expected vote is a function of district partisanship/ideology, their roll-call record, and unpredictable "year effects."

Table 8.3

Effects of Roll-Call Ideology and Presidential Vote on Incumbents'
Vote Margins: Pooled Regression, 1982–1990

	Republican Incumbents	Democratic Incumbents
Decade mean ideology[a]	−0.20	−0.15
	(−10.10)	(−9.26)
Presidential vote 1988 (inc. party)	0.72	0.61
	(14.13)	(25.10)
Year dummies		
1982	−2.02	3.97
	(−2.10)	(4.68)
1984	6.29	−1.95
	(6.87)	(−2.71)
1986	3.75	4.34
	(4.17)	(5.92)
1988	5.08	3.20
	(5.69)	(4.40)
Constant	35.85	46.08
	(13.92)	(36.76)
Adjusted R^2	0.339	0.473
SEE	7.18	7.10
N	631	857

NOTE: T-values are in parentheses.

[a]Scoring direction: conservative for Republicans; liberal for Democrats.

They also know the range of uncertainty around these expectations. Members can anticipate their next vote as:

$$Vote = E(Vote) + error$$

where E(*Vote*) is the expected vote (similar to predictions from our regression equations) and *error* represents the difference between the actual and expected votes. The *error* is a normal distribution centered around the expected vote. If members were to model their calculations from our regression analysis of Table 8.3, they would anticipate this error as a normal distribution with a mean of zero and a standard deviation of about 7.5. We obtain this estimate of uncertainty by combining the error variance from the equation predictions and the variance from unpredictable national short-term forces or year effects.[4] In intuitive terms, we can first obtain a point prediction for a member by multiplying and adding the terms of the regression equation. With the statistical rule of thumb that about 95 percent of cases fall within two standard deviations of the mean, a 7.5 standard deviation suggests that 95 percent of the time the outcome will fall within fifteen points of the expected vote. For instance, one member might see her election prospects as a best guess of, say, 65 percent of the vote, based on something like our equation. Taking into account the error in this expectation, 2.5 percent of the time the vote would be over 80 percent and 2.5 percent of the time under 50 percent. The risk of the latter possibility is of special concern to our member. Given the 7.5 estimated standard deviation, our hypothetical member's expectation is to win on average with 65 percent of the vote while anticipating a 97.5 percent chance of surviving the next election. Using the contours of the normal distribution, similar calculations can be made for other members, with differing values for their expected vote.

Congressional Responses to Constituency Ideology

Members of Congress face the task of balancing the sometimes conflicting goals of reelection and satisfying their personal ideological needs and those of their partisan supporters. We have observed the evidence that incumbents' electoral success is influenced by roll-call ideology. What does the evidence show regarding the congressional response?

Given the information contained in the regression equations of Table 8.3, we are able to estimate members' probabilities of reelection as a function of district and member ideology. The one variable that members can manipulate is their own ideological record. Thus, members could ask questions of the sort, "how can I affect my reelection chances by adjusting my ideological posture?"

In actuality, members of Congress are remarkably stable in their roll-call records, as measured by ideological group ratings. Thus, members rarely change their basic ideological stances once they have congressional experience. Small changes may be too small to be noticed by many voters and might risk the charge of ideological "flip-flopping." Members' ideological choices are made before they develop a visible ideological record.

Let us consider the decision of a new Republican freshman House member. For the sake of argument, assume that this new member's personal ideological preference would be a 100 percent conservative voting record.[5] But the member knows that by taking a public posture leftward from this ideal additional votes will be gained in the general election. Thus, the new mem-

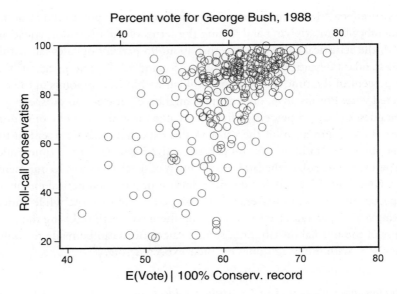

Figure 8.2. Republican roll-call conservatism by district presidential vote and expected congressional vote, 1980s.

ber must strike a tradeoff. By sticking to the far right, the member achieves maximum ideological satisfaction, but at some electoral risk. By moderating, the member can shore up the electoral base, but with a cost in terms of ideologically motivated partisans in his or her party. How the member solves this problem will depend in part on the electoral circumstances.

To provide a helpful illustration, Figure 8.2 presents a scatterplot predicting the average ideological position of 1980s Republican members, as a function of the 1988 presidential vote for George Bush in their districts, recorded as a percentage along the top margin. We observe a moderate correlation representing ideological roll-call behavior as a function of district voting for the offfice of president. This graph is more meaningful, however, if the horizontal axis is scaled not as the district vote for president but as the expected vote for Congress, given the district vote for president. Thus, we present along the bottom margin the Republican member's expected vote given average (for the 1980s) short-term forces or year effects. This expected vote is extrapolated from the Republican equation in Table 8.2, and shows the expected vote *assuming that the member voted a 100 percent conservative voting record.*

The thing to notice from Figure 8.2 is that members who are electorally threatened—whose expected vote would be near or below 50 percent with a 100 percent conservative record—are the ones who moderate. Very safe Republicans are far more likely to actually vote close to 100 percent conservative. For the sake of argument, assume that the typical Republican member's personal ideological preference would be a 100 percent conservative voting record. But our member can gain more votes by taking a public posture more leftward from this personal ideal. Thus, the member must achieve a tradeoff. By sticking to the far right, the member achieves maximum ideological satisfaction, but at some electoral risk. By moderating, the member can shore up the electoral base but with a cost in terms of ideological satisfaction. How the member solves this problem will depend in part on the electoral circumstances.

One way to demonstrate the moderation process and its electoral effect is particularly revealing. From the expected vote and the net variance around this estimate, we can estimate the probability that a member will lose in a typical election year. In Figure 8.3, the horizontal axis is the expected vote for a Republican incumbent, given a 100 percent conservative voting record, as before. The vertical axis is scaled as the probability of an incumbent victory, given the expected vote for the member's actual roll-call record *plus the net variance around this expected vote*. There are two curved lines. The lower curved line represents the probability of winning, given the expected vote and a 100 percent conservative voting record. The upper curved line represents the probability of winning given a 50 percent conservative voting record. The gap between these two lines is slight on the right-hand side of the graph, where virtually all Republicans should be safe. The gap becomes large when the expected vote (assuming a 100 percent conservative roll-call record) is in the 50–50 range. This is because when the outcome is problematic, relatively small ideological movement can make a big difference.

In Figure 8.3, the hollow dots represent the projected probabilities of reelection (vertical axis) given the actual roll-call records (not shown) and the expected vote given a 100 percent conservative voting record (horizontal axis) for House Republicans in the 1980s. Clearly, most Republican incumbents were in position to be safely reelected even with 100 percent conservative records. In the upper right-hand part of the graph we see many safe Republican incumbents whose likelihoods of winning are unaffected by moderating behavior. They need not moderate, and they do not. On the left side of the graph, however, we observe several Republican members who are likely losers if they hold to a 100 percent conservative voting record. (This result is projected from the lower curved line.) In actuality, these otherwise-threatened Republican incumbents enjoy reelection probabilities

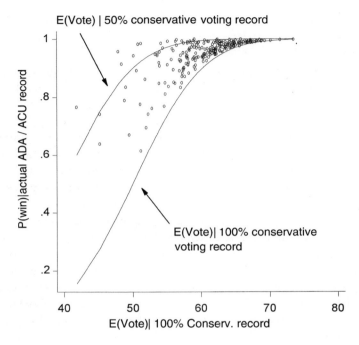

Figure 8.3. Estimated effects of roll-call moderation on the probability of winning, Republican incumbents in the 1980s.

that are rather safe. The vertical distances between the observations and the bottom curved line represent the gains in reelection probability from their roll-call moderation. The vertical distances between the observations and the top curved line represent the difference in probability of reelection between the actual roll-call record and a moderate 50 percent conservative record.

Moderating behavior accounts for an appreciable portion of incumbents' success at reelection. We can see this by the following experiment. For each Republican incumbent race over the five election years of the 1980s, we "set" the incumbent's roll-call record to 100 percent conservative. For Democratic incumbents, we make a parallel setting of the roll-call record to 100 percent liberal. We then ask: Given our equations of Table 8.2, what are the probable reelection rates for the two sets of incumbents? As our benchmark, 98 percent of all Democratic incumbents and 96 percent of all Republican incumbents got reelected during the 1980s.

From the information contained in Table 8.3, we can project each 1980s'

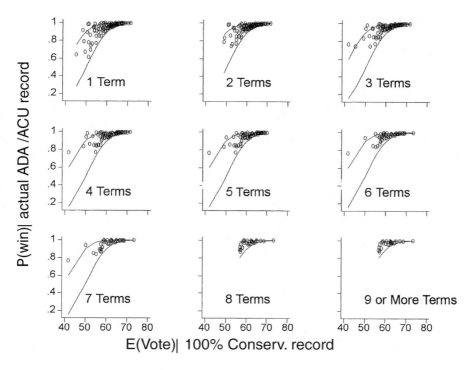

Figure 8.4. Estimated effects of moderation on the probability of winning, by seniority, Republicans in the 1980s.

incumbent's probability of winning the next election assuming a 100 percent conservative (Republicans) or 100 percent liberal (Democrats) voting record. Averaged over Republican incumbents, the probability of winning the next election with a 100 percent conservative record was 88 percent. Thus, the average risk of defeat would have tripled from 4 percent to 12 percent given a 100 percent conservative voting record. Averaged over Democratic incumbents, the probability of winning the next election with a 100 percent liberal record was 91 percent, which more than tripled the average risk. Put another way, *members of Congress cut their short-term electoral risk by as much as two-thirds by taking the ideological positions they did instead of their party's ideological extreme.*

Keep in mind that there are two related reasons why we observe few threatened Republican members who do not moderate. One is the anticipation of the likelihood of a loss if the member does not moderate. The other is that those who do not moderate do not survive long. Figure 8.4 repeats

Figure 8.3's demonstration of the relationship between expected vote (given a 100 percent conservative record) and the probability of winning the next election. This time, however, the graph is subdivided by seniority. Figure 8.4 shows that the more terms the member has served, the fewer observations there are in the range where the probability of surviving the next election is low. Among the threatened, survival is highest among those who moderate.

We have now seen several graphs that illustrate the contribution of ideological moderation for survival by congressional Republicans. We could also illustrate with congressional Democrats, showing the mirror opposite pattern. For Republicans, moderation means more liberalism. For Democrats, it means more conservatism. Among Democrats, the most electorally threatened (assuming a 100 percent liberal record) are the ones most likely to moderate in the conservative direction. And those who need to but do not are the ones who do not survive long.

Refinement: Calibrating Constituencies and Members on a Common Scale

So far, we have related constituency opinion on one scale (presidential voting) to ideological roll-call voting (ACU, ADA scales) on another. What we miss by doing this is the nuance of estimating relative ideological distances *between* members and districts. While we can say that more district conservatism generates a more conservative member, for example, we cannot say anything about the actual closeness between districts and their members.

In this section we remedy this limitation by recalibrating constituency opinion and roll-call ideology on a common scale. This common scale is the 1–7 ideological scale that the NES uses to measure citizen ideological preferences in its national surveys every election year. In NES surveys, people are asked to rate themselves on a scale that goes from very liberal (1) to very conservative (7). For midterm elections, NES also has asked its respondents to rate their congressional candidates on the same 1–7 scale. Here, for leverage, we use citizen ratings of their representatives relative to themselves.

Our first task is to recalibrate district presidential voting (the 1988 Bush-Dukakis vote) to represent the NES 1–7 scale. For instance, we ask which mean position on the 7-point scale corresponds to a 55 percent vote for Bush in 1988. To obtain an answer, we take observed respondent ideological positions for *informed* (see below) NES respondents, 1982–90. We regress the *respondents'* 1–7 ideological positions on their *district's* Bush vote. By doing this, we have an estimate of the average 1–7 scale position for every possible value of the Bush vote. In practice, the district Bush vote ranges from less than 10 percent to more than 75 percent. The corresponding scale positions are mainly in the range from three to five. In other words, the ideological distance between a very anti–Bush district and a very pro–Bush district is only about two points on the seven–point ideological scale.

Our second task is to recalibrate roll–call ideological voting, represented as percent conservative or percent liberal, as positions on the 1–7 NES scale. Here, for a set of informed respondents, we regress respondent perceptions of the member's ideology (along with member's party affiliation) on the roll–call score. It makes some difference whether we try to estimate ideological nuances for all NES respondents willing to venture a guess as to the member's ideology or whether we restrict the estimate to people defined as informed in some way. The difference is that informed respondents see sharper differences. We choose to use informed respondents measured as those who (1) see the Democratic party to the left of the Republican party when rating the *parties* on the 1–7 scale and (2) willingly rate both the incumbent and the challenger on the 1–7 scale (but not necessarily the Democrat to the Republican's right). The advantage of this restriction to informed respondents is that evaluations appear to be unaffected by the respondent's own ideological position.

With this regression of perceived member ideology on actual roll–call position and party, we have a measure of the expected ideological perception given the actual roll–call position and party. Both roll–call position and member party affiliation affect the perceptions even of informed respondents. The contribution of party affiliation to perceptions is strong evidence that members are limited by party stereotype in how much they can affect their ideological image. It is likely that virtually all Republican incumbents are perceived to their opponents' right and virtually all Democratic incumbents are perceived to their opponents' left, even in the rare instances when these ideological stereotypes are not "objectively" true.

Because we use a subset of seemingly informed respondents for the calibration of member ideological positions, we use the identical set of informed respondents for the calibration of constituency ideology. By the procedures just outlined, we have projected district presidential voting onto the 1–7 scale and done the same for member roll–call voting. We can use these projections for all races of the 1980s, not just those used in the calibration exercise.

Figure 8.5 presents the picture for Republicans. This is the same graph shown in Figures 8.2 and 8.3 as a relationship between constituency posi-

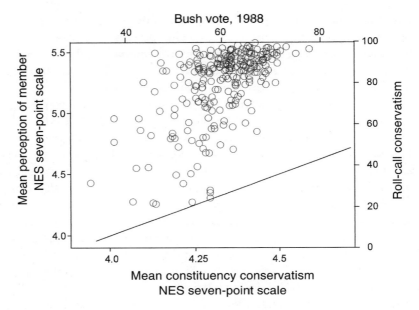

Figure 8.5. Conservatism of Republican House members by constituency ideology (using NES seven-point scale metric).

SOURCE: NES, 1982–90.

tion, the Bush vote, and roll-call position. Figure 8.5 is scaled so that (informed) constituency ideology on the NES 1–7 scale predicts (informed) perceptions of the same 1–7 scale. Constituency ideology is rescaled as (projected) mean ideology, among the informed, on the NES 1–7 scale. Member ideology is rescaled as (projected) constituent mean perceptions (among the informed) of member positions on the same 1–7 scale. The original scales are also shown along the top margin (Bush vote) and right margin (roll-call conservatism).

With the rescaling we have two powerful new observations. First, since all cases are above the diagonal line representing equivalence between constituency opinion and member perception, we observe that Republican House members are perceived to the right of their districts. This should be no surprise. Second, we see that the gap between the member and the district grows as the district becomes more conservative. This means that the more conservative the district, the more the informed constituents see their member as more conservative than themselves. This observation may be a surprise, but it has an interesting explanation. The most conservative dis-

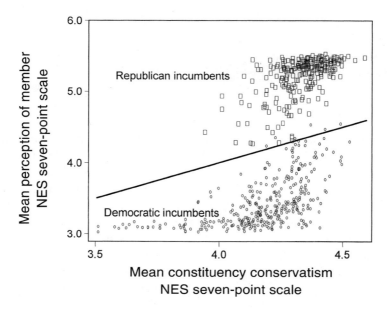

Figure 8.6. Representation as seen by the voters: Incumbents of the 1980s.
SOURCE: NES, 1982–90.

tricts are the safest for Republican candidates, which gives Republican conservative candidates more license to act out their conservatism.

The mirror image pattern can be shown for Democrats. Figure 8.6 com-
bines the graph for Republican incumbents with that for Democrats. The
horizontal axis again represents the mean position of informed voters on
the 1–7 scale. The vertical axis represents the mean perceived position of the
member on the 1–7 scale. To some extent the gap between the perceptions
of Republican and Democratic members are exaggerated by the fact that
even informed voters take into account member party affiliation.

As Figure 8.6 highlights, there is greater range of opinion among Dem-
ocratic-held districts than Republican-held districts. At each extreme of
district ideology, safe members are either perceived considerably more
conservative than their district (Republicans) or considerably more liberal
(Democrats). The battleground districts, where incumbent reelection is
more problematical, fall in the middle. Among the cases in the middle, the
ones closer to the diagonal line represent members perceived closer to the
mean (informed) voter position. In this range, the cases closer to the diagonal represent incumbents who are closer to their district and thus more likely

to win reelection. Members from competitive districts may wish to join their party's ideological extreme, but the electoral costs of doing so would be too high. Instead, most members from competitive districts take relatively moderate positions, which help their reelection chances.

Electoral Change and Representation

Our analysis so far has treated the electoral environment as static, as though the mechanisms that give rise to the representative-represented relationship have been constant through the decades. But in fact, considerable electoral change has occurred over the last twenty years, affecting the nature of and extent to which congressional constituencies receive faithful policy representation in Congress. Among the citizenry there have been changes in partisanship since the mid-1970s, with the largest changes being the dramatic growth of Republican identification, particularly in the southern states. In Congress, Republicans have gained numerical strength to the point that they have become the majority congressional party. As with voters, the Republican gain in Congress has been strongest in the South. As the South turns Republican, the two major parties have become even more polarized on issues. The blocs of conservative southern Democrats and moderate northeastern Republicans who gave each party their moderate wings are much smaller today than they were twenty years ago. Here, we address the increased ideological polarization of congressional parties, and its effect on congressional responsiveness to constituency ideology.

It has become evident to congressional observers that the Republicans and Democrats in Congress have become increasingly polarized on the basis of ideology. Figure 8.7 demonstrates this change in terms of our indicators of ideological roll-call voting. Over the last twenty years, within the Republican party, the mean-roll liberalism score has become slightly more conservative (lower scores in Figure 8.7). Meanwhile, ideology scores for Democratic members have become distinctly more liberal (scores increasing in Figure 8.7). Figure 8.7 shows that by the 1990s Democrats were consistently more liberal and Republicans more conservative than was the case in the 1970s.

At least part of the reason for this change are the gains made by the Republican party in the southern states (which have long been more conservative than other parts of the country). Figure 8.8 shows the average ideological ratings over time for each party, here shown separately for the southern and nonsouthern states. At the beginning of the period, the ideological

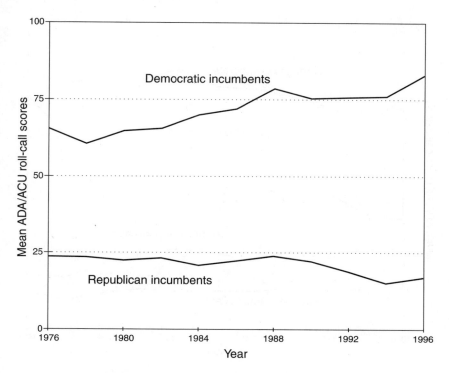

Figure 8.7. Roll-call liberalism by party, 1976–1996.

scores of southern Democrats were closer to Republicans than to nonsouthern Democrats. However, by the end of the period the remaining southern Democrats were just slightly less liberal than their northern fellow partisans. Within the Republican party we also see a trend, though less dramatic, of convergence toward greater ideological extremism. Thus, the increased polarization between the parties is a combination of members of the parties taking more divergent positions generally, but also of electoral replacement in which very conservative southern Republicans have been replacing more moderate southern Democrats.

We must ask whether increased ideological polarization in Congress that we have documented has resulted in any change in constituency representation. An initial hypothesis is that the responsiveness of members of the House to their districts has been eroded by increased ideological distances between the congressional parties. But as we will see, the punch line to this investigation is not so simple.

We can refer back to Table 8.1 for a preliminary answer. Table 8.1 shows

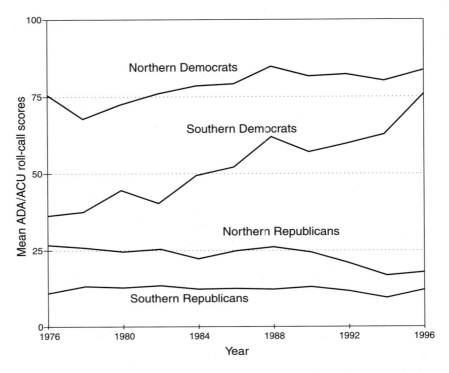

Figure 8.8. Changes in roll-call liberalism by party and region, 1976–1996.

the results of regressing roll-call liberalism on the member's party and regressing the presidential vote in the district for each election year. The
coefficients for constituency (presidential vote) show a clear pattern of decline while the coefficients for party affiliation show an increase. The pattern clearly suggests that, over the last twenty years, members have come to
pay less attention directly to their constituents and to vote more with their
party. Given the statistical controls, the increased party voting is not due to
change in the nature of Republican and Democratic districts. In some small
part it reflects representatives taking cues from their party leaders, but mainly
it reflects members' increased willingness to take ideological positions typical of their party—at the possible expense of constituency representation.

Why would party affiliation become a greater predictor of roll-call ideology at the seeming expense of constituency preferences? One reason might
be that as conflict became more polarized between the parties, members in-
dulged their personal ideological predispositions because they perceived an

acceptable level of electoral risk. One viewpoint regarding congressional elections is that as long as members take care of their districts in terms of casework and pork projects they are relatively free to take the positions they like on the broad overarching, and more ideological, issues of national politics. This strategy would be justified if voters, in fact, do not care or know about how their representatives vote bills that do not directly affect local concerns. However, as the first part of this chapter has argued, incumbents have an unmistakable incentive to heed the ideological preferences of their districts. We have no reason to believe that incumbents have come to value reelection less in the 1990s than in the 1970s, and the effective powers of the party leadership to bring about widespread loyalty—especially when votes would hurt members back home—are very limited. Thus, deserting constituency for party seems inexplicable in light of the general member goals for reelection.

In fact, even as members of Congress have voted increasingly with their party, House incumbents have continued to succeed in their reelection attempts in large part because they remain faithful to the preferences of those they represent. What has happened is a "shaping up" of party affiliation and constituency preferences over the last twenty years. As Republicans have gained ground in the South they have displaced Democrats. These southern districts are quite conservative, as reflected in their Republican tendency in presidential voting. Thus, with Republicans rather than Democrats now coming from the most conservative districts, there is a greater coherence in which most conservative districts are likely to send Republicans to the House and more liberal districts are more likely to send Democrats. Figure 8.9 shows the correlation of presidential vote and the party affiliation of incumbents over the period of our study. There is an unmistakable trend toward higher correlations; in fact the association between party and constituency preference doubled from the 1970s to the 1990s.

This shaping up, however, is not solely a function of congressional elections catching up with southern presidential voting patterns. Figure 8.10 shows the pattern of correlations between presidential vote and member's party affiliation separately for the southern and nonsouthern districts. The nonsouthern districts (darker bars in Figure 8.10) show a clear pattern of an increasing alignment of district preferences and representatives' party affiliation. The same pattern occurs among the southern districts (the lighter bars in Figure 8.10), only the trend toward greater electoral coherence is much greater. In the 1970s the party of the southern House members was only weakly related to their districts' presidential preferences (r's equal about .2),

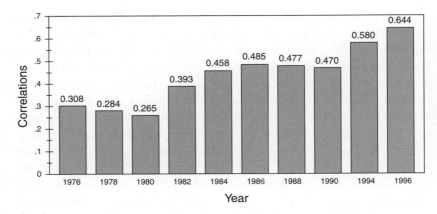

Figure 8.9. Correlation of House election outcomes and presidential vote, 1976–1996.

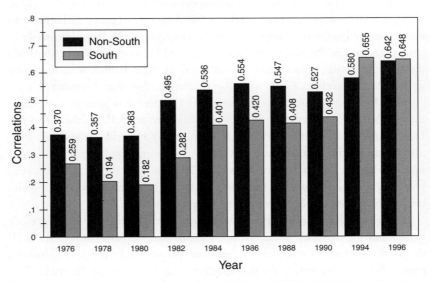

Figure 8.10. Correlations of House outcomes and presidential vote by region, 1976–1996.

but by the end of the period the pattern of alignment was much higher (*r* equals .65 in 1996) and was virtually identical to that achieved in the rest of the country. Figures 8.9 and 8.10 illustrate an element of the larger story of electoral change in documenting a clear pattern of convergence in voting for president and the House over time.

This convergence helps to answer our question about how electoral changes influence the processes of representation. As the parties become more polarized at the elite (e.g., congressional) level, constituencies increasingly elect congressional representatives based on the party affiliations of the candidates. Liberal districts more predictably elect Democrats to Congress while conservative districts more predictably elect Republicans.

With more ideologically polarized congressional parties, this increased party voting at the constituency level actually results in enhanced congressional representation. While the "direct effect" of constituency has declined (Table 8.1), the "indirect effect" of constituency (through party) has increased. Figure 8.11 shows a model of this process of constituency influence by direct (path A) and indirect (paths B and C) effects. The direct effect represents the estimated response to constituency opinion, holding the member's party constant. The indirect effect represents the ideological representation that results from constituencies voting on the basis of party. To grasp the full impact of constituency, and hence the extent of policy representation, we need to consider both direct and indirect effects of constituency ideology on roll-call voting. The logic of the calculation of these effects is shown in the bottom part of Figure 8.11.

Coefficients for direct and indirect effects are shown in Figure 8.12. The points plotted are unstandardized regression coefficients. Each indicates the estimated impact of a one percentage point difference in presidential vote on roll-call liberalism. Thus, in 1976, a one percent difference in constituency preferences (presidential vote) led to a 1.216 difference in roll-call liberalism via its direct effect, and just a 0.426 difference indirectly via the influence of constituency on party and the impact, in turn, of party on roll-call voting. These effects sum to a "total effect" for constituency preferences on roll-call liberalism equal to 1.642. The values for these effects are shown in the table in the lower part of Figure 8.12.

The pattern of effects is most easy to see graphically. The declining direct effect of constituency on roll-call voting is shown by the solid dark line. However, the dashed line, which represents the indirect effects of constituency via its effect on the party of members, shows a clear pattern of increase. The sum of the indirect and direct effects makes the total effect of

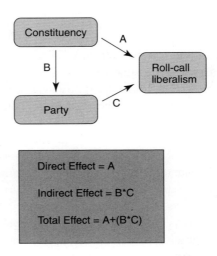

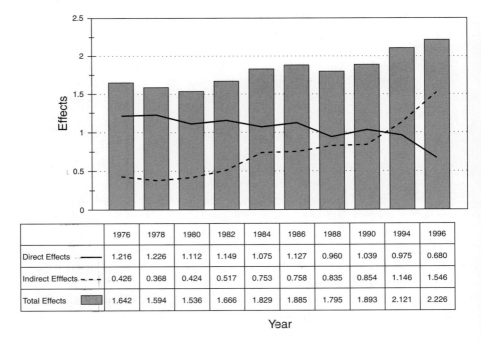

Figure 8.11. Constituency representation with direct and indirect effects.

Figure 8.12. Changing effects of constituency preferences on roll-call liberalism, 1976–1996.

constituency on roll-call ideology in this model. These total effects are shown as the bars in Figure 8.12. Their steady progression makes an important demonstration. Taking into account both direct and indirect effects, *over time constituency has a become a more important influence on members' policy voting in the House of Representatives.*

Thus, in the final analysis there is no necessary conflict between party polarization in Congress and the representation of constituency interests. Representatives throughout the period of study have produced voting patterns that align nicely with district preferences. Increasingly, however, this alignment is a function of the simple electoral coherence by which liberal districts vote for Democrats who, in the House, take liberal policy stances and conservative districts vote in Republicans who take conservative stances. Even with the increased levels of party polarization, though, we continue to see a substantial direct effect for constituency preferences, indicating that members continue to try to align their records with the ideological proclivities of their districts.

Conclusions

In this chapter, we have observed evidence of ideological representation in the U.S. House and the mechanisms by which it occurs. A good deal of political science research demonstrates the importance of a number of nonpolicy factors in voting in congressional elections. We know, for example, that name visibility is a major factor and that many citizens cannot tell us who even ran in the election, much less what the candidates stood for. In addition, we know that more of citizens' perceptions about members, particularly in the House, center on service and the successes of members in keeping in touch with their districts and in bringing home projects and benefits for the districts. We do not contest at all the importance of this strong emphasis on distributional politics that has become an important ingredient in the relationship that members forge with their districts. It is, without a doubt, an important part of the incumbency advantage.

Our point here is that by focusing only on members' advertising and service activities we ignore the fundamental theoretical aspect of representation. At least one function of Congress is to make laws, and in a democratic society we expect that what members work for will reflect, at least in broad terms, the preferences of their constituents. The distributional perspective severs this connection by seeing congressional elections only in terms of style and pork barrel issues. The analysis here shows that view is incomplete. An important component of members' electoral success comes from how they stand on issues.

We see this in several aspects of our analysis. Overall, there is a healthy correlation between constituents' preferences (as measured by presidential vote) and roll-call ideology. If electoral success were determined only by visibility, advertising, and pork projects, then we should expect no correlation at all between general constituency ideology and how members vote on bills. In addition, we show that members who are most vulnerable in terms of constituency preferences are the ones most likely to defect from their parties' ideological patterns in roll-call voting.

Even though many voters are apparently ignorant of roll-call scores, taken together our congressional electorates show considerable policy intelligence. Enough are paying attention—perhaps with others getting the message by a variety of information shortcuts—that in the aggregate, electoral moderation for incumbents clearly pays off. Thus, in competitive districts we demonstrate that electoral moderation has quite a substantial impact on the probability that a member will be reelected. Of course, moderation is less important in very liberal or very conservative districts because the party ideological positions are not far from what the average voter wants.

Finally, we addressed the issue of policy polarization in Congress. Party is clearly more strongly associated with how members vote. We can see this in the nightly news because the ideological gulf between the Democratic and Republican leadership is clearly wider than it was ten or twenty years ago. This observation suggested the hypothesis that party was becoming more important, and hence, that constituency preferences might be taking a back seat to party as a guide to members' floor behavior. Our analysis here demonstrated that even with increased party polarization in the House, the overall effects of constituency ideology have actually increased. The key here is the substantial alignment that has occurred between constituency preferences and voting. Liberal districts are much more likely to consistently vote Democratic and conservative districts are more likely to elect Republicans than was the case in the 1970s. The slow alignment, with the increases in Republican strength in the South, has actually increased overall levels of policy representation.

It is important, then, not to lose sight of the important policy connection between members and their constituents. While home style, keeping in touch, advantages in access to campaign contributors, and claiming credit are all important factors in accounting for incumbents' electoral success, so too is policy representation. Overall, members heed the general policy pref-

erences of their constituents; they lose votes—and sometimes elections—
if they stray too far ideologically. Thus, we see that in keeping members in
line with the general policy preferences of their districts, congressional elections do, in fact, perform one of their fundamental democratic functions
rather well.

Chapter 9

Differences in Legislative Voting Behavior Between Winning and Losing House Incumbents

DAVID W. BRADY, BRANDICE CANES-WRONE,

AND JOHN F. COGAN

When Jim Rowe, a White House assistant under Franklin Delano Roose-velt, pressured Representative Lyndon B. Johnson to support an administra-tion proposal on civil rights, "Johnson objected that he could only 'go so far in Texas,' and invoked the example of Maury Maverick, who, after identi-fying himself with the most progressive elements in the House, lost his con-gressional seat in 1938 after only two terms. 'Don't forget our friend Maury,' he told Rowe, 'There's nothing more useless than a dead liberal'" (Dallek 1991: 168–69).

Several recent studies of the 1994 midterm congressional elections high-light the connection between a member's voting record and his probability of reelection (Jacobson 1996d; D. W. Brady et al. 1995, 1996).[1] Democratic incumbents who voted too liberally for their districts were more likely to be defeated than those who voted in a manner consistent with their districts' preferences. While this result may seem logical to the casual observer, much of the recent literature on congressional elections would have discouraged scholars from looking for a relationship between voting and electoral out-comes.[2] Many of these studies have focused on macro-level explanations, ranging from national economic conditions to presidential coattails. Those theories that have distinguished among members have often focused on the personal vote, the strength of challengers, and district service, and the few studies that have analyzed members' voting have produced inconsistent re-sults. Only for the 1994 congressional elections has research confirmed that members' voting has electoral consequences. Given this recent finding, it seems worthwhile to pursue the relationship over time.

In this chapter, we examine the relationship between House members' voting records on major legislation and electoral outcomes during the past 40 years using different methods than those employed in previous research. We begin with a brief review of the literature on elections and comment on why this research falls short in explaining the variance in electoral losses over time. We then show that the relationship between voting and reelection initially observed in the 1994 election applies to virtually all post–World War II Congresses. Examining House elections from 1954 to 1996, we find that losing Democrat incumbents generally vote too liberally for their district and that losing Republican incumbents vote too conservative. The finding holds for both presidential and midterm election years, as well as for members of the president's party and opposition party members. In discussing these results, we hypothesize as to why members would ever deviate from their districts given the resultant increased probability of electoral defeat. We conjecture that members may exchange their votes for long–term career gains that may result from voting with congressional party leaders and, for members of the party that occupies the White House, the president. We conclude the chapter by assessing the contribution of our results to the literature on elections and proposing avenues of further research.

The Literature on Congressional Elections

The numerous studies on congressional elections can be organized along two dimensions: a micro level that studies how the actions of individual members affect their reelection chances and a macro level that examines aggregate election results. Within the first approach, there exists a literature on the relationship between members' votes and reelection probabilities, and this work has produced a wide range of conclusions. Perhaps most famously, Mayhew (1974a) contends that "position taking" by members through activities such as roll-call votes comprises a key component of the electoral connection. Mayhew provides persuasive anecdotal evidence, but does not delve into systematic analysis. For the latter, he cites the work of Erikson (1971b) and Schoenberger (1969), who both find some evidence that voting affects members' electoral percentages.

More recent analysis that has attempted to measure this effect has been less conclusive. In addition to the aforementioned research on the 1994 election, a few studies have analyzed the relationship between members' votes and elections across time. M. B. Wright (1993) and Goff and Grier (1993)

employ a two-stage residual approach to examine this matter. In each paper, the first stage consists of a regression of members' voting scores on geographic constituency characteristics, where the absolute difference between
members' actual and predicted voting scores constitutes a measure of "shirking." In the second stage of the analysis, the papers test for whether the shirking scores are correlated with a member's probability of winning reelection.
While M. B. Wright (1993) finds evidence for this relationship, the results
of Goff and Grier (1993) do not offer such support. Moreover, because both
studies equate the unexplained portion of the regression with a member's
personal ideology, they incorporate into the shirking scores the effects of any
omitted variables. Our analysis does not require shirking to include these
effects.[3]

We also use a different, and we will argue better, measure of constituency
preferences. Geographic constituency characteristics, such as the percentage
of union or unemployed workers in a district, constrain constituents within
that group to maintain similar ideological positions. While this assumption may be accurate for certain pieces of legislation, constituents within a
group may have different ideological predispositions over a variety of political matters, resulting in different preferences for candidates. For example,
while union workers may all support a higher minimum wage, they may
hold vastly different views on social issues such as abortion or school prayer.
In our analysis, we use the district vote for the presidential candidate of the
member's party to deal with this problem.

Most micro-level analysis of elections since the mid-1970s has focused on
the rise of the personal vote and the consequent decline of competitive congressional districts (Erikson 1972a; Mayhew 1974b; Cain et al. 1987; Alford
and Brady 1993, among others). According to this work, as partisanship has
declined in importance within the electorate, incumbents have come to rely
more on constituency service, personal appeal, and pure recognition to help
ensure reelection (Ferejohn 1977; Fiorina 1977a). Rare incumbent defeats
are the result of neglect on the part of the member in these areas. Members'
actual voting records are ignored as a possible causal factor affecting the odds
of reelection.

A related micro-level explanation relies on the notion of challenger quality to predict an incumbent's probability of reelection (Jacobson 1989; Jacobson and Kernell 1983). If a challenger is of high enough quality, thereby
attracting reasonable amounts of campaign financing, then the race is likely
to be close.[4] Testing the empirical importance of challenger quality is made
difficult by the fact that weak incumbents attract quality challengers. Like-
wise, the level of campaign money made available to the challenger is a func-

tion of the probability of success in defeating the incumbent, the odds of which are greater with a high-quality challenger. In sum, it is difficult to assess the independent effects of money and quality since the two are highly correlated.

The second line of research, what we call the macro-level approach, uses time series analysis to explain intertemporal variations in congressional election outcomes. Most of this literature has focused on why the president's party tends to lose seats in midterm elections and gain in presidential elections. For example, A. Campbell (1966) finds differences in the type of voters that turn out in presidential versus midterm years. Kramer (1971) and Tufte (1975) argue that dissatisfaction with the president's performance causes constituents to vote against members of his party, citing macroeconomic conditions as an important contributor to voter dissatisfaction. Offering yet another rationale, Erikson (1988) contends that the electorate votes against the president's party in midterm elections in order to create a greater "balance of power" between the branches.

Thus as a general rule, the literature on congressional elections finds little systematic support for the hypothesis that the voting behavior of incumbents affects their reelection prospects. The prime exception is the aforementioned work on the 1994 elections. Jacobson (1996d) shows that members who voted for the budget reconciliation bill that raised taxes were significantly less likely to win reelection than other members. Erikson and Wright (1995) present evidence that members' positions on issues had electoral consequences in the 1994 election. Using individual level NES data, they show that moderation was rewarded and extreme liberalism punished. These results corroborate those of D. W. Brady et al. (1995), who statistically demonstrate that incumbent voting records played a key role in determining reelection probabilities among Democratic incumbents in the 1994 election.

The finding that constituents held members of Congress accountable for their legislative votes in the 1994 elections does not mean that voters have always done so. The 1994 elections may have been an aberration. On the other hand, incumbent voting behavior may have consistently affected reelection probabilities and prior research has failed to glean the impact from the data. In the next section, we will examine post–World War II congressional election data to determine which of these hypotheses holds.

Data and Methodology

The difficulty in measuring the degree of conservatism or liberalism among a district's voters has long been recognized. As Fiorina (1974) pointed out long ago, the problem is that we do not have good measures of constituency preferences. Using moving averages of the House vote builds in the incumbent's personal vote (Fiorina 1974), while using geographic constituency characteristics misses the distinctions regarding constituencies within the geographic area (Fenno 1978).

A key component of D. W. Brady et al. (1995) and Erickson and Wright (1995) was employing a satisfactory measure of district preferences along a conservative-liberal continuum, and the approach used in this chapter is similar. To estimate the preferences of each congressional district along a liberal-conservative continuum, we use the district's vote for the presidential candidate of the representative's party.[5] This vote has the advantage of measuring voters' choices over the same national candidates in elections in which it is easy to identify which candidate is left and which is right. The measure thus establishes an ordinal ranking among congressional districts on a liberal-conservative continuum for that election. The higher the district's vote for the Democratic candidate in a given election, the more liberal the district's policy preferences at the time of that election. For example, in 1992, 47 percent of North Carolina voters in the Fourth District, which includes the college town of Chapel Hill, voted for Bill Clinton, while 39 percent voted for George Bush. Only 39 percent of voters in North Carolina's Third District, which includes relatively rural communities, voted for Clinton, with 46 percent voting for Bush (Duncan 1993). Our measure assumes that voters in the Fourth District have more liberal policy preferences than do voters in the Third District.

Operationally, for each presidential election and congressional district, we compute the proportion of the presidential two-party vote received by the presidential candidate of the member's party. Thus for Democrats, this variable equals the proportion of the two-party vote for the Democratic candidate, and for Republicans, the variable equals the proportion for the Republican candidate. When analyzing House elections during presidential election years, we use the district's vote in that year. When analyzing midterm House elections, we use the district's vote in the prior presidential election.

To measure congressional members' voting records on a liberal-conservative continuum, we use members' ADA scores. For each election year, we compute the members' ADA scores on votes taken during the congressional session immediately preceding the election year. As calculated by the ADA, the scores, which range from 0 to 100, reflect the proportion of liberal positions taken by the member on a selected number of key votes. We use this score for Democrat members, and 100-ADA for Republican members, calling our score *P_ADA*. Thus for both parties, a higher score reflects a more extreme member of the party. For the Democrats, a higher score suggests a more liberal member, and for Republicans, a higher score suggests a more conservative member. We use this transformation to provide consistency in the interpretation of coefficients across tests.

In general we use ADA scores as a preference measure because the ADA votes in any given year include the vast majority of key policy issues during that year. The scores include all of the major tax and budget votes of the 1980s and 1990s, including the 1981 Gramm-Latta Budget Reconciliation Bill, the 1986 Tax Reform Act, and the 1990 and 1993 Budget Acts. The ADA scores also include the abortion, school prayer, and labor legislation votes of the 1970s and 1980s. In addition, the scores include the key civil rights votes and votes on the Great Society programs in the 1960s. Another reason for choosing ADA scores is that the measure is widely known among members and often publicized in their districts.

To uncover the existence of systematic differences in voting behavior between winning and losing incumbents, we thus estimate a regression of the following form:

$$(1)\ P\_ADA_i = a_i + b_1 PVOTE_i + b_2 SOUTH_i + b_3 LOSE_i + e_i$$

where *P_ADA* is equal to a member *i*'s ADA score if the member is a Democrat and equals 100 minus the ADA score if the member is a Republican,

PVOTE is the proportion of the two-party presidential election vote received by the presidential candidate of member *i*'s party in *i*'s district,

SOUTH is a dummy variable that assumes a value of one if the member's district is in the southern census region and a value of zero otherwise, and

LOSE is a dummy variable that assumes a value of one for losing members and a value of zero for winning members.

Separate regressions are estimated for each political party and election year from 1952 through 1994, except for 1962.[6] Thus, twenty-one sets of parameter estimates are obtained for each political party.[7] For each test, *PVOTE* serves as a control for the policy preferences of the voters in a district. The coefficient on the dummy variable *LOSE*, b_3, measures the difference in congressional member voting behavior on policy issues between winning and losing incumbents conditional on these voter preferences.

The parameters are first estimated with OLS. Then, to improve the efficiency of the estimates, the data are pooled across election years.[8] With the OLS results, we focus on the two key estimated relationships: first, the relationship between the district's policy preferences and the representative's congressional voting record; and second, the differences in voting behavior between incumbents who were reelected and those who were defeated.

Table 9.1 reports the estimated coefficients for *PVOTE* and their standard errors[9] separately for Democrat and Republican winning incumbents.[10] The results demonstrate that, as expected, for congressional members of both political parties, voting on major policy issues is strongly related to the district policy preferences. The more liberal the district's policy preferences, the more liberal the voting record of its representative on policy issues. An increase of 10 percentage points in the district's two-party vote for the Democratic presidential candidate is associated, on average, with about an 8 percentage point increase in ADA score among Democratic representatives. For Republican incumbents, such an increase for a Republican presidential candidate is associated with about an 11 percentage point increase in our variable *P_ADA*, or an 11 percentage point decrease in ADA score.

The results are highly significant for both political parties. For Democrats, all of the annual estimates except those for the 1950s are significant at conventional levels. For Republicans, the annual estimates are significant except that for 1958. Moreover, the estimated relationship is remarkably stable over time, and the results suggest no discernable trend for either political party. This stability gives us confidence that the regression estimates are capturing an important relationship between constituent policy preferences and voting behavior on policy matters by the constituents' representative.

Turning to our second question of whether systematic differences in voting behavior exist between incumbents who win reelection and those who are defeated, we examine the parameters for the *LOSE* variable. The estimated differences in ADA voting scores between winning and losing congressional incumbents of each party are reported in Table 9.2 along with their standard errors. The results, though not generally statistically significant, are consistent with our expectations in terms of the signs of the coefficients. After controlling for the liberal-conservative preferences of congressional districts, Democratic incumbents who lost reelection bids had voting records that were more liberal than the records of Democratic incumbents who won reelection. Similarly, Republicans who lost reelection bids had more conservative voting records than those who won reelection. For Democrats, the estimated effect has the correct sign in 16 out of 21 years. For Republicans, the estimated effect has the correct sign in 14 out of 19 years.

However, the paucity of observations on losing incumbents precludes estimating individual election-year differences in ADA scores with any precision. In 11 of the 21 elections covered by our analysis, only 5 or fewer

Table 9.1

Constituent Preference and Representatives' Voting Behavior, 1954–1994

Year	DEMOCRATS		REPUBLICANS	
	PVOTE[a] Coefficient[b]	PVOTE Standard Error[c]	PVOTE Coefficient	PVOTE Standard Error
1954	4.1	1.2	11.9	2.1
1956	−0.31	1.5	12.3	2.7
1958	−0.04	1.3	5.8	3.8
1960	3.6	1.3	14.2	2.7
1962	—	—	—	—
1964	8.4	1.0	16.3	2.3
1966	8.0	0.9	8.0	1.9
1968	7.5	1.5	9.0	2.0
1970	7.5	1.2	11.8	2.3
1972	7.6	1.4	17.2	3.2
1974	7.1	1.4	10.9	3.2
1976	4.0	1.1	12.1	3.1
1978	4.8	1.4	6.8	2.6
1980	6.7	1.2	8.5	1.6
1982	6.0	1.3	9.1	1.9
1984	5.5	0.8	10.0	1.6
1986	7.6	0.9	10.9	1.8
1990	6.7	0.8	1.9	2.1
1992	11.0	1.0	10.2	2.1
1994	11.4	1.0	7.6	1.6

[a] PVOTE = proportion of two-party presidential election vote.

[b] Coefficients measure the import of a 10 percent increase in the proportion of the two-party popular vote received by the presidential candidate of the member's party.

[c] White (1980) or robust standard errors are reported.

Table 9.2

Differences in ADA Scores Between Winners and Losers of House Elections, Individual Year Analysis

Year	DEMOCRATS			REPUBLICANS		
	LOSE Coefficient[a]	LOSE Standard Error[b]	Percent Too Liberal (Losers)	LOSE Coefficient	LOSE Standard Error	Percent Too Conservative (Losers)
1954	−2.5	5.2	67 (3)	12.4	3.8	72 (18)
1956	4.6	3.6	57 (7)	15.6	4.0	100 (7)
1958	−3.7	1.8	100 (1)	−6.8	6.0	38 (34)
1960	4.1	5.3	77 (22)	−15.3	13.0	33 (3)
1962	—	—	—	—	—	—
1964	9.9	7.0	60 (5)	11.3	2.9	87 (39)
1966	6.1	3.0	64 (39)	−11.2	4.2	0 (1)
1968	3.4	12.6	60 (5)	—	—	—
1970	24.1	10.9	100 (2)	10.6	3.9	78 (9)
1972	16.0	8.5	80 (5)	5.5	8.5	67 (8)
1974	−10.5	9.8	33 (3)	10.8	2.7	89 (36)
1976	2.5	4.8	71 (7)	21.5	3.5	100 (4)
1978	2.9	5.7	53 (13)	−1.7	10.0	60 (5)
1980	13.0	5.3	76 (25)	12.1	5.9	100 (2)
1982	−1.0	2.0	0 (1)	−2.3	5.1	62 (21)
1984	8.3	4.5	68 (13)	4.4	5.0	67 (3)
1986	−17.2	1.91	0 (1)	11.0	2.9	100 (5)
1988	−4.9	2.1	0 (2)	6.3	4.0	75 (4)
1990	4.3	4.7	67 (6)	2.5	6.6	67 (9)
1992	16.8	3.4	92 (13)	4.6	6.7	83 (6)
1994	7.5	2.8	76 (34)	—	—	—

[a] LOSE = dummy variable for winning and losing candidates.

[b] Coefficients measure the average ADA difference between winning and losing incumbents after controlling for voter preferences in congressional districts and whether a member is from a Southern district. A positive coefficient suggests that Republican losers were more conservative—and Democrat losers more liberal—than the winners.

[c] White (1980) or robust standard errors are reported

Democratic incumbents lost reelection bids. Also, in 11 of the 21 elections only 5 or fewer Republican incumbents lost reelection bids. In years in which the estimated impact for Democrats is the wrong sign, the number of losers never exceeds three.

Table 9.2 also reports the estimated proportion of losing Democratic incumbents who voted more liberally than we would predict for winners in districts with identical preferences, and the analogous proportion of losing Republican incumbents who voted more conservatively. The estimated proportions are generally greater than 50 percent. Again, however, the small number of observations on losing incumbents precludes precisely estimating individual election-year differences.

To improve the precision of the estimates, we pool the data across parties and elections and estimate a time-invariant difference in voting behavior between winners and losers over all elections. This is accomplished by estimating all of the equations as a one-equation system with the same dependent and independent variables used above. Within the equation, the coefficients on the *LOSE* dummy variable are constrained to be equal across time. All other coefficients are allowed to vary intertemporally.

The estimation method is complicated by the fact that the error terms are not likely to be independent over time. Unmeasured factors, such as member ideology and constituent preferences not captured by *PVOTE*, will produce autocorrelation in the disturbances. Congressional redistricting each decade further complicates the estimation problem. The functional form of the autocorrelation is likely to be different in years that involve no redistricting as compared to those years in which redistricting does occur. Moreover, the correlation in disturbance terms across years involving redistricting is likely to vary with the amount of redistricting.

To estimate the parameters of our system of equations in the face of this statistical issue, we have specified a simple functional form that captures the main features of autocorrelation. We have assumed that the error terms followed a single first-order auto-regressive form during election years that do not involve redistricting. During each of the redistricting years in our data, 1972, 1982, and 1992, we have permitted the autocorrelation parameter to vary.[11] Thus, the form of the autocorrelation structure can be written as:

$$(2) \quad e_{it} = r_0 e_{it-1} D_0 + r_1 e_{it-1} D_1 + r_2 e_{it-1} D_2 + r_3 e_{it-1} D_3 + u_{it}$$

where r is a first order auto-regressive parameter, D_0 is a dummy variable that assumes a value of unity during non-redistricting years and 0 otherwise,

D_1 is a dummy variable that assumes a value of unity during the redistricting year 1972 and 0 otherwise,

Table 9.3

Differences in ADA Scores Between Winners and Losers
of House Elections, Pooled Regression 1954–1994

	Coefficient[a]	Standard Error[b]
LOSE	2.05	1.04
Autocorrelation Parameters		
Without Gerrymandering	0.671	0.012
1992 Gerrymandering	0.592	0.057
1982 Gerrymandering	0.569	0.056
1972 Gerrymandering	0.711	0.069

[a]The coefficient measures the average ADA difference between winning and losing incumbents after controlling for voter preferences in congressional districts and whether a member is from a southern district.

[b]Robust or White (1980) standard errors are reported.

D_2 is a dummy variable that assumes a value of unity during the redistricting year 1982 and 0 otherwise,

D_3 is a dummy variable that assumes a value of unity during the redistricting year 1992 and 0 otherwise, and

u_{it} is an error term with mean zero and is independently distributed over time.

The findings for *LOSE* and the autocorrelation terms are given in Table 9.3. As shown in Table 9.3, the coefficients and standard errors on the auto-correlation terms suggest a high level of correlation across years within a district. This correlation is strong for years with and without redistricting.

The results for the incumbent lost variable suggest that a systematic difference exists between winning and losing incumbents. House members who lose reelection bids are statistically more likely to have voted more extremely within their party than their counterparts who won reelection. For Republicans, losers are likely to have voted more conservatively, and Democrat losers are likely to have voted more liberally than winning members of the losers' parties. This difference is significant at a *p*-value of less than .05.

The value of the coefficient on the incumbent lost variable suggests that the actual difference in the voting records of the winners and losers is not that large. Losers are found to vote on average approximately 2 percent more extremely than the winners. The estimates suggest that representatives may consistently vote according to their constituents' preferences, but lose reelection because they vote out of step with their district on a few key issues. The relatively small magnitude of the estimate is in many ways not suprising. In a given election, only a limited number of issues can occupy the public debate, and strategic opposition candidates will attempt to ensure that those issues over which a member has deviated from his or her district's preferences dominate this debate. Members' votes on a few key issues may therefore affect electoral outcomes significantly.

In sum, our findings show that members' voting records *do* affect their reelection chances contingent on the distribution of preferences in the district. With few exceptions, losing incumbents are too extreme for their districts. This is true for both presidential and midterm elections, and for members of the president's party as well as opposition party members. This finding is significant because it adds the element of responsibility back into the election equation. A frequent criticism of Congress is that its members are overly concerned with reelection and yet not responsive to public opinion in policy decisions. By implication, this criticism suggests that members act to ensure their reelection independent of how they vote. That is, enough campaigning and constituency service assures incumbents of reelection. Our results indicate that a more policy-oriented electoral connection exists, with voters holding members responsible for their legislative voting records.

Discussion of Results

Although our results help elucidate congressional election outcomes, a major puzzle remains: Why would members ever vote out of step with their constituents? Previous research suggests a few answers. According to the literature on congressional careers, representatives aim to advance within the hierarchy of House leadership posts (Hibbing 1991; Cox and McCubbins 1993, among others). Such success is not only rewarding in and of itself, but may lead to further advancements outside the House, including the Senate, governorships, or cabinet positions. Recent work on parties highlights the fact that these career advances normally occur within the member's political party. Cox and McCubbins (1993) and Rohde (1991) offer general hypotheses along these lines, arguing that in the modern Congress, parties influence members' votes. A member who votes consistently against the party's leaders on positions adopted by the party caucus cannot expect to advance rapidly. The member is unlikely to get a good committee assignment and is unlikely to be offered a spot in the leadership ranks. Support for key party positions is essential for advancement.

Research on the presidency offers further insight as to why members would vote against district opinion. For example, presidents may offer executive or judicial branch appointments, or provide fellow partisan members increased party prominence. Neustadt's (1990) seminal description of the bargaining president rests upon this type of give-and-take. Similarly, Bond and Fleisher (1990) argue that a president's ability to trade political favors increases his capacity to gain members' votes. Quantitative support for this argument is provided by Sullivan (1987, 1990, 1991) and DeMarchi and Sullivan (1997), who show that presidential bargaining activities sway members' votes.

Thus, although our claims regarding members' votes and subsequent electoral consequences go against much of the previous literature, the contention that members have incentives to vote out of line with district opinion is not novel. Presidents and party officials have long sought the votes of members, and members have arguably gained career favors from obliging such leaders. For example, when Lyndon B. Johnson first went to Washington, D.C. from a moderate-to-conservative Texas district where Johnson won in spite of backing Franklin D. Roosevelt's court packing plan, the president helped him get a good committee assignment. Fred Vinson of Kentucky, a central figure on the Ways and Means Committee, explained that during dinner at the White House he "kept wondering just what it was that [the president] wanted from him. I knew it was something. Finally, he said casually—oh, very casually—'Fred, there's a fine young man just come to the House. Fred, you know that young fellow, Lyndon Johnson? I think he would be a great help on Naval Affairs'" (Dallek 1991: 164).

Two other examples illustrate this type of incentive system in recent Congresses. Democrat Jim Jones, who represented the "very Republican" (Barone and Ujifusa 1984) First District of Oklahoma from 1973 through 1986, voted ten to fifteen points more liberal than the few Democrats elected from similar districts (for example, Jack Hightower of Texas). Jones was rewarded with the chairmanship of the Budget Committee in 1981 and subsequently appointed U.S. ambassador to Mexico. Marjorie Margolies-Mezvinsky was not so lucky. Elected in 1992 in Pennsylvania's Thirteenth District, a moderate-to-conservative district, she maintained a moderate-to-conservative voting record until she voted with her party and President Clinton on the 1993 reconciliation budget bill that raised taxes. Presumably, over the long run this loyalty would have been rewarded by the president and/or party leaders. She lost the next election, however, with at least one Republican poll indicating that a majority of her constituents did not approve of her vote on the reconciliation bill.

Thus our claim that members will vote against district preferences is hardly novel. Partisan leaders, and in particular the president, have their own legislative agendas that require the support of other members. In exchange for this support, leaders can offer long-run career advancement. What is novel about our chapter is the argument, supported by evidence, that these career advancements are achieved at a risk of losing office. As with Marjorie Margolies-Mezvinsky, a member who votes at the extremes of her district's preferences significantly increases her probability of electoral defeat.

Conclusion

Our finding that members' voting is correlated with their reelection probabilities has significant implications for a wide range of the literature, beginning with research on congressional elections. Many aggregate level explanations for congressional elections have been previously offered. Economic variables, such as the rates of unemployment and inflation, and political variables, including presidential popularity, have been used to predict and explain broad trends in elections, such as presidential coattails and midterm loss (A. Campbell 1966; Tufte 1975; Erikson 1988). Recent micro-level analysis has generally distinguished members' reelection probabilities on the grounds of activities such as pork barrel constituency service and campaigning. What systematic analysis has been conducted on the relationship between members' voting and reelection probabilities over time has not produced conclusive results. Our study, which attempts to improve upon previous measures and statistical techniques, suggests that members' votes have significant electoral consequences, both for members of the president's party and the out party.

This result supports public opinion research arguing that individual voters' lack of information does not aggregate into mass electoral ignorance (Page and Shapiro 1992). If the electorate were completely uninformed about members' votes on key legislation, we would expect losing members' ADA scores to be no different than those of winning members. Our individual year regressions suggest that losers vote more extremely than winners, and our pooled time series shows that this difference is significant. Thus even if individual voters are not fully informed about candidates' voting histories, the electorate as a whole appears to make decisions based on this factor.[12]

Our study has further significance for understanding congressional members' behavior at a theoretical level. In one sense, our finding supports the claim that elections make members accountable to constituency preferences.

Yet if elections produced 100 percent accountability, incumbents should not systematically vote out of line with their districts, and we observe such behavior. How might these findings be reconciled?

We suggest a rationale for this discrepancy relating to members' long-run career goals. Our hypothesis is similar to arguments suggested by party scholars such as Cox and McCubbins (1993) and Rohde (1991) but is more directly tied to the president. In particular, we argue that the president may offer members of his party benefits such as appointments and party prominence in exchange for their votes, and that members may rationally make such trades even though they result in short-run constituency disfavor.

Our study thus provides for more coherence among the literatures on Congress, elections, and public opinion by suggesting that the electoral connection presumed to dominate American elections is different than pundits and scholars have commonly assumed. Legislators may vote out of line with their districts. Voters may lack complete information concerning all policies and their outcomes. Yet those incumbents who lose tend to have significantly more extreme voting records than winners, even accounting for partisanship of the district.

Chapter 10

The Effect of Party on Issue Emphasis
in the 1994 House Elections

DAVID L. LEAL AND FREDERICK M. HESS

This project was designed as an investigation into the use of issues and strategies by House challengers in the 1994 elections. We were long puzzled by the fact that even though issues are supposed to be at the heart of campaigns, political science has found it difficult to quantitatively analyze how issues are used and what effect they have on outcomes. The unexpected results of this particular election, however, meant that the dataset might also prove useful to understanding the dynamics involved in the change in party control of the House.

We realized that while researchers would no doubt scour the NES and other surveys, ours might be the only dataset based on interviews with House challengers and their staffs. This chapter therefore examines how partisanship affected the use of particular campaign issues and whether the use of those issues had an impact on the vote for House challengers. In this way, this chapter adds to the literature on how issues are used by political campaigns and examines why House Republican candidates were able to do so well in 1994.[1]

While many elements of congressional campaigns have been extensively researched, the use of issues is not one of them. Carmines and Stimson (1989: 3) wrote that "to speak of politics is to speak of political issues, almost invariably. We speak of them as if we knew of them. But we truly do not. We do not know why they arise, why one question rather than another comes to seem important, why it happens at a particular time, rather than another, why some last, why most do not."

Why this lack of research on such an inherently interesting topic? E. Cook et al. (1994: 188) in their study of the abortion issue in gubernatorial politics suggested that "previous research may have ignored the role of non-economic issues because it is difficult to incorporate such variables into aggregate models." Although not a few researchers have written on campaign strategy and the use of issues, most related analyses have been qualitative in orientation. We agree that incorporating the use of issues by campaigns is difficult for empirical researchers, but the research design of this chapter proposes a method of obtaining comparable data across electoral campaigns.

This chapter investigates how challengers *emphasize* issues in their electoral campaigns and whether partisanship plays a role. Investigating "issue emphasis" does not mean testing whether partisanship influenced the stance challengers took on issues, which would be fairly self-evident. Instead, we will show that Democrats were less likely than Republicans to discuss many specific issues in their campaigns, regardless of their stance on these issues. We will then show that the use of two issues had a statistically significant and positive effect on the vote for Republican challengers, which is the first aggregate finding in the literature of how a particular non–economic issue influenced voting decisions on the first Tuesday of November.[2]

Literature Review

To date, a number of scholars have surveyed or interviewed congressional campaigns to learn more about candidate strategies (Kingdon 1968; Huckshorn and Spencer 1971; Hershey 1974; Maisel 1982; Luntz 1988; Salmore and Salmore 1989; Herrnson 1995). Yet only a few researchers have attempted a quantitative examination of issue selection or the effect of issues on election results. The best example is Herrnson (1995), who asked challengers about the focus of their campaign advertising. In one of the first applications of aggregate regression analysis to campaign issue research, he found that House challengers who reported that at least one issue played an important role in their campaigns increased their vote totals (213, 275–76).

A number of scholars have attempted to understand whether issues affect election outcomes by analyzing individual-level survey data. These efforts include the previously cited work of E. Cook et al. (1994), which analyzed exit polls in ten states and found that abortion was a significant predictor of vote choice in nine. In addition, Howell and Sims (1993) analyzed survey data on Louisiana voters and found that the influence of the abortion issue depended on specific electoral and contextual factors.

Other scholars have argued that issues may not be important to challenger campaigns, however. Maisel (1982) surveyed congressional primary elections in 1978 and concluded that few campaigns emphasized issues and those that did tended to be unsuccessful. He suggested that candidates developed issue positions to maintain credibility with various elites, but that these positions were not intended to sway voters. In fact, he reported that almost all candidates perceived the voters as not caring about issue content and that the incumbent was the major campaign issue. Hershey (1974: 76) similarly found that most campaign managers and candidates in Wisconsin in 1968 did not perceive issues as significantly affecting vote totals, even though many nonetheless used national issues in their campaigns.[3]

Some research has also been conducted on the use of issues and campaign messages by Senate candidates (Franklin 1991; Sellers 1998). It has found that the use of issues can affect election outcomes. Franklin (1991) found that Senate incumbents who emphasized issues in their campaigns allowed voters to better perceive their ideological positions, whereas Sellers noted that candidates did better when they emphasized issues for which they had built records perceived favorably by the public.

A second literature relevant to this chapter is that on Republicans' electoral success in the 1994. Explanations include possible long-term shifts in ideological outlook and partisan loyalty (Abramowitz and Ishikawa 1995), a regionally and ideologically concentrated reaction against Bill Clinton's administration and House members who supported its policies (D. W. Brady et al. 1996), and an ideological movement by the public toward the Republican party in combination with declining incumbency advantages (Ferejohn et al. 1995).

This chapter takes a different but complementary look at the partisan dynamics of the election by examining whether challengers differed by party on whether or not they engaged in or avoided an issue-based electoral strategy. Such an explanation has been hinted at in the literature, but only barely. Kingdon (1968), for instance, found that many more Republican than Democratic candidates in 1964 reported no policy emphasis at all. This suggests that candidates may avoid issues when they perceive their party to be electorally vulnerable. Republicans may have acted this way in anticipation of Barry Goldwater's defeat in 1964, just as media accounts suggested that Democrats tried to distance themselves from an expected anti-Clinton vote in 1994.

Third, this chapter will also have implications for the literature on party-issue ownership. According to Petrocik (1996: 831), "Candidates will not usually engage in textbook debates with each disputing points raised by their opponents. They will not attempt to change opinions on issues. Each will focus on *their* party constituency issues." Popkin (1991: 57–58) argued that "Party candidates for office try to increase the salience of issues where their party starts out with the largest advantage. Candidates addressing an issue where their party has a strong image have the wind at their back, whereas candidates addressing an issue where their party has a weak image are running into the wind." Ansolabehere and Iyengar (1994) used experimental evidence to demonstrate that candidates do benefit from using issues in their advertising that they can claim to "own."

Candidates do so because most voters "see differences in the parties' ability to fix current problems," trusting Republicans more on issues like values, crime, foreign policy, and taxation, and Democrats more on education, social security, and unemployment (Petrocik 1996: 830).[4] In addition, these perceptions stay relatively consistent from election to election.[5]

Because this chapter examines how much candidates from the two parties emphasized a variety of issues, we must keep in mind the possibility that issue ownership is the explanation. Of the nine issues examined, six are generally considered to be Republican issues, two are Democratic issues, and one is indeterminate. The data will show, however, that this explanation cannot be the answer.

Interviews

The authors collected the dataset by conducting phone interviews with the campaign headquarters of forty-two congressional challengers in nine northeast and mid-Atlantic states during the three weeks prior to the 1994 midterm elections.[6] The study examined challengers who were opposing House incumbents, which means that open seats (where the incumbent was not seeking reelection) were not part of the sample.

Interviews were conducted between October 10 and 30, 1994. We were able to interview campaign sources at 42 of the 75 challenger campaigns in the sample. There were a variety of reasons we were unable to reach some campaigns, including unlisted numbers, unreturned phone calls, a few instances where campaigns had closed down, and two cases of respondent hostility and suspicion.

This 56 percent response rate is better than average for research in this field. In the most recent and best-known study of this kind, Herrnson (1995) received a response rate of 42 percent for his House candidate survey. The problem with incomplete response is that campaigns that did respond may somehow systematically differ from those that did not, and thus bias the results. This risk is common to all campaign research. It is also a difficult problem to solve; if a campaign does not want to respond, there is no way to force a reply.

Of the 42 interviews, 41 have been used in the analysis. One observation proved difficult to incorporate because the challenger defeated the incumbent in the Democratic primary, so there was no incumbent in the fall campaign.[7] Of the 41 challengers analyzed, 4 unseated the incumbent in their election bid.[8] The figure of 9.8 percent (4 of 41) almost exactly mirrored the 9.2 percent rate (35 of 382) at which incumbents were defeated nationwide.

When the authors contacted each campaign, they asked to speak to the candidate, press secretary, or campaign manager. Frequently the candidate responded, and in all cases we talked with one of these three people. In doing so, we followed the lead of Herrnson (1995), who found no real differences in the responses of candidates, campaign managers, treasurers, and other campaign aides in his survey of congressional campaigns.[9]

Interviews generally lasted between ten and fifteen minutes. To lengthen the interviews would have decreased the number of observations, a phenomenon well known in survey research. This was especially true in our case because the campaigns were in the final stretch and our respondents were very busy.

Respondents were asked questions that provided two sets of dependent variables (the interview instrument is included as Appendix B). The first set of questions gathered information on how much challengers used various issues in their campaigns. The second set asked about three different campaign strategies.

We asked about nine particular issues: crime, the deficit, foreign affairs, welfare, values, education, abortion, term limits, and infrastructural development. This did not encompass all possible campaign issues, but if too many questions had been asked, the longer interview time might have decreased the number of completed interviews. It is difficult to guess which of these issues will be viewed in the future as important. Still, the study of these nine issues considerably extends previous work in the field that has considered the effect of only one issue, such as those previously cited on the role of abortion.

The strategy questions asked how much emphasis the challenger placed on her own positive personal qualities, the fact of her opponent's incumbency, and the voting record of the incumbent. These give additional insight into an important but understudied area: the strategic thinking of challengers. Fowler (1993: 118) noticed that "There has been almost no empirical work on the attitudes and strategies of congressional candidates," and this chapter will test a regression model explaining the use of challenger strategies.

As mentioned above, the issue questions asked how much campaigns emphasized the above issues, regardless of the stance taken. Therefore, it did not matter for these answers whether a candidate took a position favoring or opposing abortion, for instance. This format has the important advantage of providing comparable answers across campaigns. If the campaigns were simply asked which issues (or strategies) were important, then it would be difficult to incorporate the responses into a regression model. As previously discussed, E. Cook et al. (1994) have noted this type of problem. Our format also provides a campaign a good deal of flexibility in how to respond; if none of the issues were important, for example, a campaign could have responded zero to all questions. Thus, we allowed for comparative study and provided flexibility to the campaigns in how they could respond.

We recognize the limitations inherent in a regional study but do not believe this sample introduces significant bias. This confidence is based largely on the "'deregionalization' of congressional elections" evident over recent decades, as discussed by Abramson et al. (1994: 263). There is also a great deal of variation within and between the states in our sample: included are rural areas, suburbs, and cities varying in size from small towns to New York City.

In addition, as mentioned above, the incumbent defeat rate in our dataset almost exactly mirrored the nationwide average. This similarity was especially significant in the 1994 election because all the defeated incumbents across the nation were Democrats. These results suggest that partisan dynamics in the Northeast and Mid-Atlantic regions did not significantly differ from the rest of the nation, because Republican challengers made gains here exactly as they did elsewhere.

Models and Variables

The analysis is divided into two parts. First, it tests a model that explains challenger use of particular issues. Then it examines the relative importance of issue usage on challenger performance. Because the issue variables are measured on a seven-point scale, they are analyzed using OLS regression.[10]

ISSUE AND STRATEGY USAGE

Issue and strategy selection was modeled as a function of seven factors: challenger party, Ross Perot's share of the district's 1992 presidential vote, the incumbent's performance in 1992, challenger spending, per capita income of the district, the median age of the district, and incumbent tenure.

We expected these variables to influence the use of issues and strategies in different ways. Political party might matter because of expected positive or negative coattails from President Clinton. As mentioned above, Kingdon (1968) found that in the 1964 elections many Republican candidates reported no policy emphasis. This suggests that candidates avoid issues when they perceive their party to be electorally vulnerable. Republicans may have acted this way in anticipation of Lyndon Johnson's landslide over Goldwater in 1964, just as media accounts suggested that Democrats tried to distance themselves from an anticipated anti-Clinton vote in 1994. On the other hand, issue ownership might be the correct explanation.

Poorer campaigns may well emphasize different issues than richer campaigns. With less money, and therefore less visibility, they may need to focus on issues that are more likely to attract coverage. These "bombthrower" campaigns may neglect a discussion of the deficit, for example, in favor of a more controversial topic, like abortion. The per capita income of the district may also affect the use of particular issues. Poorer communities may care less about the deficit, for example, when there are immediate pressing needs to be addressed. Furthermore, the median age of the district may affect the discussion of issues like abortion and education, for example, because they may be generally more relevant for a younger population than for an older one.

The tenure of the incumbent was expected to affect challenger emphasis on term limits. In addition, if the incumbent performed very strongly in the last election, the challenger may have felt compelled to use hot-button issues to shake up the political status quo. In areas where Perot did well in 1992, we expected the ideas he promoted to be in greater circulation, and therefore more likely to be adopted by House challengers.

Descriptive statistics for these explanatory variables are available in Table 10.1.

The model that explains issue emphasis and strategies is therefore:

$$\text{Issue/Strategy} = a + b_1\text{Party} + b_2\text{Incumbent92} + b_3\text{IncumbentTenure} \\ + b_4\text{ChallengerMoney} + b_5\text{Perot92} \\ + b_6\text{PerCapIncome} + b_7\text{Age} + e$$

Table 10.1

Descriptive Statistics for Challengers, Incumbents,
and Districts, 1992 and 1994

Variables	Mean	Standard Deviation	Minimum	Maximum
Previous political experience[a]	0.24	0.43	0	1.00
Previously run for House[b]	0.32	0.47	0	1.0
Challenger party[c]	0.39	0.49	0	1.00
Incumbent vote percentage in 1992	0.62	0.12	0.47	0.92
Clinton percentage of district's two-party vote in 1992	0.57	0.10	0.40	0.90
Spending by challengers	$220,954	$267,838	0	$1,015,330
Spending by incumbents	$622,866	$374,441	$53,187	$1,620,110
Per capita income	$17,318	$5,366	$11,060	$41,151
Median age	34.03	1.92	30.70	38.80

SOURCES: Prior political experience information was found in *Congressional Quarterly*. The campaign finance per capita income data is from *The Almanac of American Politics 1996*. Incumbent vote percentage and Clinton percentage of district's two-party vote in the 1992 election was taken from Duncan (1993). The median age variable was found in Bureau of the Census (1992).

[a] yes = 1; no = 2.

[b] yes = 1; no = 2.

[c] Republican = 1; Democratic = 0.

Several possible variables were not included because they were highly correlated with causally prior or more theoretically interesting variables. We dropped measures for incumbent campaign expenditures and ideological ratings of the incumbent. Incumbent spending was highly correlated with challenger spending (.80), and previous research in this field is divided about the role of this variable. Some research finds that incumbent spending has little impact on election outcomes (Jacobson 1978, 1985, 1990a), whereas other papers argue that incumbent spending does play a role (Green and Krasno 1988; Ansolabehere and Snyder 1996). Krasno et al. (1994) also showed that incumbent fund-raising can react quickly to well-financed opponents, but that challengers cannot react in a similar way to incumbent success. In light of these issues, it was better to exclude incumbent spending than challenger spending.

Incumbent conservatism (ratings given by the ACU) was strongly correlated (.73) with challenger party. Because multicollinearity is a larger problem in studies with fewer observations, it was not possible to include both variables in the regression and produce reliable findings. The importance of ideology as an explanatory variable is also reduced because the dependent variables addressed issue emphasis, not the direction of support or opposition.[11] Furthermore, because challenger party is not a consequence of incumbent conservatism (or liberalism), we were comfortable focusing on challenger party as the variable of primary interest.

ELECTION OUTCOMES

To explain the 1994 electoral outcomes, the following model was created. Because the dependent variable (challenger share of the two-party vote) is continuous, OLS regression is appropriate.

$$\begin{aligned} \text{Challenger2PartyVote} = {} & a + b_1 \text{ChallengerSpend} + b_2 \text{IncumbentVote92} \\ & + b_3 \text{PPE} + b_4 \text{PreviousRunHouse} \\ & + b_5 \text{IncumbentTenure} + b_6 \text{Party} + b_7 \text{Deficit} \\ & + b_8 \text{Values} + b_9 \text{Welfare} + b_{10} \text{Crime} \\ & + b_{11} \text{TermLimits} + b_{12} \text{Foreign} + e \end{aligned}$$

To test whether particular issues played any role in the election outcomes, six issues were included as independent variables. These issues all received a great deal of attention in the fall campaign, and were part of the Republican Contract with America (see Appendix C for full text) with the exception of "values."[12] Three issues on our survey that appeared to play no role in the 1994 elections were abortion, education, and infrastructure.[13] To be safe we included the issues in an earlier version of the model, but when they proved insignificant we dropped them from the final model to avoid losing degrees of freedom.

In the honed model presented here, a variable measuring incumbent spending was originally considered but ultimately dropped to avoid problems of multicollinearity. We included the dummy variable prior political experience (PPE), a commonly used proxy for challenger quality, with the expectation that more experienced candidates should do better.

We also noted whether a challenger had previously run for a House seat, although this might help or hurt the candidate depending on the competence and competitiveness of the campaign. The final variable was incumbent tenure because long-serving incumbents have demonstrated a more significant level of political skill than those in office for only a term or two.

Results: Issues

The survey questions asked campaigns how much emphasis they placed on individual issues. To reiterate, we did not ask candidates whether they supported or opposed term limits but the degree of emphasis they placed on the issue on a 1–7 scale. Table 10.2 displays mean emphasis given by House challengers to each of the nine issues and three campaign themes.

The most-discussed issues were crime (mean score of 5.88 on the seven-point scale) and the federal deficit (5.29). The least-discussed issue by challengers was foreign affairs (2.93) and the next lowest was abortion (3.08). Challengers, however, were more likely to discuss the incumbent's voting record (mean response of 6.34) and the fact of his or her incumbency (6.05) than any other single issue under investigation. They also paid a great deal of attention to their own personal qualities (5.32), which represented the least common of the three strategies.

The most striking influence on challenger issue usage in 1994 proved to be the candidate's party. Table 10.3 shows regression results for the model that explains challenger issue emphasis for all nine issues.

In the 1994 midterm elections, Republican challengers emphasized the issues of crime, term limits, welfare, values, and foreign policy substantially more than Democratic challengers did. The findings were particularly clear for welfare and values because Republicans were more than two points more likely (on a seven-point scale) to emphasize these issues ($p < .01$). The reader should keep in mind that the challenger's substantive stance on each issue is not addressed here; regardless of their substantive stance, we find Democrats were less likely to have emphasized these issues.

How were Contract with America issues in this study affected by party stratagems? Of the issues significantly affected by party membership, crime, term limits, and welfare were mentioned in the Contract, whereas values was not. One issue cited in the Contract, the federal budget deficit, was not significantly affected by challenger party membership. It is not certain whether respondents interpreted the foreign affairs issue as referring to the Contract provisions,[14] foreign policy generally, President Clinton's then-controversial Haiti policy, or to some combination. We believe it referred at least partially to the Haiti option because some respondents mentioned Haiti when asked the question.[15] These points suggest that the partisan issue emphasis effect was not limited to Contract issues, and therefore speaks to a deeper phenomenon of how candidates discussed issues in this election.

It is clear that the use of issues by House challengers in 1994 is not explainable simply in terms of issue ownership. The literature on this subject

Table 10.2

Descriptive Statistics for Respondent Answers to
Strategy and Issue Questions, 1994

Variable	Mean	Standard Deviation	Minimum	Maximum
Abortion	3.08	2.12	1	7
Crime	· 5.88	1.38	3	7
Deficit	5.29	1.76	1	7
Education	4.27	1.60	1	7
Foreign affairs	2.93	1.49	1	7
Incumbency	6.05	1.61	2	7
Infrastructure	3.88	1.85	1	7
Personal qualities	5.32	1.60	2	7
Term limits	5.00	2.00	1	7
Values	3.68	2.00	1	7
Voting record	6.34	1.06	2	7
Welfare	4.55	1.79	1	7

NOTE: Responses collected on seven-point scale, where one signifies no emphasis and seven the strongest possible emphasis.

argues that some issues attract the attention of candidates from one party but not the other. Based on the research of Petrocik (1996), the issues of crime, welfare, values, term limits, foreign affairs, and the deficit should appeal to Republican candidates, while Democrats would have more credibility on education and infrastructural development. Is this borne out by the regression results? As we saw, crime, welfare, values, term limits, and foreign policy were all emphasized more by Republican challengers. This means that all issues usually thought to be "owned" by the Republicans except the deficit were emphasized more by Republican candidates.

The Democrats, however, did not emphasize issues that traditionally work in their favor. Party was not a statistically significant explanatory factor for the discussion of education, and simple descriptive statistics show that Republican mean emphasis (4.28) was in fact slightly greater than that for Democrats (4.25). Also, cross-tabs show that while Democrats discussed infrastructural development more than Republicans (4.31 v. 3.60), this relationship does not hold up in any of the regressions. So not only did Demo-

Table 10.3
OLS Regression Model Explaining Issue Emphasis
for Nine Issues, 1994

	Abortion	*Crime*	*Deficit*	*Education*
Intercept	0.378	5.481	2.969	4.946
	(7.410)	(5.005)	(6.501)	
Party	−0.648	0.897*	0.721	0.399
	(0.727)	(0.491)	(0.638)	(0.594)
Challenger spending	−3.48e-06**	−2.25e-05*	−1.30e-06	−2.48e-06*
	(1.69e-06)	(1.14e-05)	(1.48e-06)	(1.38e-06)
Incumbent 1992	−3.728	−3.839	−7.974**	−1.987
	(4.000)	(2.702)	(3.510)	(3.266)
Perot 1992	7.867	−6.030	−0.310	−2.952
	(7.028)	(4.746)	(6.166)	(5.737)
Incumbent tenure	−0.018	−0.019	0.032	−0.010
	(0.059)	(0.400)	(0.051)	(0.050)
Per capita income	6.56e-05	6.29e-05	−1.27e-04	−4.70e-05
	(9.22-05)	(6.22e-05)	(8.09e-05)	(7.52e-05)
Median age	0.108	0.150	0.268	0.068
	(0.221)	(0.149)	(0.194)	(0.180)
Observations	41	41	41	41
Adjusted R^2	0.09	0.05	0.01	0.04

NOTE: Standard errors are in parentheses.

*p < .10

**p < .05

***p < .01

crats avoid issues usually seen as more advantageous to Republicans, but they also avoided issues that usually put Democrats in the best light.

We also analyzed the three strategy questions (how much emphasis did the challenger place on the voting record of the incumbent, her own positive personal qualities, and the fact of her opponent's incumbency?) with the same model (Table 10.4).

Democratic challengers were less likely to talk about the voting records of their opponents than were Republican challengers. This is more evidence that Democratic challengers in 1994 avoided issues. They may have thought

Foreign affairs	Infrastructure	Term limits	Values	Welfare
0.052	11.097*	5.258	9.261	2.203
(6.049)	(6.475)	(6.730)	(5.951)	(5.229)
1.533***	−0.306	1.236*	2.413***	2.260***
(0.524)	(0.635)	(0.660)	(0.584)	(0.513)
−2.39-06*	−1.57e-06	−1.15e-06	−2.13e-06	−3.66e-07
(1.22e-06)	(1.47e-06)	(1.53e-06)	(1.36e-06)	(1.19e-06)
−2.227	−9.596***	−2.037	−1.697	−1.249
(2.883)	(3.496)	(3.633)	(3.212)	(2.823)
4.147	−4.788	−5.097	12.223**	−0.046
(5.065)	(6.141)	(6.382)	(5.644)	(4.959)
0.027	0.043	0.140	−0.576	−0.079*
(0.042	(0.051)	(0.053)	(0.047)	(0.041)
6.76e-06	−1.37e-04*	−7.98e-06	−1.013e-04	−9.24e-06
(6.64e-06)	(8.05e-05)	(8.37e-06)	(7.4e-05)	(6.5e-06)
0.053	0.065	0.053	0.377**	0.118
(0.159)	(0.193)	(0.200)	(0.177)	(0.156)
41	41	41	41	41
0.07	0.11	0.18	0.34	0.38

that blaming Republicans for the perceived failures of a government under unified Democratic control was hopeless.

Taken as a whole, these findings generate two hypotheses that might explain the partisan gap in issue emphasis. One possibility is that this is a quadrennial phenomenon in which the visibility of the president permits members of the opposing party to attack incumbents on issues where the president is vulnerable. This hypothesis might help explain the well-known phenomenon of presidential midterm losses.

A second hypothesis is suggested by parallels to Kingdon's (1968) 1964

Table 10.4

OLS Regression Model Explaining Challenger Strategies, 1994

	Discuss Opponent's Voting Record	Discuss Opponent's Incumbent	Discuss Own Positive Personal Qualities
Intercept	7.699**	12.624**	−4.392
	(3.565)	(5.336)	(6.059)
Party[a]	1.137***	0.824	0.097
	(0.350)	(0.524)	(0.595)
Challenger spending[b]	0.000	−0.333***	−0.138
	(0.081)	(0.122)	(0.138)
Incumbent 1992	−0.039	−1.828	−1.469
	(1.925)	(2.880)	(3.271)
Perot 1992	−0.193	−5.034	7.901
	(3.381)	(5.061)	(5.746)
Incumbent tenure	−0.022	0.045	−0.041
	(0.028)	(0.042)	(0.048)
Per capita income[c]	0.050	−0.0672	−0.234
	(0.443)	(0.664)	(0.754)
Median age	−0.056	−0.131	0.272
	(0.106)	(0.159)	(0.181)
Observations	41	41	41
Adjusted R^2	0.18	0.34	0.04

NOTE: Standard errors are in parentheses.

*p < .10

**p < .05

***p < .01

[a]Republican = 1; Democrat = 2.

[b]In hundred thousands.

[c]In ten thousands.

study of Wisconsin political candidates. He found that 33 percent of all Republican congressional campaigns reported no policy emphasis, whereas only 13 percent of Democrats followed the same strategy. This suggests that candidates avoid issues when they perceive their party as electorally vulnerable. Republicans may have acted this way in anticipation of the 1964 Goldwater defeat, just as media accounts suggested that Democrats tried to distance themselves from an expected anti–Clinton vote in 1994. This dynamic could therefore occur in any election, midterm or otherwise.

In sum, no variable explained issue or strategy selection as consistently as challenger party. This implies that national forces had a significant effect on the issues challengers addressed in the 1994 House elections. Whether this effect has been present in other elections—or will be in the future—cannot be determined by this chapter. Future research will be necessary to test these hypotheses over time.

Because of these systematic findings, it is not important that the behavior of the incumbents in these elections was not studied. The data show that political party affects not only the likelihood that challengers will talk about the voting records of their opponents, but also how challengers emphasize particular issues. This strongly suggests that challengers are not following incumbents for their strategic cues but are responding to the national-level political context. It is also reminiscent of Herrnson (1995), who found that most challengers ignored the issue positions of incumbents.

This leaves open the question of whether partisan-based issue emphasis decisions affected electoral outcomes. We will address that question in the following section.

Results: Electoral Outcomes

The two issues most powerfully associated with electoral performance were the budget deficit and crime. Other things being equal, challengers who emphasized these two issues fared better than those who did not (Table 10.5).

For each issue, a one-point increase on the 1–7 scale (moving from two to three, for instance) was associated with an increased vote percentage of 1.7 percent. Thus, the candidate who focused strongly on the deficit or crime (reported a seven), other things being equal, received 8.5 percent more of the two-party congressional vote than a candidate who almost ignored the deficit (reported a two). This focus on the deficit and/or crime had a very significant impact on the election, and was especially important because it was under the control of the candidate.

Challenger spending, as expected, also influenced challenger performance. The average challenger spent $160,000 in the 1992 elections. Therefore, if a challenger increased his or her spending by 25 percent ($40,000), he or she increased vote share by about 0.5 percent, and a doubling of spending was associated with a 2-percent vote increase.

Incumbent performance in the last election was also related to current

Table 10.5

OLS Regression Model Explaining Percentage of Challenger Two-Party Vote in 1994 House Elections

Variable	Coefficient
Intercept	0.341 ***
	(0.110)
Challenger spending[a]	0.011 *
	(0.006)
Incumbent vote in 1992 elections	−0.328 **
	(0.125)
Prior political experience[b]	0.078 **
	(0.038)
Previously ran for House seat[c]	−0.003
	(0.023)
Length of incumbent tenure	0.002
	(0.002)
Party[d]	0.032
	(0.033)
Deficit	0.017 **
	(0.007)
Values	−0.000
	(0.007)
Welfare	−0.007
	(0.008)
Crime	0.017 *
	(0.009)
Term Limits	−0.001
	(0.006)
Foreign affairs	−0.006
	(0.009)
Adjusted R^2	0.62
Observations	41

NOTE: Issues collected on a seven-point scale, where one signifies no emphasis and seven the strongest possible emphasis. Standard errors are in parentheses. The same regression was rerun without the five insignificant issue variables and the results were the same.

*p < .10

**p < .05

***p < .01

[a] In hundred thousands.

[b] Yes = 1.

[c] Yes = 1.

[d] Republican = 1.

incumbent performance. For every 10 percent of the vote the incumbent won in 1992, other things being equal, her 1994 vote share increased just over 3 percent. Prior political experience, as anticipated, positively influenced challenger vote totals by almost 8 percent. Previous campaigns for a House seat, however, had little impact on the vote.

The independent effect of party was insignificant. When party is inserted into the model of 1994 election outcomes, the results are statistically insignificant, whereas the other variables do not change and the corrected R^2 remains the same. This implies that the significant issue variables—crime and the deficit—are not serving as a conduit for the influence of party. Regardless of challenger party, use of these issues served to increase the challenger's vote share; one of the issues was more likely to be used by Republicans than Democrats.

Conclusions

Issues are often thought to be at the heart of campaigns and elections, yet political scientists know surprisingly little about how they are used. This chapter shows that political party was significantly associated with issue emphasis in the 1994 House elections, and thus argues that the way challengers discuss issues is not a matter of random taste or experimentation. In addition, we present evidence that the discussion of two particular issues (crime and the deficit) positively affected the vote for challengers on election day. One of these issues (crime) was more likely to be used by Republicans than Democrats. Put together, we see how part of the explanation for so many Republican victories in 1994 could lie in the greater likelihood of Republican candidates to have waged issue-based campaigns.

More specifically, political party affected the use of crime, term limits, welfare, values, and foreign affairs, but not the deficit, abortion, education, and infrastructure. In all five cases, Democrats were less likely to have emphasized those issues than were Republicans. In addition, Democratic challengers were less likely to adopt the general strategy of emphasizing the voting records of their opponents. This further suggests that Democratic challengers in 1994 were less enthusiastic about issue-based campaigning than were their Republican counterparts.

Of the issues affected by political party, three (crime, term limits, and welfare) were mentioned in the Republican Contract with America, while values was not. Foreign policy appeared to refer more to the United States involvement in Haiti than to the Contract provisions. One Contract issue, the deficit, was unaffected by partisanship.[16] This shows that the partisan effect on issue emphasis was not limited to Contract items and therefore speaks to a deeper phenomenon of how candidates discussed issues. We similarly show that the theory of issue ownership does not explain the emphasis candidates placed on issues; whereas Republicans generally emphasized issues for which they are seen by the public as most competent, Democrats passed up the opportunity to emphasize issues for which they hold greater public trust.

We discuss two hypotheses that might help explain the partisan gap in issue emphasis. The first is suggested by parallels to Kingdon's (1968) study of Wisconsin political candidates in 1964. He found that 33 percent of all Republican congressional campaigns reported no policy emphasis, whereas only 13 percent of Democrats followed the same strategy. This finding suggests that candidates avoid issues when they perceive their party to be electorally vulnerable. Republicans may have acted this way in anticipation of the 1964 Goldwater debacle, just as media accounts suggested that Democrats tried to distance themselves from an expected anti-Clinton vote in 1994. This dynamic could therefore occur in any election, midterm or otherwise.

The second possibility is that this is a quadrennial phenomenon, in which the visibility of the president permits members of the opposing party to attack incumbents on issues for which the president is vulnerable. If true, this hypothesis would help explain the phenomenon of presidential midterm losses.

We do not believe the findings are an artifact of a regional study. As previously discussed, the incumbent defeat rate in the sample almost exactly mirrors the nationwide average. This finding is especially significant for the 1994 election because all the defeated incumbents across the nation were Democrats. These similarities suggest that partisan dynamics in the area bounded by Maryland, Canada, and Lake Erie did not significantly differ from the rest of the nation because Republican challengers made gains here the same as they did elsewhere. This is further evidence of the "'deregionalization' of congressional elections" discussed by Abramson et al. (1994: 263).

A national sample would obviously have been preferable. Had we known in advance the historic outcome of the elections we might have used a more extensive national research design. We are nevertheless lucky that this survey took place at such an interesting time and thereby provided a unique look at a key election that has only recently received comprehensive empirical academic attention.

Chapter 11

The Electoral Connection Between Party and Constituency Reconsidered: Evidence from the U.S. House of Representatives, 1972–1994

MELISSA P. COLLIE AND JOHN LYMAN MASON

The growth of partisanship since the 1970s in the U.S. House of Representatives has coincided with renewed scholarly attention to the importance of the congressional parties (Aldrich 1995; Sinclair 1985, 1997b; Patterson and Caldeira 1988; R. H. Davidson 1988; Kiewiet and McCubbins 1991; Rohde 1991; Cox and McCubbins 1993). While increased partisan rancor has been manifest in a variety of aspects of House politics, one of its more obvious indicators has been the rise in party conflict on floor votes, which was higher during Ronald Reagan's administration than any time in the prior 30 years. In the same period, party unity on votes where majorities of the two parties opposed one another climbed in both parties, though more dramatically among the Democrats, for whom it reached 88 percent in 1987 and 1988, a level unmatched since the Joseph Cannon speakership, 1909–11. Together with a strengthened party leadership in the House, the higher incidence of party conflict and unity (on opposition votes) has become synonymous with a "remarkable resurgence" (Rohde 1991: 14) in partisanship, which has hardly dissipated in more recent Congresses. Indeed, partisanship became the signature feature of the 104th Republican-led House, as Speaker Newt Gingrich extended his own and, more generally, the majority party's control into the committee system and the legislative process (Evans and Oleszek 1997; Smith and Lawrence 1997; Sinclair 1997a, 1997b).

In explaining the variation in partisan floor voting in the House, scholars have traditionally examined the impact of a variety of electoral and legislative factors (Mayhew 1966; D. W. Brady et al. 1979; Cooper and Brady 1981; Crook and Hibbing 1985; Patterson and Caldeira 1988; Rohde 1991; Ward 1993). Until recently, the conventional wisdom has been that polarization in the legislative party system of the House is primarily a combination of the homogeneity of interests within each party's constituency base and the distinctiveness between them. This relationship has been obvious in studies of electoral change, party voting, and policy innovation in the House during periods of realignment (Brady 1988; Brady and Stewart 1982). Other research has demonstrated that partisan polarization in the House has been highly sensitive to the magnitude of external party conflict for much of the post–World War II period (Patterson and Caldeira 1988).

This perspective has been challenged in recent research. One alternative perspective is that the long-held connection between party-in-the-electorate and party-in-government (Key 1964; Sorauf and Beck 1988), which is the basis for the hypothesized relationship between polarized partisan constituencies and partisan polarization in the legislature, is misconceived. Rather, voters ought to be regarded as consumers of party platforms and policies, not as an integral part of political parties themselves (Aldrich 1995). A second alternative perspective is that the cohesion within parties and the conflict between them is more directly and importantly a function of party leaders' use of institutional prerogatives, such as their ability to shape the legislative agenda and manipulate rewards and sanctions (Cox and Mc-Cubbins 1993; Kiewiet and McCubbins 1991).

Though presented as challenges, these perspectives are not incompatible with the existence of a strong relationship between characteristics of the parties' constituency bases and partisan behavior in the legislature. Even if voters are regarded as consumers of party programs, we would expect them to register their approval (or disapproval) of these programs with changes in their own preferences, in much the same way that we would expect consumers who find Dial soap commercials convincing as to freshness and cleanliness to endorse Dial soap. The key distinction between this perspective and the conventional one is whether changes in constituency preferences precede or follow changes in legislative behavior. Also, despite the obvious importance of party leaders in the contemporary House, research continues to suggest that the House as an institution characteristically has a low tolerance for the centralization that comes with strong party leaders (Dodd and Oppenheimer 1997a; Dodd and Oppenheimer 1997b). Rather, the enhancement of party leaders' institutional powers is a function of the increased homogeneity in rank-and-file preferences that is tied to increased similarities in the constituency bases of the parties (Cooper and Brady 1981). For example, the recent upsurge in partisan conflict has been attributed to the homogenizing aftereffects of VRA on Democratic and Republican constituencies, which set into motion institutional reforms and party leader behavior conducive to partisanship (Rohde 1991). In this perspective, then, the causal order between changes in the constituency bases of the parties and the parties' response to these changes resembles that of the conventionally interpreted direct impact on party behavior; however, there is a presumptive lag connected to the enhancement of party leaders' institutional powers and their use of these institutional powers to legislate.

Thus the important distinctions among the three perspectives concern the temporal (and thus causal) ordering of changes in the constituency preferences associated with each party's electoral base, the shifts in the preferences of the parties' rank and file, the enhancement and application of party leaders' prerogatives, and the changes in the partisan conflict registered in floor votes. Nonetheless, each perspective incorporates some direct or indirect relationship between changes in the constituency bases of the parties and changes in the behavior of the legislative parties.

The purpose of this article is to evaluate whether the resurgence of partisan voting behavior in the House during the last two decades has been associated with changes in the constituency bases of congressional Democrats and Republicans. While we do not directly investigate the temporal distinctions that differentiate the three perspectives discussed above, we examine something more fundamental, namely, whether a case can be made that any changes in the congressional parties' electorates have accompanied the dramatic changes that have been observed at the institutional level. Given the changes that have been observed at the institutional level, our expectations are that each congressional party's constituency base has become more homogeneous and more differentiated from the other's over time. Based on NES data, our results indicate that the electorates associated with the congressional parties have undergone only marginal changes over the period in question. We conclude by discussing how marginal changes in the electorate can produce dramatic changes in the legislature.

Party Voting Behavior in the House

Because our expectations regarding changes in the constituencies of the congressional parties follow from the changes that have occurred in the legislative parties' voting behavior over time, we first document the rise of parti-

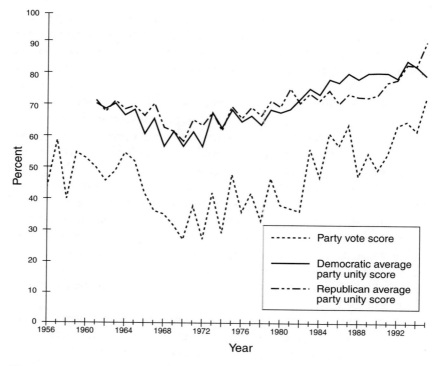

Figure 11.1.   Party vote scores and average party-unity scores in House, 1956–1995.

SOURCE: Ornstein et al. 1996, Carney 1996.

NOTE: Data show average party unity scores within parties. Party unity scores reflect the percentage of party unity votes on which a member supported his or her party. Party unity votes are those roll calls on which a majority of a party votes on one side of the issue and a majority of the other party votes on the other side. The percentages are normalized to eliminate the effects of absences, as follows: party unity = (unity)/(unity + opposition).

san voting in the House (1956–95) in terms of two conventional statistics. In Figure 11.1, the party vote score is a measure of conflict between the parties, and the average party unity score is a measure of the typical party loyalty in each party on party votes.[1] Together the two illustrate the degree to which the parties are polarized in a given House, the extreme example being when the parties are internally unified and consistently opposed to one another.

As the party vote scores show in Figure 11.1, party conflict declined consistently after 1964 and reached its low for the period in 1970 and 1972, when party majorities opposed each other on only 27 percent of recorded votes in both years. Thereafter, it climbed erratically and has only twice (1988 and 1990) dipped slightly below 50 percent in the last decade. Loyalty within both parties also increased during the same period, dramatically for the Democrats 1978–88 and for the Republicans after 1988. Combined, the average party unity scores and the party vote scores indicate that the polarization between the congressional parties during the 1990s has been greater than at any time during the prior four decades.

This polarization is more directly captured in Table 11.1, which shows changes over time in the mean and median Democratic and Republican ACU scores.

The increase in the difference between the mean Democratic and Republican scores indicates that the ideological "center" of each legislative party has grown more distant from the other over time. The decreasing standard deviations indicate an increased clustering around these ideological centers.

While the means and standard deviations provide important information on the distribution of scores over time, the changes in the median Democratic and Republican scores are of theoretical importance in light of research implying that the legislative party's median voter determines the party's program (Kiewiet and McCubbins 1991; Cox and McCubbins 1993; Aldrich and Rohde 1996; Dodd and Oppenheimer 1997b). If the median Democratic and Republican positions can be taken as proxies for the parties' legislative agendas, then the increase over time in the difference between the parties' medians indicates a substantial increase in the ideological difference between the two parties' legislative agendas.

Thus a variety of indicators of party behavior all point in the same direction: toward increased ideological confluence and agreement within each party and increased opposition and ideological distance between them. If this polarization has been associated with changes in the electorate—as it should have been according to all three perspectives—we should expect to find increases over time in the homogeneity and distinctiveness of the parties' constituency bases. Accordingly, we turn now to our analysis of the congressional parties' electorates.

Data and Methodology

Despite the intuitive appeal of a connection between party-in-the-electorate and party-in-government (Sorauf and Beck 1988), linking the two empirically has been difficult, mainly because of the problems associated with

Table 11.1

ACU Scores for Members of House by Political Party, 1971–1994

Year	REPUBLICANS			DEMOCRATS			Difference in means	Difference in medians
	Mean	Standard dev.	Median	Mean	Standard dev.	Median		
1971	71.06	27.43	79.00	39.14	33.80	27.50	31.91	51.50
1972	68.21	24.55	75.00	35.41	30.61	26.00	32.80	49.00
1973	70.42	20.16	74.00	30.79	24.41	24.00	39.63	50.00
1974	60.43	24.09	63.00	28.14	25.73	20.00	32.29	43.00
1975	71.72	24.89	81.50	27.54	26.36	15.00	44.18	66.50
1976	73.32	24.39	81.00	27.07	26.82	18.00	46.25	63.00
1977	78.72	20.58	85.00	27.58	25.04	19.00	51.14	66.00
1978	78.39	18.62	83.50	29.15	24.71	21.00	49.24	62.50
1979	76.99	22.46	68.00	26.03	24.55	17.00	50.96	51.00
1980	68.04	23.98	72.00	26.80	23.80	16.50	41.24	55.50
1981	89.68	12.91	93.00	23.43	27.06	13.00	66.25	80.00
1982	71.41	24.33	77.00	26.52	24.20	18.00	44.89	59.00
1983	76.88	22.52	86.00	21.60	25.26	17.00	55.29	69.00
1984	67.73	23.68	74.00	23.01	21.58	17.00	44.72	57.00
1985	75.61	17.38	81.00	23.12	22.14	14.00	52.49	67.00
1986	74.01	21.22	81.00	20.47	22.55	10.00	53.54	71.00
1987	73.69	23.09	82.00	11.03	15.40	5.00	62.66	77.00
1988	78.80	23.32	89.00	18.27	20.83	11.00	60.53	78.00
1989	79.47	17.68	85.00	18.72	20.51	11.00	60.74	74.00
1990	73.52	19.63	79.50	20.02	19.00	13.00	53.50	66.50
1991	82.04	17.34	85.00	17.69	19.90	11.00	64.35	74.00
1992	83.58	14.96	87.50	18.52	19.84	12.00	65.06	75.50
1993	83.38	15.22	88.00	18.93	17.86	13.50	64.45	74.50
1994	85.34	15.81	90.00	20.44	20.13	15.00	64.90	75.00

SOURCE: ACU.

measuring the homogeneity of the parties' constituencies. In prior research, scholars have used a number of measures to capture the homogeneity of the parties' constituency bases as well as the differences between them. One alternative has been to assess changes in the parties' representation of different regions and socioeconomic interests (such as agricultural v. industrial), the latter measured by district-level characteristics (Brady et al. 1979; Cooper and Brady 1981; Patterson and Caldeira 1988; Fleisher 1993). Other measures of external effects more indirectly related to the parties' constituency bases have included the proportion of new members elected, issue differences in party platforms during presidential election years, and presidential support in the district as well as the House (Brady et al. 1979; Patterson and Caldeira 1985).

Each of these measures has its advantages and disadvantages. In the absence of data on constituency opinion, for example, historical research must necessarily rely on district-level socioeconomic indicators or their surrogate, regional representation in the parties. The use of such data becomes more problematic as the complexity and size of the policy agenda expands beyond simple dichotomies, such as agricultural or industrial representation, or the variety of interests within regions becomes more differentiated. Similarly, party platforms, which reflect more directly presidential politics, and especially during the contemporary period, the ephemeral, candidate-driven grassroots politics now associated with presidential election years, can be questioned as the appropriate operationalization of the legislative parties' constituencies.

Our advantage in this study is that national election study data are available for the period we wish to examine. Still, determining the constituency base of the congressional parties is tricky. Our approach extrapolates from the insights of Mayhew (1974a) and Fenno (1978), both of whom emphasize the importance of House members' district orientation.

Accordingly, to identify each congressional party's constituency base, we begin by separating NES respondents into districts according to whether a Democratic or a Republican incumbent is running for reelection. We then focus on Democratic respondents in Democratic districts (i.e., districts where an incumbent Democrat is running for reelection) and on Republican respondents in Republican districts (i.e., districts where an incumbent Republican is running for reelection).[2] By differentiating districts and respondents in this way we can examine voters who are likely to be a part of each incumbent's reelection constituency and thus, by aggregation, each legislative party's constituency base in a particular Congress.[3] By aggregating across Democratic districts for each election year we construct a longitudinal profile of the congressional Democrats' constituency base, and like-wise for congressional Republicans' constituency base. A comparison of these profiles then enables the analysis of any changes that have occurred in the homogeneity within each constituency base or in the difference be-tween them.

We focus on these sets of voters for several reasons. One is that legislators who want to be reelected have a nuanced perspective of their districts and are especially attentive to their reelection constituency as opposed to their geographic constituency (Fenno 1978). A second reason is that the reelec-tion constituency of any given incumbent is composed at least of the dis-trict's partisans who identify with the incumbent's party. Third, most in-cumbents who run for reelection in the general election are reelected.

To determine the homogeneity and distinctiveness of each party's con-stituency base, we first examine the ideological position of the relevant respondents in Democratic and Republican districts over time.[4] Whether ideology constitutes a fully elaborated and consistent system of political val-ues and policy positions or an affective response to symbols and reference groups[5] is less important here than whether the increases in the polarization of the congressional parties have an ideological rationale in the electorate. Based on the results we presented earlier on the ideological positions of con-gressional Democrats and Republicans, our expectation is that ideological dispersion within the two parties' constituency bases decreases. Based on these same results, we additionally expect the distance to increase between the mean (median) ideological positions of voters in the two parties. To-gether, such results would indicate an increase in the homogeneity and dis-tinctiveness of the parties' constituency bases, thus establishing a foundation in the electorate for the party behavior observed at the institutional level.

Especially with respect to the Democratic constituency, our expecta-tion is related to a blurring over time of differences between northern and southern Democratic districts, due both to the infusion of southern blacks with largely liberal leanings into the Democratic electorate and the exodus of disaffected southern white conservatives into the Republican electorate (Rohde 1991). Conforming to the decreased difference between northern and southern Democratic voting habits in the Congress (Rohde 1991; Poole and Rosenthal 1991), our expectation is that the distinction between north-ern and southern Democratic electorates also declines.

In view of the policy differences between congressional Democrats and Republicans that emerged during the Reagan years and have since persisted, we also investigate voter responses on four issue areas: government protec-tion of jobs and standard of living, aid to minorities, government spending, and women's equality.[6] Our expectation is that diversity of viewpoint within each party, whether ideological or issue-related, declined over the period in question and that ideological and issue-related distinctions between each party's constituency grew.

Partisan Polarization in the Electorate?

We first examine the distributions of the ideological positions of Democratic respondents in Democratic districts and Republican respondents in Republican districts. Table 11.2 presents means and standard deviations associated with the ideological position of Democratic respondents in districts with incumbent Democrats and Republican respondents in districts with Republican incumbents.[7]

Based on the changes that occur over time in the mean ideological position of Democrats, there appears to be no sustained movement to the left in the party's constituent base. In fact, the sharpest change occurred between 1992 and 1994, when the mean shifted from 3.56 to 3.80, indicating increased conservatism rather than liberalism. Overall, the changes between elections appear marginal. The mean ideological position of Republicans grew rather steadily more conservative during the period 1972–86, thereafter fluctuating around a period high.[8]

In Table 11.2 the most direct indication of an increase in party homogeneity is a decrease over time in the standard deviation around the mean ideological position of partisan constituents in Democratic and Republican districts. Such a decrease is not apparent for Democrats in Democratic districts, where only marginal changes occur in the standard deviation (sometimes in the wrong direction). Changes in the standard deviations for Republicans in Republican districts display a different pattern. The standard deviations increased until 1980, when there was a relatively sharp decrease. With the exception of 1984, standard deviations remained below levels characteristic of the 1970s throughout the period 1980–94.

To test for a trend effect that can be obscured in year-to-year comparisons, we regressed the means and standard deviations corresponding to the sets of voters identified in Table 11.2 on time. If the Democratic electorate grew more liberal over time, the coefficient should be negative and statistically significant. If the Republican electorate grew more conservative, the coefficient should be positive and statistically significant. For Democrats, the coefficient was $-.0026$ ($p = .447$) and not statistically significant. For Republicans, the coefficient was $.0137$ ($p = .029$), which is statistically significant at the .05 level. If ideological homogeneity in the parties' constituent

Table 11.2

Ideology of Partisans in Democratic and Republican Districts, 1972–1994

Year	DEMOCRATS IN DEMOCRATIC DISTRICTS[a] Mean(St.Dev.)N Skewness	REPUBLICANS IN REPUBLICAN DISTRICTS[b] Mean(St.Dev.)N Skewness	Difference in means[c]
1972	3.77(1.30)483 −0.087	4.65(1.14)246 −0.469	0.87
1974	3.72(1.34)322 0.045	4.65(1.19)164 −0.43	0.92
1976	3.82(1.33)427 0.068	4.83(1.20)200 −0.512	1.00
1978	3.74(1.31)503 0.136	4.86(1.25)227 −0.614	1.12
1980	3.81(1.42)299 0.08	4.99(1.07)135 −0.229	1.18
1982	3.83(1.32)259 0.173	4.97(1.07)158 −0.625	1.14
1984	3.68(1.30)544 0.125	4.94(1.21)250 −0.84	1.26
1986	3.84(1.27)515 0.121	4.83(1.08)320 −0.37	0.99
1988	3.77(1.37)395 0.081	5.09(1.10)255 −0.439	1.32
1990	3.75(1.33)473 0.045	4.76(1.07)222 −0.294	1.01
1992	3.56(1.36)539 0.171	4.88(1.10)268 −0.24	1.32
1994	3.80(1.28)348 0.033	5.16(1.12)268 −0.807	1.36

SOURCE: Unless otherwise noted, all tables in Chapter 11 are based on the NES.

[a] Includes strong Democrats, weak Democrats, and Independents who lean Democratic in districts where a Democratic incumbent ran for reelection in year of analysis.

[b] Includes strong Republicans, weak Republicans, and Independents who lean Republican in districts where a Republican incumbent ran for reelection in year of analysis.

[c] Significant at the 0.001 level.

bases increased over time, the coefficient on time should be negative and statistically significant. In Democratic districts, this coefficient was $-.0004$ ($p = .44$). In Republican districts, the coefficient was $-.004$ ($p = .09$) for Republicans.

Corroborating the year-to-year comparisons, the regression results imply little to no change in the ideological position or homogeneity of the congressional Democrats' constituent base. In contrast, there is weak statistical evidence that the congressional Republicans' constituent base grew slightly more conservative over time and slightly more homogeneous. We note parenthetically that this test is a conservative one, in that it basically tests whether there is a statistical difference between the means and standard deviations, respectively, at the beginning of the time series and at the end. Even given the conservative nature of this test, only a weak case can be made for an ideological shift in the parties' constituent bases over time, and then more easily for that of the congressional Republicans than Democrats.

Turning from the ideological position and distribution of each congressional party's electorate, we examine ideological distinctions between the two. The right-hand column of results in Table 11.2 presents differences in the mean ideological position of Democrats in Democratic districts and Republicans in Republican districts. Our expectation is that the ideological difference in the two parties' electorates increased over time, indicated by an increase over time in the difference of means. As Table 11.2 shows, the difference in the mean ideological position of Democrats in Democratic districts and Republicans in Republican districts gradually increased from 1972 to 1980. Beginning with 1980, there was a fluctuation associated with midterm elections, which lasted until 1992. During the period, presidential elections apparently had a polarizing effect that dissipated in off-year elections.

This fluctuation notwithstanding, the time series has lower values at its beginning and higher ones most recently, indicating that the ideological distance between the two congressional parties' constituent bases increased over time. The trend is confirmed by regressing the differences in means on time; the coefficient is .017 and significant at the .01 level. This shift amounts to a half-unit increase on the ideological scale in the difference between the two parties' constituencies over the 1972–94 period.[9] Whether this increase is a large or a small change in the ideological distance between the congressional parties' electorates can be debated. To interpret its importance, two additional points are relevant. First, as Table 11.2 indicates, the mean ideological positions of the electorates associated with the two congressional parties were statistically different from one another throughout the period, not just in the later years when partisan conflict in the House became more pronounced. Second, the change over time in the difference between the ideological positions of the congressional parties' electorates was far less than the change that occurred over time in the mean (median) ideological position of congressional Democrats and Republicans, whether calculated for the overall period or on a year-to-year basis. That is, between the 1970s and the 1990s there was a 7 percent increase in the difference between the mean ideological position of respondents in Democratic districts and that in Republican districts, which can be contrasted with the 33 percent increase in the difference in the mean ideological positions and 23.5 percent increase in the median ideological positions of congressional Democrats and Republicans.

The evidence of the at-best marginal changes that have taken place in the congressional Democrat and Republican electorates is further substantiated in Table 11.3, which presents the summary statistics of the ideological positions of strong partisans only in Democratic and Republican districts.

As Table 11.3 shows, there was no sustained movement to the left or growth in homogeneity among Democrats in Democratic districts. The story was much the same for strong Republicans in Republican districts; like the more inclusive measurement of the parties' constituencies in Table 11.2, there was a consistently significant difference between the mean ideological position of Democrats in Democratic districts and Republicans in Republican districts. Still, a trend toward either increasing homogeneity within the parties' electorates or increasing distance between them is not confirmed statistically (at the .05 level). Neither trend emerges in regressions of the means, standard deviations, and differences of means on time.

We next focus specifically on the northern and southern electorates of the congressional Democrats. Table 11.4 reports summary statistics on voter ideology in northern and southern Democratic districts. Based on a comparison of means, these results indicate that northern Democratic districts were more liberal than southern Democratic districts throughout the period examined. This finding comports with the widely acknowledged tendency of northern Democratic House members to vote more liberally than their southern Democratic counterparts (Poole and Rosenthal 1991).

Yet based on the voting behavior of northern and southern Democrats in the House and in keeping with the account of the changes in the Democratic party's electorate since the 1970s, our expectation is that the ideological distinction between the northern and southern constituent wings of the Democratic party has declined over time. Table 11.4 also reports differences in the mean ideological position of Democrats in northern and southern Democratic districts. An indication that the ideological distinctiveness of the northern and southern Democratic electorates declined is a decrease over

Table 11.3
Ideology of Strong Partisans in Democratic and Republican Districts, 1972–1994

Year	DEMOCRATS IN DEMOCRATIC DISTRICTS[a] Mean(St.Dev.)N Skewness	REPUBLICANS IN REPUBLICAN DISTRICTS[b] Mean(St.Dev.)N Skewness	Difference in means[c]
1972	3.47(1.35)128 0.184	4.80(1.19)74 −0.639	1.33
1974	3.59(1.46)116 0.358	5.05(1.13)56 −0.495	1.46
1976	3.65(1.44)124 0.233	5.28(1.05)64 −0.767	1.63
1978	3.69(1.44)142 0.241	5.31(1.17)61 −1.147	1.62
1980	3.61(1.54)100 0.206	5.36(1.17)33 −0.902	1.75
1982	3.83(1.41)106 0.266	5.58(.835)50 −1.687	1.75
1984	3.68(1.49)170 0.203	5.18(1.25)89 −1.174	1.50
1986	3.75(1.40)189 0.229	5.09(1.16)111 −0.897	1.34
1988	3.52(1.44)144 0.201	5.7(.94)100 −0.938	2.18
1990	3.73(1.45)199 0.133	5.21(1.12)66 −1.324	1.48
1992	3.49(1.49)207 0.381	5.26(1.10)96 −0.489	1.77
1994	3.60(1.40)128 0.322	5.60(1.12)110 −1.797	2.00

[a]Includes strong Democrats in districts where Democratic incumbents ran for reelection in year of analysis.

[b]Includes strong Republicans in districts where Republican incumbents ran for reelection in year of analysis.

[c]Significant at the 0.001 level.

Table 11.4
Democratic Ideology in Southern and Northern
Democratic Districts, 1972–1994

Year	SOUTHERN DEMOCRATS[a] Means(St.Dev.)N Skewness	NORTHERN DEMOCRATS[b] Mean(St.Dev.)N Skewness	Difference in means
1972	4.06(1.34)166 −0.157	3.62(1.25)317 −0.108	0.45***
1974	4.01(1.35)140 −0.097	3.50(1.29)182 0.118	0.51***
1976	4.14(1.32)142 −0.096	3.67(1.31)285 0.146	0.47***
1978	3.99(1.33)193 0.037	3.58(1.27)310 0.179	0.41***
1980	4.04(1.46)115 −0.128	3.66(1.39)184 0.199	0.38*
1982	4.13(1.41)90 0.153	3.67(1.24)169 0.083	0.46**
1984	4.04(1.33)120 −0.034	3.52(1.26)332 0.155	0.52***
1986	4.07(1.28)189 0.255	3.70(1.25)326 0.022	0.38***
1988	3.99(1.36)131 −0.06	3.66(1.37)264 0.155	0.33*
1990	4.26(1.43)128 0.03	3.56(1.24)345 −0.107	0.70***
1992	3.96(1.40)121 0.038	3.44(1.33)418 0.189	0.52***
1994	4.00(1.23)115 0.318	3.70(1.29)233 −0.064	0.30*

[a]Includes strong Democrats, weak Democrats, and Independents that lean Democratic from districts in the original eleven states of the Confederacy, Kentucky, or Oklahoma.

[b]Includes strong Democrats, weak Democrats, and Independents that lean Democratic from districts not in the original eleven states of the Confederacy, Kentucky, or Oklahoma.

*Significant at the 0.05 level.

**Significant at the 0.01 level.

***Significant at the 0.001 level.

time in the difference in the mean ideological position of voters in the two regions. On the one hand, there was no steady decrease in the difference in means over time. Indeed, the difference in the mean ideological positions of Democrats in northern districts and southern Democratic districts increased over its prior levels in 1974, 1982, 1984, and 1990. While the smallest difference (0.30) in the mean ideological position of Democrats in northern and southern Democratic districts occurred in 1994, the largest (0.70) was in 1990.

In general, the results in Table 11.4 do not provide a straightforward story of ideological convergence between the northern and southern wings of the Democratic congressional electorate. In this respect, the results provide additional evidence that the Democratic electorate has not undergone any systematic ideological shift in the last several decades, which was also implied by the results in Table 11.2 and 11.3. This interpretation is supported by a test regressing the differences of means for the two groups of voters in Table 11.4 on time. For Democrats, this coefficient was $-.0005$ ($p = .916$).

We examine finally the means and standard deviations of Democrats in Democratic districts and Republicans in Republican districts in four issue areas: government protection of jobs and standard of living, government aid to minorities, women's equality, and government spending. These results are presented in Table 11.5.

As noted in Table 11.5, the mean positions of Democrats (in Democratic districts) and Republicans (in Republican districts) were significantly different from one another in three issue areas each year. The exception was women's equality, on which there was no statistically significant difference between the mean positions in 1972, 1984, and 1988–94.

To test for trend, we regressed both the means and standard deviations associated with the issue positions of Democrats and Republicans on time. If Democrats became more liberal over time, the coefficient of time with respect to the mean should have been negative and statistically significant. If Republicans became more conservative over time, the coefficient should have been positive and significant. Such results would indicate an increased distinction between the congressional parties' constituent bases over time in these issue areas. If the congressional parties' constituent bases became more homogeneous over time, the coefficient of time with respect to the standard deviations should have been negative and statistically significant.

On the basis of this test, the only indication of trend in the mean position of Democrats is in the issue area of women's equality. On this issue, the coefficient was $-.0456$ ($p = .0001$), which is significant at the .001 level. Trend is indicated for the mean position of Republicans in two issue areas:

Table 11.5
Democratic and Republican Positions on Four Issues, 1972–1974

Year	GOVERNMENT JOBS* DEMOCRATS[a] Mean(St.Dev.) N	GOVERNMENT JOBS* REPUBLICANS[b] Mean(St.Dev.) N	AID TO MINORITIES* DEMOCRATS Mean(St.Dev.) N	AID TO MINORITIES* REPUBLICANS Mean(St.Dev.) N	WOMEN'S EQUALITY** DEMOCRATS Mean(St.Dev.) N	WOMEN'S EQUALITY** REPUBLICANS Mean(St.Dev.) N	GOVERNMENT SPENDING* DEMOCRATS Mean(St.Dev.) N	GOVERNMENT SPENDING* REPUBLICANS Mean(St.Dev.) N
1972	3.86(2.07) 656	4.98(1.73) 294	3.87(2.10) 614	4.59(1.69) 288	3.39(2.33) 787	3.45(2.17) 337	—	—
1974	3.87(2.01) 392	5.03(1.68) 178	4.04(2.15) 406	4.77(1.68) 181	3.05(2.09) 440	3.56(2.03) 195	—	—
1976	3.92(2.08) 557	5.11(1.72) 208	3.99(2.04) 564	4.65(1.85) 214	3.07(2.10) 496	3.48(2.06) 216	—	—
1978	4.26(1.91) 554	5.28(1.47) 230	4.21(2.04) 639	4.78(1.55) 251	2.86(2.12) 663	3.26(2.01) 265	—	—
1980	3.75(1.92) 410	5.06(1.61) 173	4.07(1.73) 409	5.15(1.22) 182	—	—	2.89(1.72) 401	4.43(1.78) 172
1982	3.94(1.82) 360	4.98(1.61) 191	4.05(1.78) 355	4.84(1.36) 192	2.67(1.95) 385	3.24(1.83) 198	3.65(1.67) 330	4.84(1.29) 179
1984	3.52(1.73) 557	4.90(1.54) 241	3.56(1.65) 567	4.60(1.48) 249	2.69(1.77) 597	2.80(1.78) 251	3.38(1.48) 547	4.66(1.40) 244
1986	3.96(1.97) 337	5.32(1.57) 177	3.76(1.72) 323	4.80(1.36) 167	—	—	3.07(1.58) 641	4.33(1.54) 345
1988	3.83(1.89) 502	5.09(1.57) 283	3.78(1.94) 268	4.73(1.46) 151	2.65(1.94) 565	2.76(1.83) 299	3.34(1.51) 457	4.44(1.41) 268
1990	3.65(1.90) 631	4.77(1.61) 256	4.16(1.91) 657	4.87(1.49) 268	2.47(1.81) 333	2.83(1.92) 133	3.20(1.58) 606	4.14(1.50) 251
1992	3.88(1.75) 655	5.19(1.34) 292	4.32(1.86) 682	5.05(1.45) 290	2.13(1.64) 724	2.25(1.54) 304	3.44(1.47) 615	4.63(1.48) 282
1994	3.68(1.75) 434	5.21(1.53) 293	4.14(1.80) 432	5.28(1.44) 299	2.32(1.76) 431	2.47(1.67) 287	3.72(1.49) 396	4.88(1.57) 288

[a] Includes strong Democrats, weak Democrats, and Independents leaning Democratic in Democratic districts.

[b] Includes strong Republicans, weak Republicans, and Independents leaning Republican in Republican districts.

* Difference in means significant at .001 level for all years.

** Difference in means significant at .05 level for only 1974–78 and 1982.

aid to minorities, where the coefficient was .0177 ($p = .0434$) and significant at the .05 level, and women's equality, where the coefficient was $-.0543$
($p = .001$) and significant at the .001 level, but, we add, in the wrong (i.e.,
liberal) direction. Surprisingly, the only issue on which trend was evident
for both parties' constituent bases—women's equality—was one in which
the statistical difference in the means disappeared over time and both parties'
electorates moved in a liberal direction.

With respect to trend in the standard deviations, the results indicate a statistically significant relationship between time and the decreasing standard
deviation in Democratic and Republican issue positions. The two exceptions were Republicans on aid to minorities and on government spending.
While such a decrease is evidence of greater homogeneity in each party's
constituent base, the size of the coefficients was small, ranging from $-.014$
for the Democrats on government spending to $-.021$ for the Republicans
on women's equality. Thus change in the homogeneity of the congressional
parties' electorates appears to have been marginal, which is all the more evident from the year–to–year comparisons.

In sum, our findings on change in the issue positions of the two congressional parties' electorates indicate that there has been a statistically significant, though marginal, increase over time in the homogeneity of Democrats in all four issue areas and of Republicans in two of the four. The results
also show a statistically significant difference between the parties' mean positions throughout the period in three of the four issue areas, women's equality 1984–94 being the exception. There is little evidence, however, that
the congressional parties' electorates grew more differentiated over time. No
trend is evident in the mean position of either congressional party's electorate in two of the four issue areas: government jobs and government spending. In a second, aid to minorities, a trend toward conservatism appears in
the Republican electorate while no trend is evident among Democrats. In
the fourth, women's equality, a statistically significant trend is apparent for
each party but in both is toward liberalism.

The Electoral and Institutional Disjunction

This analysis has examined whether the dramatic increase in partisan polarization on House floor votes since the 1970s has been associated with an increase in the homogeneity and distinctiveness of the congressional parties'
electorates. Our findings indicate no statistically significant increase over
time in the ideological homogeneity or liberalism of the Democratic congressional electorate. While we find weak evidence of an increase in the

ideological homogeneity and conservatism of the Republican congressional electorate, the change has been marginal, whether calculated on a year-to-year basis or for the entire period. Throughout the period, there has been a statistically significant difference in the mean ideological positions of the two parties' electorates, and this difference has increased over time. Here again, however, the change has been slight in absolute terms when compared to the changes that have taken place in institutional behavior. Our results on the issue positions of the congressional parties' electorates show that homogeneity increased slightly over time among Democrats in each of four issue areas and among Republicans in two. While there was a statistically significant difference in the mean positions of the two parties' electorates throughout the period, in no issue area did the two electorates' mean positions grow more differentiated over time. Indeed, in the only issue area where both electorates exhibited trend, women's equality, the trend was in the same direction.

Thus we are left explaining the disjunction between the obvious and pronounced change over time that has taken place in the congressional parties' internal cohesion and opposition to one another and the surprisingly modest shifts that have occurred in the Democratic and Republican congressional electorates. One possibility is that the change in floor voting patterns has resulted from the more successful manipulation of rewards and sanctions by majority party leaders (Kiewiet and McCubbins 1991; Cox and McCubbins 1993). While this explanation might account for an increase in the internal cohesion of the majority party, it cannot account for increases in the cohesion of the minority party or its increased opposition to majority party legislative proposals. Recognizing the importance of legislative structure and procedure to congressional operations, we remain reluctant to subordinate the impact of voter effects on institutional behavior too quickly.

A second possibility is that even marginal changes in the electorates can produce dramatic changes in the behavior of the legislature. This possibility has not been explored in the literature but is one, as we shall argue below, that is crucial to identify the connection between the preferences of the electorate and the behavior of representatives in the national legislature.

For clarity's sake, we begin with Figure 11.2, which depicts the distribution of two legislative parties' ideological positions at different points in time. The upper graph shows significant dispersion in the ideological positions of members within each legislative party and ideological overlap between the two parties. This scenario is one in which some members of both parties may be easily enticed to vote with the other party. In the lower graph, the

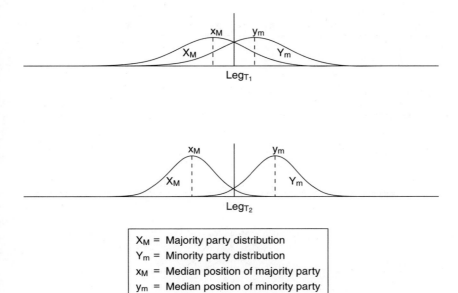

Figure 11.2. Two hypothetical configurations of the congressional parties.

ideological distance between the median legislator of the two parties is increased and the dispersion of ideological preferences of members within each party is reduced. In short, the parties in the legislature have become more polarized.

The difference in these two graphs represents the change that has taken place in the congressional parties. We believe that the key to explaining how marginal shifts in the electorate's preferences can produce such a change in the legislature is the impact of the single-member district system.

To illustrate, Figure 11.3 shows voter ideological positions in six different hypothetical districts. Three of these districts elect legislators, x_1-x_3, to the majority party. The ideological positions of these legislators is located at the position of the median voter in the relevant distribution. The other three districts elect members, y_1-y_3, to the minority party. The ideological positions of these legislators is located at the position of the median voter in the relevant distribution.

Given the districts in Figure 11.3, the outcome of the electoral process is a legislature in which there is ideological dispersion within each party and ideological overlap between the two, such as represented previously by

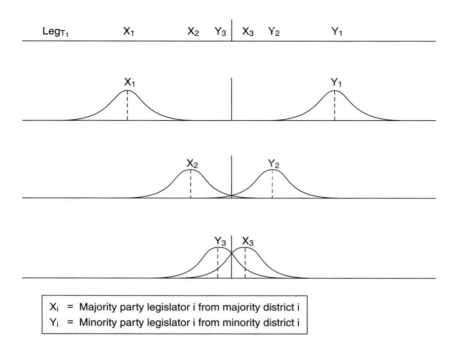

Figure 11.3.   Hypothetical district distributions and a legislature without strong partisanship.

Leg$_{TI}$ of Figure 11.2. The ideological positions of majority and minority party members are represented in Figure 11.3 on the line corresponding to Leg$_{TI}$.

Figure 11.4 reproduces Figure 11.3 and shows the change at Time 2 that has taken place in the distribution of voter ideological positions associated with each district. In the upper majority and minority party districts, there is virtually no change in the distribution of ideological positions of voters. In the middle two districts, there is a minor degree of change. In the lower two districts, the distribution of ideological positions in both the majority and minority party districts changes dramatically. The location of legislators elected by all of these districts again corresponds to the median voter of the relevant district. The ideological positions are represented at the top of the figure by the broken line at Leg$_{T2}$.

Given the amount of change that has occurred in these districts and the presence of the single-member district system, the legislative outcome at Time 2 is that the ideological dispersion within each congressional party is

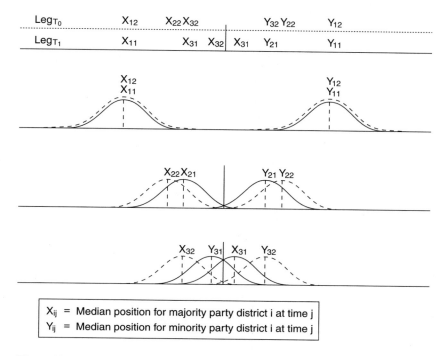

Xᵢⱼ = Median position for majority party district i at time j
Yᵢⱼ = Median position for minority party district i at time j

X_{ij} = Median position for majority party district i at time j
Y_{ij} = Median position for minority party district i at time j

Figure 11.4.   Hypothetical district distributions and two legislatures.

substantially reduced and the ideological distance between the median legislator in the two parties is substantially increased. Relative to the legislature
at Time 1, the legislature at Time 2 has become polarized along partisan lines.

Our point here is to illustrate how relatively minor adjustments in the
congressional electorate can, because of the aggregative effects of the single-
member district system, produce a dramatic shift in behavior at the institutional level. That is, in only a third of the districts associated with each party
was there a significant shift in voter ideological positions. Aggregated across
the other districts, this dramatic change washes out and the change in each
party's congressional electorate appears far more modest. Indeed, rather than
absolute increases in the homogeneity associated with each party's constituent base, it is the aggregative function of the single-member district system
that may better account for changes in the behavior of congressional parties.

In this regard, consider Figure 11.5, which shows that the distribution
of voter preferences can look quite different across districts but result in
the election of legislators with identical ideological positions. As Figure 11.5

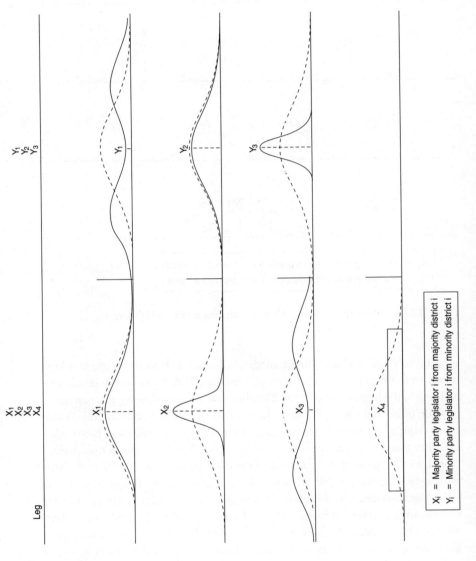

Leg

X_1
X_2
X_3
X_4

Y_1
Y_2
Y_3

X_1

X_2

X_3

X_4

Y_1

Y_2

Y_3

X_i = Majority party legislator i from majority district i

Y_i = Minority party legislator i from minority district i

Figure 11.5. Hypothetical distributions of majority and minority party districts.

shows, together these hypothetical district distributions yield a legislature in which majority party legislators have identical ideological positions and minority party legislators have identical ideological positions.

While this hypothetical legislature conforms and is indeed an exaggeration of a legislature in which the congressional parties are cohesive internally and opposed to one another, the members of each party have been elected from districts with obviously different voter distributions. Thus Figure 11.5 shows that a polarized congressional party system at the institutional level is not necessarily the result of a homogeneity or similarity of voter preferences at the district level. Interestingly, the majority party in this hypothetical legislature has no incentive to compromise with the minority party; rather it proposes the policy on which its members all agree and wins.

In sum, to understand the growth of partisan polarization in the House, we need not rely exclusively on explanations that emphasize the manipulation of internal procedure, polarization in the electorate, or even increases in the homogeneity across districts. Rather, we need also look to the effects that a single-member district system has on the translation of district preferences into institutional behavior.

Conclusion

In this chapter, our purpose has been to examine whether the well-documented growth in the polarization of the congressional parties in the House has been connected to an increase in the homogeneity and distinctiveness of the congressional parties' electorates. Our empirical findings show that changes in the ideological and policy positions of the electorate have been marginal at best. Thus we are led to explore whether marginal changes in the electorate can produce dramatic changes at the institutional level. We have argued that the aggregative function of the single-member district system is the mechanism through which slight changes in the electorate translate into far more important shifts at the institutional level.

This explanation suggests that polarization at the institutional level does not necessarily spring from a parallel polarization at the level of the electorate. In this respect, it suggests that partisan realignments of the electorate (Burnham 1970) are not necessarily or exclusively the precipitating factor behind profound changes in institutional behavior and public policy. Indeed, our research suggests the wisdom of Key's (1961) insight on secular realignment as opposed to critical elections. In general, our explanation comports with the sensitivity to popular sentiment classically associated with the House as a legislative institution. It is moreover what we might expect to see in an era in which candidate-centered elections have produced representatives with the incentive to scrutinize their constituencies meticulously and the technology to do so. It also is consistent with research indicating a correspondence between changes in public attitudes and changes in public policy wrought at the institutional level (Stimson et al., 1995).

Still, our explanation casts the representative connection between the electorate and the institution in a more ominous light insofar as demands from the public for slight change result in wildly exaggerated shifts in public policy. If indeed the connection between party-in-the-electorate and the congressional parties' institutional behavior is now such that marginal perturbations in the electorate produce drastic changes at the institutional level, we suspect that the widely acknowledged stability in American public policy is, in the immediate future at least, in jeopardy.

Epilogue

1998 and Beyond

DAVID W. BRADY, JOHN F. COGAN,
MORRIS P. FIORINA

Continuity and change receive equal billing in the title of this collection, but the emphasis in the essays leans toward change. Continuity is about the familiar, and for that reason somewhat dull; change is about differences, and for that reason more interesting. Moreover, over and above the normal human interest in novelty, the striking changes embodied in the 1994 elections—so unexpected against the backdrop of continuity in the preceding decades—were important by almost any standard. The Republican majority is now in the fifth year of what will be at least a six-year run and associated with it are important policy consequences, such as the end of the federal welfare entitlement, and important political consequences, such as the impeachment of a president for the second time in our history.

The essays in this volume do a comprehensive job of surveying changes in campaigns, elections, and representation associated with the 1994 and 1996 House elections. But whenever changes are identified, the usual questions arise. Do new developments represent permanent changes or are they aberrations? Will cessations of existing trends prove to be only temporary pauses when examined a few years hence? Will newly emergent trends continue or will they revert to familiar equilibria? While logical arguments and indirect evidence can support speculations about such matters, only the passage of time truly can tell whether elections of the early twenty-first century will look more like those of the mid-1990s or more like those of earlier decades. Still, time already has marched on since the contributions to this collection were prepared, and another election has occurred. The 1998 elections provide further—albeit preliminary—data relevant to the changes discussed in this volume. This wrap-up essay reviews the contributions of the preceding chapters in light of the 1998 elections.

The 1980s Equilibrium: Incumbency and Insulation

The "continuity" in the title of this collection refers first and foremost to the era of incumbency and insulation described in detail by nearly two decades of research.[1] In retrospect, the era began to take shape by the late 1960s after social, economic, and technological changes weakened the organizational bases of the parties, and new issues called into question citizen identifications with the parties. By the mid-1970s the earlier scholarly portrait of House elections appeared dated and inaccurate. That portrait pictured House elections as low-information, party-line affairs (Stokes and Miller 1962). Voters knew little about the candidates, the votes they cast, or the positions they espoused, and voted largely in accord with long-standing party affiliations, especially in midterm elections. Presidential coattails and reactions to presidential performance injected an element of national responsiveness into House election results, but it was easy to overestimate the strength of that response (Miller 1955) as well as its policy content (A. Campbell 1960).

By the late-1970s this sketch of House elections appeared increasingly out of line with the facts. Erikson (1972a) and Mayhew (1974b) had called attention to a growing electoral advantage of incumbency, and succeeding studies documented frenetic activities of incumbents that on their face were inconsistent with beliefs that members were invisible to constituents or unable to affect their electoral fortunes through their personal behavior. By the early 1980s a torrent of research was painting a new portrait of House elections, one in which incumbents largely controlled their own fates. According to the new consensus, so long as they kept their issue positions within a broad range appropriate to their districts and kept clear of scandal, incumbents should rarely lose. By diligent constituency service, extensive personal contact, faithful communications, and other ways limited only by their imaginations (and that of their staffs), they could create personal constituencies that would stick with them even when presidential votes were moving toward the other party. Expanding fund-raising advantages later were added to the already impressive array of advantages of incumbency. Contrary to the expectations of the Framers, the House became a bastion of stability.

Periodically, elections raised questions about the new portrait. In 1974, for example, 40 incumbents were defeated, but nearly all were Republicans, an outcome attributable to the Watergate scandal and President Richard Nixon's subsequent resignation—a unique circumstance. Proper order was restored in 1978 as statistical models of midterm losses based largely on data from the old era badly overestimated Democratic seat losses, while researchers working with newer data were close to the mark (Fiorina 1978). Again, the 1980 elections suggested that the Republicans had "nationalized" the election, defeating 27 Democratic incumbents while losing only three of their own; moreover, a relatively large midterm seat loss followed in 1982. But a few years later incumbency returned with a vengeance as only six incumbents were defeated in both 1986 and 1988, and statistical estimates of the incumbency effect soared to an all-time high of 13 percent in 1986 (Figure 7.8). The incumbency era had reached its apogee.

Along with studies of the advantage of incumbency came studies of declining responsiveness to national events and conditions such as the state of the economy and the performance of the president. The Congress seemed to be becoming insulated from national social and economic conditions and issue debates. Although research into incumbency quickly took on a life of its own, much of the initial impetus for the attention to the growing advantage of incumbents reflected the natural surmise that waxing incumbency had negative implications for electoral responsiveness. This concern is stated clearly in Mayhew (1974b: 295) and Fiorina (1977b: 12–13), and Burnham titled a 1975 article "Insulation and Responsiveness in Congressional Elections." Briefly, if incumbent electoral margins were increasing so that fewer found themselves in the marginal range of the vote distribution, then the coattails of a popular presidential candidate would pull fewer challengers of his party into office, and fewer incumbents would be defeated by reactions to an unpopular candidate or president of their own party. Moreover, if ticket-splitting was increasing as personal votes grew larger, then House elections increasingly reflected a set of factors—local or district—different from presidential elections, which largely reflected national considerations. As a consequence of both these changes, empirical studies reported that presidential coattails had shortened, that midterm reactions against the party of the incumbent president had become muted, and that the swing ratio— the rate at which votes translate into seats—had dropped (e.g., Ansolabehere et al. 1992).

One consequence of these changes was the development of a persistent state of divided government. Throughout the 1970s and 1980s the Republicans enjoyed an advantage on national issues, reflected in repeated wins by their presidential candidates. But this advantage was not reflected in

Congress—save for Republican control of the Senate from 1981 to 1986. By the late 1980s a respected political commentator was comparing the Democratic-dominated House of Representatives to the Soviet Politburo (Broder 1988), and more general arguments about divided government and gridlock had become commonplace.

In sum, in the incumbency and insulation equilibrium that extended from the late 1970s to the early 1990s members of the House held their electoral fates in their own hands. Electoral defeat was a rarity, reflecting laziness, scandal, or an avoidable political mistake. Consequently, retirement had replaced elections as the principal source of turnover in House seats. Electoral accountability in the broad national sense eroded as the Democratic majorities in the House flourished despite the electoral failures of their presidential candidates and the failed Jimmy Carter presidency. Most elections showed modest changes in the House, and these changes were statistically quite predictable.

A Move to a New Equilibrium?

For students of congressional elections the 1994 outcome was comparable to a paleontologist seeing a dinosaur walk by the window. The vote shifts and seat swings of that year were thought to be things of the past. In retrospect, as the articles in this volume show, there were clear intimations of change in earlier elections, although they were not yet notable enough to call into question the prevailing portrait of House elections.

Still, even in the aftermath of the 1994 results, most students of the subject were not eager to abandon the old portrait, and when the dust cleared, some familiar features of the old appeared simultaneously with the new. Despite the bloodbath suffered by Democratic incumbents in 1994, 90 percent of all the incumbents who ran, won. Moreover, statistical estimates of the incumbency advantage were actually higher in 1994 than in 1990, the previous midterm election.[2] For approximately a year the new House focused almost exclusively on matters of national policy, but after the politically disastrous government shutdowns, electorally nervous Republicans reverted to tried-and-true formulas, distancing themselves from the unpopular Newt Gingrich, and emphasizing their efforts on behalf of their districts.

The Republican majority survived in 1996, but chastened Republicans behaved somewhat differently in the 105th Congress. Transportation Committee chair Bud Shuster rolled over the Republican leadership, putting together a coalition that passed what has been called the largest pork barrel bill in history, a distinction that may have been surpassed in the omnibus appropriations bill negotiated by the leadership itself at the end of the session. The result of this more traditional approach to elections was an incumbency-dominated outcome in 1998 that was reminiscent of 1986 and 1988. Of 401 incumbents seeking reelection, only five lost for an all-time record incumbent reelection rate of 98.5 percent.

To be sure, this apparent reversion to the pre-1994 pattern was completely overwhelmed in popular and scholarly commentary by a new development: for only the second time since the Civil War, the party of the president gained seats in the midterm election. For whatever reason—a reaction to Republican emphasis on the Monica Lewinsky scandal, the lack of a positive policy agenda, economic boom times, or whatever—the 1998 results put Bill Clinton alongside Franklin Roosevelt (1934) in the pantheon of electoral giants.

Thus, we have yet another election that shows significant change from what has gone before, but change that appears to overlay considerable continuity. At least, that is the impression given from a quick consideration of the general results. More detailed consideration of more specific aspects of the 1998 elections might revise that initial impression. Hence, in the remainder of this chapter, we revisit the essays in this volume, viewing their conclusions in light of the 1998 results.

Nationalization in 1998

The essays by Jacobson and by Brady, D'Onofrio, and Fiorina present evidence that House elections in the 1990s have become increasingly nationalized, meaning that they move consistently with each other and with presidential election results. At first glance the 1998 results appear strikingly at odds with those findings: incumbents were more successful at winning reelection than ever before in history. Moreover, the winning incumbent's average margin has crept back up to 10 percent after falling in the earlier elections of the 1990s. But as pointed out by Brady, D'Onofrio, and Fiorina, there is not a one-to-one tradeoff between the estimated national and local components of the House vote. Extending the regression results in their article reveals that in the 1998 regression the coefficient for the 1996 presidential vote was somewhat smaller than the coefficient for the 1992 presidential vote was in the 1994 regression. Still, the coefficient is larger than the corresponding coefficient for any midterm election except 1994 and 1982. Thus, the findings indicate that the heightened nationalization evident in 1994 and 1996 continued in 1998, albeit at a slightly reduced level.

Other evidence supports this interpretation. Although incumbent margins crept up in 1998, the standard deviation of the vote swing in the districts contested in both 1996 and 1998 was 7.4 percent, lower than that between 1992 and 1994 (7.9 percent). This comparison suggests more uniformity in the House vote than a look at incumbent success would have led us to expect. It is too early for survey evidence about individual voting decisions to be available, but fragmentary evidence is consistent with the aggregate patterns.

Jacobson too reports important continuities amid the changes.[3] He points out that a key difference between 1998 and preceding elections in the 1990s was the low level of competition. The 95 uncontested districts matched the record set in 1950, and neither party nominated especially strong challengers, thus contributing to the banner year for incumbents. An important part of the explanation is that before the Lewinsky scandal broke, expectations pointed to a status quo election. Given the expected midterm losses, strong Democratic challengers were not anxious to run, and with a popular president and booming economy expected to minimize those losses, strong Republican challengers did not look on 1998 as an especially propitious time to run either. When the initial revelations failed to shake public approval of the president, those minimalist expectations held, resulting in a middling collection of challengers.

But despite the runaway success of incumbents, Jacobson notes lurking indications of continued nationalization. Of the seventeen seats that switched party control, thirteen went to the party whose presidential candidate carried the district in 1996. Thus, the aggregate tendency for House and presidential votes to become more closely aligned continued in 1998.

House Votes and Representation

One of the national sources of movement in the House election vote is reaction to policies considered by the Congress. Four essays in this volume consider the electoral impact of positions taken by House candidates, especially incumbents. Brady, Canes-Wrone, and Cogan show that over the past four decades defeated incumbents were marginally out of step ideologically with their districts: Democrats were on average 2 percent "too liberal," and Republicans 2 percent "too conservative." In the 1998 elections very few incumbents were defeated, but three of the four defeated Republicans were too conservative—by a relatively large 8 percent.[4] Also of interest, the 31 Democrats who voted in the autumn of 1998 to proceed with impeachment hearings ran about three points better than the Democrats who opposed proceeding, according to one analysis, and five points better, according to a second.[5]

Collie and Mason conclude that the increasing polarization of the congressional parties has not been caused by or even accompanied by significant polarization at the constituency level. Rather, if the polarization within Congress has constituency roots at all, it apparently stems from the capacity of the single-member district system to exaggerate small changes in popular sentiment. It is interesting to look at the Republican drive to impeach President Clinton in light of their argument. Despite large popular majorities in favor of the more moderate stance of censuring the president, House Republicans pushed on with impeachment. Critics have charged that Republicans were defying popular sentiment. House Republicans have responded that they are not driven by public opinion polls, but have a duty to follow their consciences and the Constitution, however unpopular such actions might be. Political scientists have suggested that despite first appearances, electoral considerations may still be important. A widely offered explanation for the Republicans' behavior is that impeachment sympathizers are concentrated within Republican districts; thus, congressional Republicans are following popular sentiment *within their districts*, not defying it, as misleadingly suggested by aggregate polling figures. If Collie and Mason are correct, however, we might find less polarization at the district level than the preceding explanation presumes. Of course, without time series data it is problematic to judge how much polarization is more or less than expected.

Erikson and Wright have a somewhat different take on the polarization of the congressional parties. Their analysis shows that the positions representatives take clearly are reflective of the center of gravity of constituency opinion, subject to the qualifying influence of electoral security: safe Democrats and Republicans are more liberal or conservative than their districts' opinions would indicate. For Erikson and Wright, the explanation of increased polarization lies in the increasing nationalization of elections discussed earlier. As more and more districts align their congressional and presidential votes, fewer representatives are cross-pressured by having a district that supported the presidential candidate of the other party. Why this development has no reflection in the analyses reported by Collie and Mason, however, remains something of a puzzle.

Leal and Hess focus on challengers rather than incumbents, reporting that Republican challengers in 1994 emphasized issues more than Democratic challengers did. One possible explanation is that in midterm elections candidates of the out-party find it easy to raise issues on which the president's party is vulnerable. This explanation appears to presume some variant of negative voting—voters pay more attention to negative issues raised by the out-party than to positive issues that could be raised by the in-party candidates. A second more general explanation is that electorally vulnerable parties avoid issues and electorally advantaged parties raise them. In 1994 both of these hypotheses pointed to heavier Republican issue emphasis.[6]

Interestingly, in 1998 the Republicans made a perhaps fateful decision late in the campaign to focus on the Lewinsky scandal, spending about $10 million on ads explicitly mentioning President Clinton and the scandal. This decision raised many eyebrows at the time, and when the Republicans actually lost seats it was held up as an example of what not to do by critics who charged that congressional Republicans had failed to develop any positive program, relying instead on anti-Clinton sentiments to do their work for them. Newt Gingrich's subsequent fall was a resounding reflection of such sentiments. To the extent that scholarly analyses confirm charges like these, such results would contradict both of the hypotheses suggested by Leal and Hess to explain the 1994 findings: the Republicans still were the out-party in 1998 and the Democrats were thought to be vulnerable. Perhaps the general explanation for both cases is a variation of the old political maxim that you can't beat somebody with nobody—any reasonable program beats no program at all.

Money in 1998

Most of the popular commentary about campaign finance in the past few years has focused on soft money and independent expenditures, especially in the 1996 Clinton presidential campaign. In contrast, most of the discussion prior to 1996 focused on congressional campaign finance, PACs in particular. The features of PAC giving that provoked concern have not changed; they have only been buried in the spate of criticism of large soft money contributions to parties, and "independent" media buys by parties and groups. Ansolabehere and Snyder document the growth of the incumbency advantage in campaign finance, especially in PAC contributions, and conclude from a sophisticated statistical analysis that most of the advantage reflects the institutional importance of the members receiving contributions. A more colloquial illustration of their findings is provided by the reversal of the fortunes of Republican and Democratic members of Congress in the aftermath of the 1994 Republican takeover (Salant and Cloud 1995).

Nineteen ninety-eight was a very good year for incumbents, and the incumbency advantage in money paralleled the incumbency advantage in votes. According to the October Federal Election Commission filings (the latest available as we write) incumbents held a 4 : 1 advantage in spending, the highest ratio since the late 1980s, and a reversal of the pattern of declining ratios from 1990 to 1996. Financial disparities like these have fueled the cry for reform for two decades, but Congress has shown little inclination to implement any of the proposals on the table. Hence, some reformers have turned to the states as vehicles for campaign finance reform. In the late 1980s and early 1990s states began experimenting with low contribution limits as a mechanism for limiting the electoral advantage derived from office, but the courts soon put an end to such experimentation. Consistent with its previous rulings, the Supreme Court in 1998 struck down an Arkansas law that set a very low limit on the size of contributions. The Court held that low limits restrict the free expression of donors.

The 1998 elections signaled a new direction in campaign finance reform. Several states passed initiatives providing for generous public funding for campaigns that accepted spending limits. If such reforms "work," they will remove one of the key electoral advantages incumbents derive from office—private money. Whether a voluntaristic public financing system proves successful, however, depends on how it affects the status of candidates, especially incumbents, and thereby their decisions to opt in or out of the system. Maine, Massachusetts, New Jersey, and other public financing states will be the laboratories of campaign finance reform over the next decade.

The South in 1998

In his chapter Bullock chronicles the contribution of political change in the South to the new Republican congressional majorities. Despite presidential-level breakthroughs in the 1950s and 1960s, success in congressional elections was slower coming. Not until the early 1980s for the Senate, and the mid-1990s for the House, did the long-standing Democratic edge in congressional voting disappear. Today, of course, the South, and especially the Deep South, has become the region that most strongly supports Republicans, a development that underlies many discussions of the "southernization" of the contemporary Republican party.

The 1998 elections resulted in only minimal partisan change in the southern delegations to the House and Senate. In the House, no southern incumbent was defeated and only two open seats changed party control—one for each party—resulting in no net change. In the Senate, Republican incumbent Launch Faircloth of North Carolina was defeated, and several Democratic seats thought to be in danger remained Democratic. To be sure, no one expected Republican gains to continue at a pace comparable to that from 1992 to 1996: after the 1996 elections only fourteen Republican president/Democratic House districts remained, and it is districts like these that have produced the 1990s Republican surge in the region. Still, there is no denying that—relative to their expectations—southern voting in 1998 was a disappointment for the Republicans.

Interestingly, Bullock (1999) notes that redistricting after the 2000 census may contribute to further Republican congressional gains. As a result of majority-minority redistricting and continued Republican gains in southern state legislatures, African Americans and Republicans now constitute a majority in every southern state legislative chamber except the Arkansas Senate and House, the Louisiana House, and the North Carolina Senate. If they work together, as they did in 1990s redistricting across the nation, Republicans could gain seats at the expense of white Democrats (see below).

Race in 1998

Epstein and O'Halloran conclude that while majority-minority districts clearly increase the descriptive representation of ethnic and racial minorities, they do so at the cost of decreased substantive representation of minority interests. Concentrating minorities into a small number of majority-minority districts inevitably produces majority-*majority* districts that are whiter—and more likely to elect Republicans—and the Democrats whom such districts elect are somewhat less supportive of policies blacks favor (the former "election" effect is much stronger than the latter "representation" effect). Epstein and O'Halloran suggest that because racially polarized voting has been declining, districts no longer need to be overwhelmingly minority in order to give minority candidates equal opportunities of victory. In particular, the judicial standard of 60–65 percent for the South could be reduced to 45 percent minority today.

Consistent with their analysis, in 1998 all four African-American representatives elected in 1996 from minority-minority districts won reelection. So was Mel Watt of North Carolina, whose reconfigured district (because of court-ordered redistricting) was only 36 percent minority. The point of equal opportunity in the South, defined as the percent of the black voting age population at which a minority and a white candidate have equal estimated probabilities of election, is now below 40 percent for the first time. Of particular interest was Georgia's Sanford Bishop, who won reelection in a rural, racially conservative district by opposing gun control and supporting a balanced budget and peanut subsidies—policies popular among white constituents, racially conservative or not.

While the time span is too short and the numbers too small to draw firm conclusions, the results of recent elections provide grounds for optimism in an area where pessimism often reigns. If racial bloc voting is declining, and whites are becoming more willing to vote for minority candidates, then the need for majority-minority districts to assure descriptive representation will decrease. Such districts have provided a floor for minorities in recent decades, but they have also constructed something of a ceiling as well. As the need for the floor lessens, the ceiling for minorities will rise.

The Image of Congress in 1998

Republicans found popular reaction to the events of 1998 little short of infuriating. President Clinton, mired in scandal, enjoyed continued high approval ratings. Meanwhile, the Republican Congress ranked about twenty points lower than Clinton in popular evaluations, and lower still when its handling of the Lewinsky matter was specifically at issue. Many commentators attributed the almost unprecedented 1998 outcome to the negative image of the Republican Congress. While the evidence to test such speculations is not yet available, they are consistent with the Hibbing and Tiritilli contribution to this volume.

Hibbing and Tiritilli argue that there are conditions under which public dissatisfaction with Congress as an institution can hurt the House majority party. The 1994 elections appear to be a near-perfect illustration: a high level of popular disapproval of Congress interacted with a much higher than usual popular appreciation that the Democrats were the majority party. Hibbing and Tiritilli suggest that 1994 probably was unusual in that these two basic conditions were seized upon by opposition political elites: an energetic Republican leadership set out to nationalize the election, attacking Congress itself and blaming the Democrats for its sorry condition. Ross Perot also contributed by exhorting his supporters to give Republicans a chance to run things.

The 1998 elections suggest that the 1994 results may not be as unusual as Hibbing and Tiritilli thought. Popular dissatisfaction with Congress for its fixation on impeachment was high, and there was no doubt that it was a *Republican* Congress that was so fixated. Granted, only six incumbents lost, but five of the six were Republicans, and this in a year when Republicans were expected to make the normal midterm gains. In the open-seat contests, narrow races consistently were decided against the Republicans. Consistent with arguments from the older responsible parties tradition, in an era of distinct parties and strong partisanship among political elites voters may find it relatively easy to hold parties accountable for their performance—not only for the personal performance of their presidents, but also for the collective performance of their representatives. If so, we may need to revise our list of which factors influence House elections and which factors can be safely ignored.

As this collection went to press, the Republicans in Congress had provided us with another test of the Hibbing and Tiritilli argument. After the conclusion of the impeachment proceedings, popular approval of Congress reached a low ebb. Unless memories are short, or popular evaluations rise dramatically, the 2000 congressional elections will provide another test of the electoral relevance of party and institutional responsibility.

Reference Matter

FIXED-EFFECTS REGRESSIONS

PREDICTING INCUMBENT RECEIPTS

Variable	Total	PAC	Other
Incumbent party strength	59,719	−152,542	212,416
	(126,252)	(47,284)	(100,102)
Challenger spending	0.519	0.161	0.359
	(0.022)	(0.008)	(0.017)
No challenger spending	−15,073	−6,653	−8,439
	(12,924)	(4,840)	(10,247)
No challenger	−65,033	−26,218	−38,800
	(12,470)	(4,670)	(9,887)
Challenger is TV celebrity	−44,445	18,675	−63,132
	(37,218)	(13,939)	(29,509)
Challenger is wealthy	−47,608	−18,049	−29,578
	(25,064)	(9,387)	(19,873)
Challenger previous office: state office	36,276	21,147	15,134
	(14,542)	(5,446)	(11,530)
Challenger previous office: local office	65,986	16,696	49,275
	(15,450)	(5,786)	(12,250)
Challenger previous office: judicial/law enforcement	−12,274	−8,243	−4,039
	(30,348)	(11,366)	(24,062)
Opponent spending in incumbent's primary	0.141	0.017	0.123
	(0.028)	(0.011)	(0.023)
No opponent spending in incumbent's primary	−44,982	−18,393	−26,584
	(11,687)	(4,377)	(9,267)
Incumbent in scandal	44,711	22,691	22,033
	(19,578)	(7,332)	(15,523)
Freshman	57,460	33,614	23,841
	(12,150)	(4,550)	(9,633)
Party leader	637,814	287,844	349,969
	(39,954)	(14,963)	(31,678)
Committee leader	55,755	39,904	15,877
	(19,319)	(7,235)	(15,317)
Good committee assignment	42,689	75,634	−32,927
	(22,165)	(8,301)	(17,574)

Bad committee assignment	−28,891	−1,296	−27,576
	(14,468)	(5,419)	(11,472)
Pivotal	587,215	491,240	95,667
	(494,355)	(185,145)	(391,962)
Constant	373,230	141,214	231,995
	(64,033)	(23,981)	(50,770)
Number of observations	3,450	3,450	3,450

NOTE: Individual and party-year fixed effects not reported. Standard errors in parentheses.

Appendix B

SECTION OF INTERVIEW INSTRUMENT

Please indicate on a 1 to 7 scale, how much each of the following statements describes your campaign strategy, where 1 means it is not a part of your strategy at all and 7 means it reflects the primary focus of your strategy:

9. We are focusing on our candidate's positive personal qualities.

10. We are emphasizing our opponent's incumbency and the need for a change.

11. We are focusing on how our opponent's voting record in Congress does not serve the district's interests.

12. I'm now going to read you some issues. How much has the candidate focused on each following issue, where 1 means not at all and 7 means a great deal? This question does not ask whether you support the issue, just how much you emphasize it:

    A. Foreign affairs
    B. The deficit
    C. Education
    D. Infrastructural development of the district
    E. Values and morality
    F. Reforming welfare
    G. Abortion
    H. Term limits
    I. Crime

Appendix C

THE CONTRACT WITH AMERICA

1. Balanced Budget Amendment/Line Item: The Fiscal Responsibility Act: A balanced budget/tax limitation amendment and a legislative line-item veto to restore fiscal responsibility to an out-of-control Congress, requiring them to live under the same budget constraints as families and businesses.

2. The Taking Back Our Streets Act: An anti-crime package including stronger truth-in-sentencing, good faith exclusionary rule exemptions, effective death penalty provisions, and cuts in social spending from this summer's "crime" bill to fund prison construction and additional law enforcement to keep people secure in their neighborhoods and kids safe in their schools.

3. The Personal Responsibility Act: Discourage illegitimacy and teen pregnancy by prohibiting welfare to minor mothers and denying increased AFDC for addition children while on welfare, cut spending for welfare programs, and enact a tough two-years-and-out provision with work requirements.

4. The Family Reinforcement Act: Child support enforcement, tax incentives for adoption, strengthening rights of parents in their children's education, stronger child pornography laws, and an elderly dependent care tax credit to reinforce the central role of families in American society.

5. The American Dream Restoration Act: A $500 per child tax credit, begin repeal of the marriage tax penalty, and creation of American Dream Savings Accounts to provide middle-class tax relief.

6. The National Security Restoration Act: No U.S. troops under U.N. command and restoration of the essential parts of our national security funding to strengthen our national defense and maintain our credibility around the world.

7. The Senior Citizens Fairness Act: Raise the Social Security earnings limits which currently forces seniors out of the workforce, repeal the 1993 tax hikes on Social Security benefits, and provide tax incentives for private

long-term care insurance to let Older Americans keep more of what they have earned over the years.

8. The Job Creation and Wage Enhancement Act: Small business incentives, capital gains cuts and indexation, neutral cost recovery, risk assessment/cost-benefit analysis, strengthening the Regulatory Flexibility Act, and unfunded mandate reform to create jobs and raise worker wages.

9. The Common Sense Legal Reform Act: "Loser pays" laws, reasonable limits on punitive damages, and reform of product liability laws to stem the endless tide of litigation.

10. The Citizen Legislature Act: A first-ever vote on term limits to replace career politicians with citizen legislators.

SOURCE: "Republican's Initial Promise: 100 Day Debate on Contract." *Congressional Quarterly Weekly Report*. November 11, 1994, pp. 3216–19.

Chapter 1

1. The journals were the *American Journal of International Law*, *American Journal of Political Science*, *American Political Science Review*, *International Organization*, *Journal of Politics*, *Philosophy and Public Affairs*, *Political Science Quarterly*, *Public Opinion Quarterly*, and *World Politics*.

Chapter 2

1. Democrats had won 204 seats in 1994 but went into the 1996 election with only 198 because of party switches and a special election loss.

2. Here and throughout this chapter, I define decades by reapportionment cycles; for example, the 1980s include 1982 through 1990; the 1990s (so far), 1992 through 1996.

3. The Gallup series consists of 176 observations from July 1974 through September 1995; in addition to a 5.1 point swing to the Republicans in late 1984, the poll shows an earlier swing of 6.0 points in their direction at the time of the 1980 elections. The series shows no consistent trend toward either party after 1984. The NES series has a single observation for each election from 1952 through 1994; it shows no change at the time of the 1980 election, but a sustained shift of 6.1 points to the Republicans commencing in 1984. The CBS News/*New York Times* series contains 119 observations from January 1981 through October 1996; it shows a sustained shift of 4.8 percentage points to the Republican party in November 1984, with no subsequent trend. All of these measurements are from regression equations using dummy variables to examine temporal changes in the distribution of partisan identifiers. The NES and CBS News/*New York Times* data classify leaners toward a party as partisans; the Gallup data treat them as independents.

4. At least according to the Gallup and CBS News/*New York Times* polls. The jury is still out on the NES, which did show an increasingly Republican electorate in 1994; although the results of House elections in 1996 and 1998 returned increasingly narrow majorities, the electorate did not become more Republican in identification.

5. The average district-level two-party vote for the Democratic presiden-

tial candidates in 1988 and 1992 in the states that lost seats was 52.5 percent; in states that gained seats, 48.8 percent, a difference that is significant at $p < .01$.

6. The coefficient for 1992 has a t-value of 1.78, making it significant at $p < .10$ on a two-tailed test and $p < .05$ on a one-tailed test.

7. It takes 218 of the House's 435 seats for majority control.

8. I define the South as the eleven states of the Confederacy: Alabama, Arkansas, Florida, Georgia, Louisiana, Mississippi, North Carolina, South Carolina, Tennessee, Texas, and Virginia.

9. The Republican gains among southern Senate seats have been even more spectacular. As late as 1960 the party held none of the twenty-two seats in states of the old Confederacy. As recently as 1990, it held only seven of these seats. After gains in 1992, 1994, and 1996, it now holds fourteen (64 percent) after the 1998 elections.

10. I include in the categories of western plains and Mountain States Arizona, Colorado, Idaho, Kansas, Montana, Nebraska, Nevada, New Mexico, North Dakota, Oklahoma, South Dakota, Utah, and Wyoming.

11. For 1952 through 1958, I have used the mean district presidential vote in 1952 and 1956; for 1960, the mean presidential vote in 1956 and 1960; for 1962 and 1964, the 1964 presidential vote; for 1966 through 1970, the 1968 vote; for 1972, the 1972 vote; for 1974 through 1980, the 1976 vote; for 1982, the mean of 1976 and 1980; for 1984 through 1990, the mean of 1984 and 1988; and for 1992 through 1996, the mean of 1988 and 1992.

12. The years are 1948, 1958, 1964, 1974, and 1982.

13. On average from 1946 through 1990, the Republicans won 180 House seats; from 1958 through 1992, their total never exceeded 192; the 1996 election left the Democrats with 207 seats, 11 shy of a majority.

14. The "sophomore surge" and "retirement slump" are, respectively, the additional share of votes a party typically adds when its candidate first runs as an incumbent and loses when the seats become open, compared to the party's average swing for the election year (Alford and Brady 1988). Districts redrawn since the previous election are omitted, leaving too few for analysis in election years following the decennial reapportionment.

15. This despite the fact that far fewer incumbents have run unopposed in the 1990s than in earlier decades (see below); in general, the fewer incumbents who run unopposed, the higher should be the average vote for incumbents, because more of the relatively safe seats figure into the calculations.

16. The same pattern appears if we define "marginality" at 55 percent instead of 60 percent of the two-party vote.

17. Only once since the Civil War has the president's party not been weakened in the House at the midterm; that was in 1934, during the New Deal realignment. A review of the Senate seats up in 1998 gave Democrats little hope of making gains there and the results yielded no change, i.e., 55 Republicans and 45 Democrats (Jacobson 1997a).

18. According to the national exit poll, voters who made their decision in the last few days before the election went for Dole over Clinton, 40 percent to 35 percent (*Los Angeles Times*, Nov. 7, 1996, A22). An additional 1 percent of the vote would have given Democratic candidates over 50 percent in 11 House districts, giving them a bare majority in the House; 2 percent would have given Democrat candidates over 50 percent in 22 districts.

19. Reported in *Hotline*, Nov. 15, 1996.

20. *Los Angeles Times*, Dec. 31, 1995, A13.

Chapter 3

1. In the House, Majority Leader Dick Armey and Majority Whip Tom DeLay are southerners, as is Senate Majority Leader Trent Lott.

2. Republicans won House seats in Alabama, Georgia, and Mississippi in 1964 and picked up a Senate and House seat in South Carolina through conversion. Prior to 1964, the only GOP presidential victory in the Deep South came in Louisiana in 1956.

3. In portions of the South, the white vote goes to Republicans running for offices below the U.S. House. For example, in Florida Republicans had majorities in both chambers of the state legislature in 1997. The GOP also controlled both of North and South Carolina's houses and the Texas state senate after the 1996 elections. It is reasonable to assume that Republicans are winning the bulk of the white vote in state legislative elections they win. In addition, they may win the white vote in states they lose if the black vote is high enough.

4. Districts at least 30 percent black with GOP legislators in the 102d Congress were: Alabama's First and Second, Louisiana's Fourth and Eighth, South Carolina's First and Second, and Virginia's First and Third. Virginia's Third District was represented in the 102d Congress by Republican Thomas Bliley, the current incumbent in the Seventh District, which incorporates much of the white population in the old Third District (Bullock 1995).

5. The three-judge federal panel that redrew Georgia's congressional districts when the state legislature proved unable to make adjustments mandated by the Supreme Court in *Johnson v. Miller* (1995) consciously tried to return to the outlines of the plan used during the 1980s. Of course, adjustments for population shifts and the assignment of an eleventh seat to the state necessitated a number of changes from the plan of the 1980s (ibid).

6. After the 1992 election, Bustamante and his wife were indicted for bribery and racketeering.

7. The Rim or Peripheral South is comprised of Arkansas, Florida, North Carolina, Tennessee, Texas, and Virginia. Alabama, Georgia, Louisiana, Mississippi, and South Carolina are the Deep South.

8. The Louisiana district underwent an open seat transition in 1996 so it may be less susceptible to a GOP challenge, although the elimination of the

all-comers primaries that Louisiana has used for a generation may improve GOP prospects. In 1996, the two candidates who advanced from the primary to runoff were both Democrats. In the future, Republicans will be able to get one of their own into the general election.

9. It should be noted that the number of nonsouthern seats has declined over time. In the 1950s and 1960s, 329 seats were outside the South. That number fell to 327 with the 1970s reapportionment and to 319 in the 1980s. Since 1992, there have been 310 northern seats and 125 in the South.

10. The state of Virginia is appealing the decision striking down its 64 percent black Third District; the necessity of redrawing districts in the other states has been settled.

11. Cleo Fields (D-La.) did not run for reelection following the redesign of his district; all other African Americans won additional terms.

12. The First District received Savannah's African-American population that had been in McKinney's district when she represented the Eleventh. The Democrat challenging Republican Jack Kingston raised little money, campaigned ineffectively, and polled less than one-third of the vote. The weak Democratic performance in the First resulted in the Democrat doing less well among white voters than did the Democratic nominees in the four districts included in Table 3.7.

13. Most of Bell's more than $500,000 came from out-of-state sources (Pace 1997).

14. These represent the bulk of the new majority-black districts that had biracial contests. Missing are Florida's Twenty-Third, South Carolina's Sixth, and Alabama's Seventh.

15. Population shifts almost certainly mean that in the Fourth District the voting age population currently exceeds 40 percent black because at the time of the 1996 election African Americans constituted 42 percent of the registered voters. Black registration in the Second District stood at 35 percent in 1996.

Chapter 4

1. An excellent summary of this research is presented in Sorauf 1992.

2. This argument has been expressed in various ways. Gary Jacobson's important works point to the quality or abilities of the challengers, as opposed to the resources of incumbents as determinative. In particular, see Jacobson 1978 and Jacobson and Kernell 1983. Two recent thought-provoking analyses are Gerber 1996 and Zaller 1998.

3. The victory rate of the highest quality challengers is only one in three.

4. One problem with the 1978 data is a very high nonfiler rate. Data for subsequent years are much more reliable, so we omit 1978 from subsequent statistical analyses.

5. This quantity equals .08 times log(630,000) − log(255,000).

6. This estimate is derived from a simple regression of vote on lagged vote plus a dummy variable for incumbent contested elections. See Gelman and King 1990.

7. The daily averages are probably low since they assume that fund-raising occurs 365 days a year from the day after one election to the day of the next.

8. This is true of the median as well as the average. In the median race, the incumbent spends $651,000 and the challenger spends $408,000.

9. A number of studies are relevant here, notably Fenno 1974; Grier and Munger 1991; Milyo 1997; and Romer and Snyder 1994.

10. As a social scientific matter, it is hard to measure the proximity of an individual to the median. The literature here is extensive. Over the last two decades several procedures have been developed for scaling roll-call votes that seem to work reasonably well. We use the ratings issued by the Americans for Democratic Action (ADA), which seem to perform reasonably well.

11. We estimated the regressions with the dependent variables measured in three different scales: linear, log, and square root. The scale did not matter for the quantities reported in Table 4.5, though the square root scale seems to be the least susceptible to skews in the variables and extreme cases. Our estimates of the absolute differences in receipts comes from the regression with the linear version of the dependent variables. Our estimates of the percent change in receipts comes from the logarithmic regressions.

Chapter 5

1. We will discuss the construction and distribution of this latter variable in more detail below.

2. It is interesting to compare these conditions with the three-pronged test for vote dilution established by the Supreme Court in *Thornburg v. Gingles* (1986): (1) the minority group must be "sufficiently large and geographically compact" to make up a majority in at least one single member district; (2) the minority must be "politically cohesive;" i.e., it must vote as a bloc; and (3) the majority must also vote "sufficiently as a bloc to enable it . . . usually to defeat the minority's preferred candidate." The first prong is a threshold requirement that the minority involved be sufficiently large and compact to merit any further investigation. The other two prongs identify the existence of competing blocs of voters of unequal size, such that the outcome of the political process is consistently disadvantageous to the smaller group. The three *Gingles* conditions therefore effectively identify the bloc voting situation in the first part of Figure 5.2.

3. This is one of Guinier's (1994) arguments in favor of alternative voting schemes, such as cumulative voting, that might help ensure fairer outcomes for minorities in the political process.

4. See Davidson and Grofman (1994) for a state-by-state analysis of these gains.

5. In addition, two majority Hispanic districts—the California Twentieth and Twenty-sixth—have recently elected white representatives.

6. In fact, blacks are now in an analogous position to that of southern Democrats early in the century. Blacks have been accruing seniority within the Democratic party, so that they are now poised to occupy leadership positions should the Democrats return to a majority.

7. We have undertaken the standard procedure for attendance-correcting, eliminating from the total possible votes those measures on which a member did not actually cast a ballot. In the cases where a member was replaced through retirement or death, we calculated the average district support score.

8. In 1975, the VRA was amended to include language minorities (mostly Hispanic), as well as racial minorities.

9. See Epstein and O'Halloran (1999) for a more detailed exposition of this estimation procedure.

Chapter 6

Most of the data utilized in this study came from the biennial NES. We employed the NES CD-ROM containing the results of all elections from 1948 to 1994.

1. For inspections of longitudinal variations in approval of Congress, see Durr et al. 1997; and Patterson and Caldeira 1990.

2. Although it may seem as though people could achieve a success rate of 50 percent just by guessing one of the two major parties, this is not the case because upwards of a third of all respondents did not even venture a guess when confronted with this question. The results in Figure 6.1 are for all respondents, whereas the rest of the results presented herein deal with voters only. If Figure 6.1 is restricted to voters only, the patterns across years remain essentially the same, but the percent knowing the majority party, not surprisingly, is somewhat elevated.

3. The actual NES question on approval permits four options: strongly approve, approve, disapprove, and strongly disapprove. We have treated the variable as dichotomous because we noticed some intransitivities when the four-point scale was employed. The important distinction seems to be between those who approve and those who disapprove regardless of how strongly people claim to have these opinions.

4. The variables are standardized so that they are accorded equal weight when combined in the interactive term. After computing the z-score, we added a constant to all scores so that there were no negative numbers, thus giving the interactive term the desired qualities.

5. For simplicity's sake, we make linear assumptions regarding party

identification, district type, and economic perceptions. In other words, we assume that it hurts probabilities of voting Democratic about as much to go from an open seat to a Republican incumbent seat as it does to go from a Democratic incumbent seat to an open seat. We have looked at the results with this assumption removed (by substituting dummy variables for each possible value) and, while the linearity is not perfect, the assumption for all three variables is close enough for us to conclude that the addition of numerous separate terms for all the specific categories of these variables is not warranted. The results are available from the authors.

6. This procedure is necessary because probit results are not constant (linear), so it is necessary to set each variable to a concrete value.

Chapter 7

1. Another possibility is that Democratic elites inadvertently followed strategies that nationalized the elections.

2. The electoral swing in 1994 was 6.83 percent away from the Democrats, with a variance of 12.9. This was the smallest variance since the 1970 House election, making the 1994 election the most uniform in terms of swing in twenty-four years. Likewise, the 52-seat Democratic loss in 1994 was far greater than economic models would have predicted (Tufte 1973), for the economy was quite healthy heading into the election. Similarly, the losses were greater than surge and decline models would have forecast (A. Campbell 1966), given the fact that there was no Democratic surge two years prior. Democrats actually lost ten seats in the House while winning the presidency in 1992.

3. The covariances were sufficiently small that Stokes omitted them and focused only on main effects (1965: 66–67).

4. Stokes (1973) replied that such effects would show up in covariance terms, which had generally been small in the analyses he had done.

5. For units of analysis, they substituted counties for congressional districts and regions for states. In addition, they included uncontested districts, while Stokes's analysis excluded almost the entire South.

6. In all the analyses in this chapter, we use the Democratic percent of the two-party vote as a measure of presidential support in the district.

7. Two other chapters in this volume (Brady, Canes-Wrone, and Cogan; Erikson and Wright) also use presidential vote in the district as an indicator of district ideology. We interpret ideology as a national-level force, albeit a long-term one compared to the short-term national forces of economic conditions, and characteristics of the presidential candidates.

8. Thanks to the work of Ansolabehere and Snyder, presidential vote in whole-county districts is available back to 1872. We are currently working with a longer, if less complete, series.

9. From 1968 to 1996, these data are from *The Almanac of American Politics*.

From 1952 to 1966, the returns are from the United States Congressional District Data Books. To its credit, the *Almanac* provides recalculated presidential district level votes for reapportionment years, mapping the pre-redistricting party vote totals onto the new districts in 1972, 1982, and 1992. Unfortunately, similar mapping for the House vote was only done for 1980 onto 1982 districts (by *Congressional Quarterly*), hence this is the only reapportionment year we can include in our analysis.

10. We define uncontested seats as those in which there is only one major party candidate. Third-party winners are excluded from the analysis.

11. The imputation process simply generates random probabilistic estimates of what the vote share in an uncontested race would have been had the race been contested. These estimates share the same limit, and are more consistent than estimates obtained by simply assigning some fixed vote share to uncontested winners. See King's web page http://gking.harvard.edu/stats.shtml for detailed information about the JudgeIt software and sample applications.

12. Like Gelman and King (1990), we used a single incumbency variable, given that even in 1994 the coefficients for the two parties were not significantly different.

13. Using the four-year lagged vote seems to stretch the credibility of presidential vote as a proxy for the national component of the current House vote. For example, it makes little sense to analyze the nationalization of the 1968 House vote using as an indicator the vote totals from Lyndon Johnson's defeat of Barry Goldwater four years earlier.

14. The correlation between the two variables is −.34.

15. In 1954, there were 61 contested seats out of 133 total seats, but by 1996 there were 130 contested races out of 148 total seats.

16. The South is defined as the eleven states of the old Confederacy. We do not report a separate analysis for the South alone because of the small number of observations and the large temporal changes in the number and distribution of uncontested districts.

17. It certainly seems likely that some of the underlying factors in the southern transition to House competitiveness and Republican dominance are related to the nationalization process. Our results simply indicate that, in the aggregate, changes in the South do not account for the national trends. For a similar finding regarding the increased relationship between district presidential vote and partisan identity of the winning House candidate see the contribution by Erikson and Wright in this volume.

18. For both Democrats and Republicans, the mean ADA score was calculated for the first session of the 83d to 104th Congresses (1953–95). The ADA is a score that ranges from 0 (extremely conservative) to 100 (extremely liberal). The variance of each distribution was also calculated, and it is this number that we use as a proxy for party homogenization. For 1953 to 1981,

the average variance was 29.0 for Democrats and 19.7 for Republicans. However, for 1983 to 1995, the average variance dropped to 22.6 for the Democrats and 14.7 for the Republicans.

19. Of course, whether members of Congress absorb and use such information is another matter. There is not much evidence suggesting that they do.

Chapter 8

1. For some of our previous writing on congressional representation, see Erikson (1971b); Erikson and Wright (1980, 1997); G. C. Wright (1978, 1989).

2. Any possible exceptions are not likely to be perceived by the constituents anyway. By reputation, Republicans are on the right and Democrats are on the left. Even the rare Republican candidate who takes positions to the left of the median constituent would still be seen by most voters to their right because of the strong ideological cue that the candidate is a Republican.

3. In the rare instance where a conservative Democrat is to the constituency's right or the liberal Republican is to the district's left, any potential for electoral damage would be muted by the fact that the constituency's perception of its candidate's record would be filtered by the constituency's knowledge of the candidate's party and ideological affiliation.

4. Technically speaking, $\text{Var}(error) = \text{SEE}^2 + \text{Var}(\text{year effects})$. The standard deviation of *error* is the square root of $\text{Var}(e)$.

5. If one prefers, consider the ideological motivation of the member to be derived from the preferences of others. The hypothetical Republican member may prefer a 100 percent conservative voting record because of the views of the local party constituency and the need to prevail in the primary rather than from personal preferences.

Chapter 9

The authors would like to thank participants of the 1997 Hoover Institution of War and Peace Elections Conference, Robert D'Onofrio, John Lott, and Tom MaCurdy for helpful comments and conversations. All mistakes are our responsibility.

1. In addition, Erikson and Wright (1997) show that a member's positions over issues affected his or her electoral results.

2. For a complementary analysis of how a member's positions affect his re-election prospects, see the Erikson and Wright chapter in this volume.

3. For other problems with the two-stage residual approach, see Bender and Lott (1996).

4. See the Ansolabehere and Snyder chapter of this book for related work on the effect of incumbency in garnering campaign contributions.

5. This measure is also employed in Erikson and Wright (1993, 1997).

6. The extensive reapportionment that followed the Supreme Court decision in *Baker v. Carr* (1962) has prohibited the mapping of the 1960 presidential vote onto the new 1962 congressional districts.

7. In two years, 1994 and 1966, no incumbent Republicans lost. Hence, for Republicans, nineteen parameter estimates of the difference in voting behavior between winning and losing incumbents were obtained.

8. We also estimated the parameters using logistic analysis in which the dependent variable was transformed to equal the natural log of the odds ratio, $LN(ADA/100 - ADA)$. These results were substantively similar.

9. Because regressions with proportions as dependent variables generally have heteroskedastic errors, we report White (1980) or robust standard errors for all regressions based on equation (1).

10. The parameter estimates for *LOSE* are reported in Table 9.2. All other results from the regressions can be obtained from the authors upon request.

11. Specification analysis rejects constraining autocorrelation coefficients across redistricting and non-redistricting years.

12. Bartels (1996) finds that aggregating across voters reduces but does not eliminate the electoral consequences of individual voters' lack of information. We do not claim to prove that the electorate behaves as if fully informed, only that some level of informed behavior is present.

Chapter 10

The names of the authors appear in random order. This chapter was an equal collaboration.

1. Because our data encompass only one year, we cannot compare the dynamics of 1994 to immediately prior House elections. We therefore cannot explain change, but we can suggest how particular election dynamics may have affected the outcome. We will, however, be able to compare the results to those of the 1964 House elections because of Kingdon's (1968) study on candidates and campaigns for that year. As will be shown, the similar role of party is striking.

2. Although see Leal (1998) for aggregate-level research on the role of non-economic issues on gubernatorial election outcomes.

3. Hershey (1974: 48, 71) found that over 85 percent of campaign managers believed that candidate image affected the vote more than issues or even party identification and that a majority of candidates felt the same way.

4. As Popkin (1991: 56) put it, "Analysis of party images shows that voters reason about the relative ability of parties to deal with different issues. They do not assume that the same party is uniformly good at representing all groups or dealing with all issues."

5. Petrocik (1996: 826) wrote that "Perceptions of a party's issue competence probably change very slowly, when they change at all."

6. These were Connecticut, Maryland, Massachusetts, New Hampshire, New Jersey, New York, Pennsylvania, Rhode Island, and Vermont.

7. State Senator Chakka Fattah defeated incumbent Lucien Blackwell in the Democratic primary in the Second District of Pennsylvania.

8. In our sample, Michael Forbes (R) defeated George Hochbrueckner (D) in New York's First District; Charles Bass (R) defeated Dick Swett (D) in New Hampshire's Second District; John Fox (R) defeated Marjorie Margolies-Mezvinsky (D) in Pennsylvania's Second District; and Bill Martini (R) defeated Herb Klein (D) in New Jersey's Eighth District. See Kaplan and Gruenwald (1994: 3232).

9. Herrnson (1995: 263, 270), in describing his own survey of congressional campaigns, wrote that "No distinctions were drawn between the response of candidates, campaign managers, treasurers, and other campaign aides. . . . There are several reasons for treating these responses equally. First, since campaign decision making is a cooperative endeavor involving a small group of decision makers, these individuals can be expected to have similar perceptions of the important factors in and determinants of the campaign. Second, during pretests of the questionnaire, several members of the same campaign provided responses that were nearly identical. Third, in almost a dozen cases a copy of the survey was received from a candidate and a campaign advisor of the same campaign, and, as was the case in the pretests, the responses of the two campaigners mirror each other closely."

10. The benefits of ordered probit diminish with the more categories found in the dependent variable. Because there are seven possible categories, we use the simpler OLS technique.

11. For example, it is reasonable to expect that strong liberals and strong conservatives would have emphasized abortion, although for different reasons. More interesting is whether challengers of one party tended to talk more about certain issues.

12. We included "values" because the word is commonly used in contemporary political rhetoric. According to a *New York Times* article on Robert Dole's declaration of candidacy for the presidency, "Aides to Mr. Dole said the points about values and reigning in Government registered especially well in tests with groups of potential Republican voters who were asked about versions of the speech in recent days. That helps explain why Mr. Dole repeated the word values nine times in the speech today" (Berke 1995). This is not just an issue for moderate Republicans trying to move to the right, however. According to neoconservative Ben Wattenberg (1995: 10), "I believe that the values situation in America has deteriorated. I believe that government has played a big role in allowing values to erode. I *think* that values are

our most potent *political* issue. I know that *values* are our most important *real* issue."

13. Education and infrastructure appeared to be drowned out in a campaign that became an aggressive referendum on Clinton's presidential performance and the proposed Republican Contract with America. Abortion did not emerge as a major campaign issue (as evidenced by the 3.08 mean score on issue emphasis, see Table 10.2), which may have been because candidates sought to avoid such a divisive issue. Avoiding abortion was a key part of the Republican strategy, and the topic was one of the social issues studiously avoided in the Contract.

14. The national security section of the Contract with America (point six) reads: "The National Security Restoration Act: No U.S. troops under U.N. command and restoration of the essential parts of our national security funding to strengthen our national defense and maintain our credibility around the world."

15. Some experts found that Republican challengers emphasized foreign affairs much less than Republicans traditionally have. Former Bush administration National Security Advisor Brent Scowcroft said, "[For] a lot of the freshmen congressmen . . . foreign policy didn't figure in their campaigns, they didn't get elected on it, their interest is other than foreign policy. They are young and don't have a deep background. In that sense they are not natural, if you will, traditional Republicans who put foreign policy up front" (Kranish 1995).

16. As discussed previously, it is not certain whether respondents interpreted foreign affairs in the context described in the Contract with America.

Chapter 11

Prepared for *Congressional Elections in the Post WWII Era: Continuity and Change*. David W. Brady and John F. Cogan, eds. December 1998. An earlier version of this article was presented at the Annual Meeting of the American Political Science Association, San Francisco, August 31–September 2, 1996.

We wish to thank the participants of the Hoover Institution Symposium on Congressional Elections in the Post–World War II Era. We wish to extend special thanks to Sunil Ahuja, Gary Cox, Morris Fiorina, Marc Hetherington, Tse-min Lin, Irwin L. Morris, Phil Paolino, Daron Shaw, Joseph Smith, and Terry Sullivan for their comments and suggestions.

1. The party vote score is the percentage of recorded votes on which a majority of Democrats opposed a majority of Republicans. For each party member, the party unity score is the percentage of times the member voted with the majority of his or her party on a party vote.

2. Respondents are classified as Democrats whether they report themselves

as strong Democrats, weak Democrats, or Independents leaning Democratic. Respondents are classified as Republicans in a comparable way. While there is controversy in electoral studies over whether to classify "leaners" as partisans or Independents, we erred toward a partisan classification because of our interest in capturing the likely supportive constituents of the incumbent House member (Fenno 1978), which themselves become part of the legislative party's constituent base. Based on evidence that leaners behave many times as closet partisans (Keith et al. 1992), we classified them as such.

3. The only respondents that are systematically eliminated from both Democratic and Republican districts are "pure" Independents. We recognize that a case can be made that Independents can become swing voters in some districts and thus ought to be included in estimations of some incumbents' reelection constituencies. In earlier versions of this article (Collie and Mason 1996), we included results on Independents for this reason. We omit discussion of them here for two main reasons. First, it is unclear in which districts Independents become swing voters and for how long. Second, their inclusion had virtually no substantive impact on the interpretation of our other results reported here. We are happy to provide these results upon request.

4. Ideological self-placement is on the standard seven-point scale ranging from liberal (low values) to conservative (high values).

5. For example, see Conover and Feldman (1981), H. E. Brady and Sniderman (1985), Fleishman (1986), and Lyons and Scheb (1992).

6. We selected these issue areas because of their continuing importance in the policy agenda and because NES wording on questions about them remained largely consistent over the period we analyze.

7. In Tables 11.2, 11.3, and 11.4 we report skewedness of our sample distributions to indicate that the distributions around the mean are normal, which enables the mean to serve as a proxy for the median in the two types of districts. It is possible to recover specific median values beyond the simple median integer (Aldrich et al. 1989). We chose the mean instead of precise medians because the sample mean values are close to the median values given the minor skewedness of our sample distributions. Skewedness is calculated as follows:

$$n/(n1)(n2)\Sigma^*(x_i - |x)^3 s^3$$

In 1984, the skew in the distribution of ideological predispositions for Republican respondents ($-.84$) was the most severe of any sample across the years of analysis. The median ideology rating for the respondents in the sample was 5.17 on the seven-point scale. The mean ideology score for respondents in the sample was 4.95, less than a quarter of a point different from the recovered median. The skew in the distribution of the ideological predispositions for Democratic respondents of the 1982 survey (.173) was the most severe for

Democrats across the election years analyzed. The recovered median for this sample distribution was 3.86, 0.03 of a point away from the sample mean of 3.83. The small differences between the sample means and the sample medians convince us that the former is good proxy for the median ideological position, which becomes a point of interest later in our discussion. In any case, the mean is the convergent equilibrium in multicandidate spatial models of quadratic Euclidean distance (Hinich 1978; Lin and Enelow n.d.).

8. We compared these results to comparable summary statistics on verified voters and found only marginal differences between them. For example, the mean ideological positions for all Democratic respondents were 3.77, 3.72, 3.82, 3.74, and 3.81 from 1972 to 1980, and for verified voter Democratic respondents were 3.65, 3.73, 3.74, 3.68, and 3.77. Furthermore, we question whether members of Congress limit their attention only to voters as opposed to voters and potential voters (Fiorina 1974; Arnold 1990). The more conservative option, we believe, is to base our analysis on the more inclusive set of respondents, thus not limiting our sample to voters.

9. The low value, .87, conveniently coincides with 1972, and the high value, 1.36, with 1994.

Epilogue

1. This research is ably synthesized in Jacobson (1997b), and earlier editions of the same textbook.

2. Because of redistricting we cannot use the Gelman-King formula for calculating the incumbency advantage in 1992.

3. For elaboration see Jacobson (1999).

4. The lone defeated Democratic incumbent was an insignificant one ADA point "too liberal."

5. The first figure is from an unpublished analysis by John Cogan; the second is reported in Jacobson (1999). There is an interesting asymmetry here: Democrats who took a public stand against Clinton were, if anything, rewarded at the polls, whereas post-election commentary suggests that Republicans as a party may have been punished. If, after further investigation, these claims stand up, the most plausible explanation is that Democratic opposition was regarded as evidence of independence, whereas Republican opposition was regarded as evidence of partisanship.

6. Of course, it is possible that in general Republicans are more likely to raise issues than Democrats. This possibility seems less likely given the discussion of 1998 in the text.

Abramowitz, Alan I., and Suzie Ishikawa. 1995. "Explaining the Republican Takeover of the House of Representatives: Evidence from the 1992–94 NES Panel Survey." Paper presented at the annual meeting of the American Political Science Association, Chicago, Aug. 31–Sept. 3.

Abramson, Paul, John Aldrich, and David Rohde. 1994. *Change and Continuity in the 1992 Elections*. Washington, D.C.: Congressional Quarterly Press.

Aistrup, Joseph A. 1996. *The Southern Strategy Revisited*. Lexington: University of Kentucky Press.

Aldrich, John H. 1995. *Why Parties? The Origin and Transformation of Political Parties in America*. Chicago: University of Chicago Press.

Aldrich, John H., and David Rohde. 1996. "The Republican Revolution and the House Appropriations Committee." Paper presented at the annual meeting of the Southern Political Science Association, Atlanta, Nov. 7–9.

Aldrich, John H., John L. Sullivan, and Eugene Borgida. 1989. "Foreign Affairs and Issue Voting: Do Presidential Candidates 'Waltz Before a Blind Audience?'" *American Political Science Review* 83: 123–41.

Alford, John R., and David R. Brady. 1988. "Partisan and Incumbent Advantage in U.S. House Elections, 1846–1986." Working Paper Number 11. Center for the Study of Institutions and Values, Rice University.

———. 1993. "Personal and Partisan Advantage in U.S. Congressional Elections, 1846–1990." In Lawrence C. Dodd and Bruce I. Oppenheimer, eds., *Congress Reconsidered*, 5th ed., pp. 141–57. Washington, D.C.: Congressional Quarterly Press.

Alford, John R., and John R. Hibbing. 1981. "Increased Incumbency Advantage in the House." *Journal of Politics* 43 (Nov.): 1042–61.

Ansolabehere, Stephen, David Brady, and Morris Fiorina. 1992. "The Vanishing Marginals and Electoral Responsiveness." *British Journal of Political Science* 22: 21–38.

Ansolabehere, Stephen, and Alan Gerber. n.d. "Incumbency Advantage and the Persistence of Legislative Majorities." Manuscript, MIT and Yale.

Ansolabehere, Stephen, and Shanto Iyengar. 1994. "Riding the Wave and Claiming Ownership Over Issues: The Joint Effects of Advertising and News Coverage in Campaigns." *Public Opinion Quarterly* 58: 335–57.

Ansolabehere, Stephen, and James M. Snyder Jr. 1996. "Money, Elections and Candidate Quality." Unpublished manuscript, MIT.

Arnold, Douglas. 1990. *The Logic of Congressional Action*. New Haven: Yale University Press.

Bailey, Michael. 1998. "Information, Strategy and Representation: A Strategic Actor Model of Representation." Unpublished manuscript, Georgetown University.

Barone, Michael, and Grant Ujifusa. 1983. *The Almanac of American Politics 1984*. Washington, D.C.: National Journal.

Bartels, Larry M. 1996. "Uninformed Voters: Information Effects in Presidential Elections." *American Journal of Political Science* 40: 194–230.

Bartley, Numan V., and H. D. Graham. 1975. *Southern Politics and the Second Reconstruction*. Baltimore: The Johns Hopkins University Press.

Beck, Paul Allen. 1977. "Partisan Dealignment in the Postwar South." *American Political Science Review* 71: 477–97.

Bender, Bruce, and John R. Lott Jr. 1996. "Legislator Voting and Shirking: A Critical Review of the Literature." *Public Choice* 87: 67–100.

Berelson, Bernard R., Paul F. Lazarsfeld, and William N. McPhee. 1954. *Voting: A Study of Opinion Formation in a Presidential Campaign*. Chicago: University of Chicago Press.

Berke, Richard L. 1995. "Now Officially Dole is Making a Run for '96." *New York Times*, Apr. 11: A1.

Bernstein, Robert A. 1989. *Elections, Representation and Congressional Voting Behavior: The Myth of Constituency Control*. Englewood Cliffs, New Jersey: Prentice Hall.

Black, Earl. 1976. *Southern Governors and Civil Rights*. Cambridge: Harvard University Press.

Black, Earl, and Merle Black. 1973. "The Wallace Vote in Alabama: A Multiple Regression Analysis." *Journal of Politics* 35 (Aug.): 730–36.

———. 1987. *Politics and Society in the South*. Cambridge: Harvard University Press.

———. 1992. *Vital South*. Cambridge: Harvard University Press.

Bond, John R., and Richard Fleisher. 1990. *The President in the Legislative Arena*. Chicago: University of Chicago Press.

Born, Richard. 1986. "Strategic Polls and Unresponsive Voters." *American Political Science Review* 80: 599–612.

———. 1990. "The Shared Fortunes of Congress and Congressmen." *Journal of Politics* 52 (Nov.): 1223–41.

Bott, Alexander. 1991. *Handbook of U.S. Election Laws and Practices*. Westport, Conn.: Greenwood.

Boucher, Robert L., Jr., and Albert D. Cover. 1996. "The Changing Impact of Institutional Assessments on Vote Choice in Congressional Elections." Paper presented at the annual meeting of the American Political Science Association, San Francisco, Aug. 29–Sept. 1.

Brady, David W. 1988. *Critical Elections and Congressional Policy Making*. Stanford: Stanford University Press.

Brady, David W., John F. Cogan, Brian Gaines, and R. Douglas Rivers. 1996. "The Perils of Presidential Support: How the Republicans Took the House in the 1994 Midterm Election." *Political Behavior* 18: 345–67.

Brady, David W., John F. Cogan, and R. Douglas Rivers. 1995. "How the Republicans Captured the House: An Assessment of the 1994 Midterm Elections." The Hoover Institution Essays in Public Policy.

Brady, David W., Joseph Cooper, and Patricia A. Hurley. 1979. "The Decline of Party in the U.S. House of Representatives, 1887–1968." *Legislative Studies Quarterly* 4: 381–407.

Brady, David W., L. Sandy Maisel, and Kevin M. Warsh. 1994. "An Opportunity Cost Model of the Decision to Run for Congress: Another Contributor to Democratic Hegemony." Paper presented at the annual meeting of the American Political Science Association, New York, Sept. 1–4.

Brady, David W., and Joseph Stewart. 1982. "Congressional Party Realignment and Transformation of Public Policy in Three Realignment Eras." *American Journal of Political Science* 26: 333–60.

Brady, David W., and Craig Volden. 1998. *Revolving Gridlock: Politics and Policy from Carter to Clinton*. Boulder, Colo.: Westview.

Brady, Henry E., and Paul M. Sniderman. 1985. "Attitude Attribution: A Group Basis for Political Reasoning." *American Political Science Review* 79: 1061–78.

———. 1991. "The Likability Heuristic." In Paul M. Sniderman, Richard A. Brody, and Philip E. Tetlock, eds., *Reasoning and Choice: Explorations in Political Psychology*, pp. 93–119. New York: Cambridge University Press.

Broder, David. 1988. "Housecleaning is Needed." *San Jose Mercury News*, June 1: 11b.

Brownstein, Ronald. 1986. "Still No Breakthrough." *National Journal* 18 (Sept. 20): 2228–32.

Bullock, Charles S., III. 1983. "The Effects of Redistricting on Black Representation in Southern State Legislatures." Paper presented at the annual meeting of the American Political Science Association, Chicago, Sept. 1–4.

———. 1984. "Racial Crossover Voting and the Election of Black Officials."
Journal of Politics 46 (Feb.): 238–51.

———. 1988. "Creeping Realignment in the South." In Robert H. Swan-
brough and David M. Brodsky, eds., *The South's New Politics: Realignment and Dealignment*, pp. 220–37. Columbia: University of South Carolina Press.

———. 1995. "The Evolution of Redistricting Plans in Georgia in the 1990s."
Paper presented at the annual meeting of the Association of American
Geographers, Chicago, Mar. 14–18.

———. 2001. "The Contemporary South and the 1988 Elections." In John
Kuzenski, Laurence Moreland, and Robert Steed, eds., *Eye of the Storm:
The South in the Postreform Congress*. Westport, Conn.: Praeger.

Bureau of the Census. 1992. *Population and Housing Characteristics for Congressional Districts of the 103rd Congress*. Washington, D.C.: Department of
Commerce.

Burnham, Walter Dean. 1965. "The Changing Shape of the American Political Universe." *American Political Science Review* 59: 7–28.

———. 1970. *Critical Elections and the Mainsprings of American Politics*. New
York: Norton.

———. 1975. "Insulation and Responsiveness in Congressional Elections."
Political Science Quarterly 90: 411–35.

Butler, David, and Donald Stokes. 1969. *Political Change in Britain*. New York:
St. Martin's.

Cain, Bruce E. 1992. "Voting Rights and Democratic Theory: Toward a
Color-Blind Society." In Bernard Grofman and Chandler Davidson,
eds., *Controversies in Minority Voting*, pp. 261–77. Washington, D.C.:
Brookings Institute.

Cain, Bruce E., John Ferejohn, and Morris Fiorina. 1987. *The Personal Vote:
Constituency Service and Electoral Independence*. Cambridge: Harvard University Press.

Calvert, Randall L. 1985. "Robustness of the Multidimensional Voting
Model: Candidate Motivations, Uncertainty, and Convergence." *American Journal of Political Science* 29: 69–95.

Cameron, Charles, David Epstein, and Sharyn O'Halloran. 1996. "Do
Majority-Minority Districts Maximize Substantive Black Representation in Congress?" *American Journal of Political Science* 90: 794–812.

Campbell, Angus. 1960. "Surge and Decline: A Study of Electoral Change."
Public Opinion Quarterly 24: 397–418.

———. 1966. *Elections and the Political Order*. New York: Wiley.

Campbell, Angus, Philip Converse, Warren Miller, and Donald Stokes. 1960.
The American Voter. New York: John Wiley.

Campbell, James E. 1993. *The Presidential Pulse of Congressional Elections.* Lexington: University Press of Kentucky.

———. 1997. "The Presidential Pulse and the 1994 Midterm Congressional Election." *Journal of Politics* 59: 830–57.

Carmines, Edward G., and Geoffrey C. Layman. 1997. "Issue Evolution in Postwar American Politics: Old Certainties and Fresh Tensions." In Byron E. Shafer, ed., *Present Discontents: American Politics in the Very Late Twentieth Century*, pp. 89–134. Chatham, N.J.: Chatham House.

Carmines, Edward G., and James Stimson. 1989. *Issue Evolution: Race and the Transformation of American Politics.* Princeton: Princeton University Press.

Carney, Dan. 1996. "As Hostilities Rage on the Hill, Partisan-Vote Rate Soars." *Congressional Quarterly Weekly Report*, Jan. 27: 199.

Claggett, William, William Flanigan, and Nancy Zingale. 1984. "Nationalization of the American Electorate." *American Political Science Review* 78: 77–91.

Cohen, Richard. 1994. "A Few More Chips Off the 'Solid South.'" *National Journal* 26 (Apr. 16): 910.

Collie, Melissa P., and John L. Mason. 1996. "Party-in-the-Electorate and Party Behavior in the House, 1972–94." Paper presented at the annual meeting of the American Political Science Association, San Francisco, Aug. 29–Sept. 1.

Conover, Pamela Johnston, and Stanley Feldman. 1981. "How People Organize the Political World: A Schematic Model." *American Journal of Political Science* 28: 95–126.

Converse, Philip E. 1966. "The Concept of a Normal Vote." In Angus Campbell, Philip E. Converse, Warren E. Miller, and Donald E. Stokes, *Elections and the Political Order*, pp. 9–39. New York: Wiley.

Converse, Philip E., Aage R. Clausen, and Warren E. Miller. 1965. "Electoral Myth and Reality: The 1964 Election." *American Political Science Review* 59: 321–36.

Converse, Philip E., Warren E. Miller, Jerold G. Rusk, and Arthur C. Wolfe. 1969. "Continuity and Change in American Politics: Parties and Issues in the 1968 Elections." *American Political Science Review* 63: 1083–105.

Cook, Elizabeth, Ted Jelen, and Clyde Wilcox. 1994. "Issue Voting in Gubernatorial Elections: Abortion and Post-Webster Politics." *Journal of Politics* 56: 187–89.

Cook, Rhodes. 1994. "Incumbent Advantage Lost in November." *Congressional Quarterly Weekly Report*, Dec. 31: 3694.

———. 1997. "Actual District Votes Belie Ideal of Partisanship." *Congressional Quarterly* 55 (Apr. 12): 859–62.

Cooper, Joseph, and David W. Brady. 1981. "Institutional Context and Leadership Style: The House from Cannon to Rayburn." *American Political Science Review* 75: 411–25.

Cooper, Joseph, David W. Brady, and Patricia A. Hurley. 1977. "The Electoral Basis of Party Voting: Patterns and Trends in the U.S. House of Representatives, 1887–1969." In Louis Maisel and Joseph Cooper, eds., *The Impact of the Electoral Process*, pp. 133–65. Beverly Hills, Calif.: Sage.

Cox, Gary W., and Jonathan N. Katz. 1996. "Why Did the Incumbency Advantage in U.S. House Elections Grow?" *American Journal of Political Science* 40: 478–97.

Cox, Gary W., and Matthew D. McCubbins. 1993. *Legislative Leviathan: Party Government in the House*. Berkeley: University of California Press.

Crook, Sara Brandes, and John R. Hibbing. 1985. "Congressional Reform and Party Discipline: The Effects of Changes in the Seniority System on Party Loyalty in the U.S. House of Representatives." *British Journal of Political Science* 15: 207–26.

Cummings, Milton C., Jr. 1966. *Congressmen and the Electorate: Elections for the U.S. and the President*. New York: Free Press.

Dallek, Robert. 1991. *Lone Star Rising: Lyndon Johnson and His Times, 1908–1960*. New York: Oxford University Press.

Davidson, Chandler, and Bernard Grofman, eds. 1994. *Quiet Revolution in the South: The Impact of the Voting Rights Act, 1965–1990*. Princeton: Princeton University Press.

Davidson, Roger H. 1988. "The New Centralization on Capitol Hill." *Review of Politics*: 345–64.

DeMarchi, Scott, and Terry Sullivan. 1997. "Presidential Bargaining Through Time: Persuasion, Incomplete Information, Budget and Tenure." Paper presented at the annual meeting of the American Political Science Association, Washington, D.C., Aug. 28–31.

Dodd, Lawrence C., and Bruce I. Oppenheimer. 1997a. "Revolution in the House: Testing the Limits of Party Government." In Lawrence C. Dodd and Bruce I. Oppenheimer, eds., *Congress Reconsidered*, 6th ed., pp. 29–60. Washington, D.C.: Congressional Quarterly Press.

———. 1997b. "Congress and the Emerging Order: Conditional Party Government or Constructive Partisanship?" In Lawrence C. Dodd and Bruce I. Oppenheimer, eds., *Congress Reconsidered*, 6th ed., pp. 390–413. Washington, D.C.: Congressional Quarterly Press.

Downs, Anthony. 1957. *An Economic Theory of Democracy*. New York: Harper and Row.

Duncan, Philip, ed. 1993. *Politics in America*. Washington, D.C.: Congressional Quarterly Press.

Durr, Robert H., John B. Gilmour, and Christina Wolbrecht. 1997. "Explaining Congressional Approval." *American Journal of Political Science* 41 (Jan.): 175–207.

Edsall, Thomas. 1984. *The New Politics of Inequality.* New York: Norton.

Edwards, George C., III. 1980. *Presidential Influence in Congress.* San Francisco: W. H. Freeman.

Epstein, David, and Sharyn O'Halloran. 1999. "Measuring the Electoral and Policy Impact of Majority-Minority Voting Districts." *American Journal of Political Science* 43: 367–95.

Erikson, Robert S. 1971a. "The Advantage of Incumbency in Congressional Elections." *Polity* 3: 395–405.

———. 1971b. "The Electoral Impact of Congressional Roll Call Voting." *American Political Science Review* 65: 1018–103.

———. 1972a. "Malapportionment, Gerrymandering, and Party Fortunes in Congressional Elections." *American Political Science Review* 66: 1234–45.

———. 1972b. "A Reply to Tidmarch." *Polity* 4: 527–29.

———. 1978. "Constituency Opinion and Congressional Behavior: A Reexamination of the Miller-Stokes Representation Data." *American Journal of Political Science* 22: 511–55.

———. 1988. "The Puzzle of Midterm Loss." *Journal of Politics* 50: 1011–29.

Erikson, Robert S., and Gerald C. Wright. 1980. "Policy Representation of Constituency Interests." *Political Behavior* 2: 91–106.

———. 1995. "Voters, Candidates and Issues in Congressional Elections." In Lawrence C. Dodd and Bruce I. Oppenheimer, eds., *Congress Reconsidered*, 5th ed., pp. 91–114. Washington, D.C.: Congressional Quarterly Press.

———. 1997. "Voters, Issues, and Candidates in Congressional Elections." In Lawrence C. Dodd and Bruce I. Oppenheimer, eds., *Congress Reconsidered*, 6th ed., pp. 132–51. Washington, D.C.: Congressional Quarterly Press.

Evans, C. Lawrence, and Walter J. Oleszek. 1997. "Congressional Tsunami? The Politics of Committee Reform." In Lawrence C. Dodd and Bruce I. Oppenheimer, eds., *Congress Reconsidered*, 6th ed., pp. 193–211. Washington, D.C.: Congressional Quarterly Press.

Fenno, Richard F. 1974. *Congressmen in Committees.* Boston: Little, Brown.

———. 1975. "If, as Ralph Nader Says, Congress is 'The Broken Branch,' How Come We Love Our Congressmen So Much?" In Norman J. Ornstein, ed., *Congress in Change: Evolution and Reform*, pp. 24–57. New York: Praeger.

———. 1978. *Home Style: House Members in Their Districts.* Boston: Little, Brown.

Ferejohn, John A. 1977. "On the Decline of Competition in Congressional Elections." *American Political Science Review* 71: 166–76.

———. 1998. "A Tale of Two Congresses: Social Policy in the Clinton Years." In Margaret Weir, ed., *The Social Divide: Political Parties and the Future of Activist Government*, pp. 49–82. Thousand Oaks, Calif.: Sage.

Ferejohn, John A., and Randall L. Calvert. 1984. "Presidential Coattails in Historical Perspective." *American Journal of Political Science* 28: 127–46.

Ferejohn, John A., Brian Gaines, and Douglas Rivers. 1995. "The Failure of Incumbency: Why the Democrats Lost the House in 1994." Paper presented at the annual meeting of the American Political Science Association, Chicago, Aug. 31–Sept. 3.

Fiorina, Morris P. 1973. "Electoral Margins, Constituency Influence, and Policy Moderation: A Critical Assessment." *American Politics Quarterly* 1: 479–98.

———. 1974. *Representatives, Roll Calls, and Constituencies*. Lexington, Mass.: Lexington Books.

———. 1977a. "The Case of the Vanishing Marginals: The Bureaucracy Did It." *American Political Science Review* 71: 177–81.

———. 1977b. *Congress, Keystone of the Washington Establishment*. New Haven: Yale University Press.

———. 1978. "The Incumbency Factor." *Public Opinion* (Sept./Oct.): 42–44.

———. 1982. "Congressmen and their Constituencies: 1958 and 1978." In Dennis Hale, ed., *Proceedings of the Thomas P. O'Neill Jr. Symposium on the U.S. Congress*, pp. 33–64. Boston: Eusey Press.

———. 1983. "Who Is Held Responsible: Further Evidence on the Hibbing-Alford Thesis." *American Journal of Political Science* 27 (Feb.): 158–64.

———. 1996. *Divided Government*. 2d ed. Boston: Allyn and Bacon.

Fleisher, Richard. 1993. "Explaining the Change in Roll-Call Voting Behavior of Southern Democrats." *Journal of Politics* 55: 327–41.

Fleishman, John A. 1986. "Trends in Self-Identified Ideology from 1972 to 1982: No Support for the Salience Hypothesis." *American Journal of Political Science* 30: 517–41.

Fowler, Linda. 1993. *Candidates, Congress, and the American Democracy*. Ann Arbor: University of Michigan Press.

Franklin, Charles H. 1991. "Eschewing Obfuscation? Campaigns and the Perception of U.S. Senate Incumbents." *American Political Science Review* 85: 1193–214.

Frymer, Paul A. 1996. "The 1994 Electoral Aftershock: Dealignment or Realignment in the South." In Philip A. Klinkner, ed., *Midterm: The Elections of 1994 in Context*, pp. 99–113. Boulder, Colo.: Westview.

Gais, Thomas, and Michael Malbin. 1997. *The Day After Reform: Sobering Campaign Finance Lessons From The American States*. Albany, N.Y.: Rockefeller Institute Press.

Geer, John, ed. 1998. *Politicians and Party Politics*. New Haven: Yale University Press.

Gelman, Andrew, and Gary King. 1990. "Estimating Incumbency Advantage Without Bias." *American Journal of Political Science* 34 (Nov.): 1142–64.

Gerber, Alan. 1995. "Campaign Spending and Senate Election Outcomes: Using 'Cost Shifters' to Reestimate the Effects." Unpublished manuscript, Yale University.

———. 1996. "Rational Voters, Candidate Spending, and Incomplete Information." Unpublished manuscript, Yale University.

Giles, Michael W., and Melanie Buckner, 1995. "David Duke and the Electoral Politics of Racial Threat." In John C. Kuzenski, Charles S. Bullock III, and Ronald Keith Gaddie, eds., *David Duke and the Politics of Race in the South*, pp. 88–98. Nashville: Vanderbilt University Press.

Gilmour, John B., and Paul Rothstein. 1993. "Early Republican Retirement: A Cause of Democratic Dominance in the House of Representatives." *Legislative Studies Quarterly* 18 (Aug.): 345–65.

Goff, Brian L., and Kevin B. Grier. 1993. "On the (Mis)measurement of Legislator Ideology and Shirking." *Public Choice* 76: 5–19.

Green, Donald P. 1990. "Rebuttal to Jacobson's 'New Evidence for Old Arguments.'" *American Journal of Political Science* 34: 363–72.

Green, Donald P., and Jonathan S. Krasno. 1988. "Salvation for the Spendthrift Incumbent: Reestimating the Effects of Campaign Spending in House Elections." *American Journal of Political Science* 32: 884–907.

Grier, Kevin, and Michael Munger. 1991. "Committee Assignments, Constituent Preferences, and Campaign Contributions." *Economic Inquiry* 29: 24–43.

Groseclose, Timothy, Steven Levitt, and James M. Snyder. 1999. "Comparing Interest Group Scores Across Time and Chambers: Adjusted ADA Scores for the U.S. Congress." *American Political Science Review*, forthcoming.

Guinier, Lani. 1994. *The Tyranny of the Majority: Fundamental Fairness in Representative Democracy*. New York: Free Press.

Gujarati, Damodar. 1988. *Basic Econometrics*. 2d ed. New York: McGraw Hill.

Hadley, Charles S. 1985. "Dual Partisan Identification in the South." *Journal of Politics* 47 (Feb.): 254–68.

Hager, George. 1995. "GOP Ready to Take Debt Limit to the Brink and Beyond." *Congressional Quarterly Weekly Report*, Sept. 23, 2865.

Handley, Lisa. 1996. "Liability Issues in *Moon v. Meadows*: Racially Polarized

Voting in Virginia Elections." Submitted to the court in *Moon v. Mead-ows*, C.A. No. 3: 95CV942 (E.D. Va., 1996).

Herrnson, Paul. 1995. *Congressional Elections: Campaigning at Home and in Washington*. Washington, D.C.: Congressional Quarterly Press.

Hershey, Marjorie Randon. 1974. *The Making of Campaign Strategy*. Lexington, Mass.: Lexington Books.

————. 1984. *Running for Office: The Political Education of Campaigners*. Chatham, N.J.: Chatham House.

Hibbing, John R. 1991. *Congressional Careers: Contours of Life in the U.S. House of Representatives*. Chapel Hill: University of North Carolina Press.

Hibbing, John R., and John R. Alford. 1981. "The Electoral Impact of Economic Conditions: Who is Held Responsible?" *American Journal of Political Science* 25 (Aug.): 423–39.

Hibbing, John R., and Elizabeth Theiss-Morse. 1995. *Congress as Public Enemy*. Cambridge: Cambridge University Press.

Hill, Kevin A. 1995. "Does the Creation of Majority Black Districts Aid Republicans? An Analysis of the 1992 Congressional Elections in Eight Southern States." *Journal of Politics* 57 (May 1995): 384–401.

Hinich, M. J. 1978. "The Mean Versus the Median in Spatial Voting Games." In P. Ordeshook, ed., *Game Theory and Political Science*, pp. 357–74. New York: New York University Press.

Hinckley, Barbara. "Interpreting House Midterm Elections: Toward a Measurement of the In-Party's 'Expected' Loss of Seats." *American Political Science Review* 61: 694–700.

Holmes, Robert A. 1982. "The Politics of Reapportionment, 1981: A Case Study of Georgia." *Urban Research Review* 8: 1–4.

Howell, S. E., and R. Sims. 1993. "Abortion Attitudes and the Louisiana Governors Election." *American Politics Quarterly* 21: 54–64.

Huckshorn, Robert, and Robert Spencer. 1971. *The Politics of Defeat: Campaigning for Congress*. Amherst: University of Massachusetts Press.

Jackson, Brooks. 1990. *Broken Promise: Why the Federal Election Commission Failed*. New York: Priority Press.

Jacobson, Gary C. 1978. "The Effects of Campaign Spending in Congressional Elections." *American Political Science Review* 72: 469–91.

————. 1980. *Money in Congressional Elections*. New Haven: Yale University Press.

————. 1981. "Incumbents' Advantages in the 1978 U.S. Congressional Elections." *Legislative Studies Quarterly* 6 (May): 183–200.

————. 1985. "Money and Votes Reconsidered: Congressional Elections, 1972–1982." *Public Choice* 47: 7–62.

———. 1987. "The Marginals Never Vanished: Incumbency and Competition in Elections to the U.S. House of Representatives, 1952–1982." *American Journal of Political Science* 31: 126–41.

———. 1989. "Strategic Politicians and the Dynamics of House Elections, 1946–1986." *American Political Science Review* 83 (Sept.): 773–93.

———. 1990a. "The Effect of Campaign Spending in House Elections: New Evidence for Old Arguments." *American Political Science Review* 34: 334–62.

———. 1990b. *The Electoral Origins of Divided Government: Competition in U.S. House Elections, 1946–1988.* Boulder, Colo.: Westview.

———. 1990c. "Meager Patrimony: The Reagan Era and Republican Representation in Congress." In Larry Berman, ed., *Looking Back on the Reagan Presidency*, pp. 288–316. Baltimore: The Johns Hopkins University Press.

———. 1991. "The Persistence of Democratic House Majorities." In Gary W. Cox and Samuel Kernell, eds., *The Politics of Divided Government*, pp. 57–83. Boulder, Colo.: Westview.

———. 1993. "Reversal of Fortune: The Transformation of the U.S. House Elections in the 1990s." *Political Science Quarterly* 108: 375–402.

———. 1996a. "Divided Government and the 1994 Elections." In Peter F. Galderisi, ed., *Divided Government: Change, Uncertainty, and the Constitutional Order*, pp. 61–84. Lanham, Md.: Rowan and Littlefield.

———. 1996b. "House Elections in Perspective." *Political Science Quarterly* 111: 203–23.

———. 1996c. "The 1994 House Elections in Perspective." In Philip A. Klinkner, ed., *Midterm: The Elections of 1994 in Context*, pp. 1–20. Boulder Colo.: Westview.

———. 1996d. *The Politics of Congressional Elections.* 4th ed. Boston: Little, Brown.

———. 1997a. "Congress: Unprecedented and Unsurprising." In Michael Nelson, ed., *The Elections of 1996*, pp. 143–66. Washington, D.C.: Congressional Quarterly Press.

———. 1997b. *The Politics of Congressional Elections.* 4th ed. New York: Longman.

———. 1999. "The 1998 Congressional Elections." *Political Science Quarterly*.

Jacobson, Gary C., and Michael A. Dimock. 1994. "Checking Out: The Effects of Overdrafts on the 1992 House Elections." *American Journal of Political Science* 38 (Aug.): 601–24.

Jacobson, Gary C., and Samuel Kernell. 1983. *Strategy and Choice in Congressional Elections.* 2d ed. New Haven: Yale University Press.

Jacobson, Gary C., and Thomas P. Kim. 1996. "After 1994: The New Politics of Congressional Elections." Paper presented at the annual meeting of the Midwest Political Science Association, Chicago, Sept. 2–5.

Kaplan, Dave. 1994. "This Year Republicans Gamble that All Politics is National." *Congressional Quarterly Weekly Report* 52 (Oct. 22): 3005–10.

———, and Juliana Gruenwald. 1994. "Longtime 'Second' Party Scores a Long List of GOP Firsts." *Congressional Quarterly Report* 52 (Nov. 12): 3232–39.

Katz, Richard S. 1973a. "The Attribution of Variance in Electoral Returns: An Alternative Measurement Technique." *American Political Science Review* 67: 817–28.

———. 1973b. "Rejoinder to 'Comment' by Donald E. Stokes." *American Political Science Review* 67: 832–34.

Kawato, Sadafumi. 1987. "Nationalization and Partisan Realignment in Congressional Elections." *American Political Science Review* 81: 1235–50.

Keith, Bruce E., David B. Magleby, Candice J. Nelson, Elizabeth Orr, Mark C. Westlye, and Raymond E. Wolfinger. 1992. *The Myth of the Independent Voter*. Berkeley: University of California Press.

Key, V. O., Jr. 1949. *Southern Politics*. New York: Knopf.

———. 1955. "A Theory of Critical Elections." *Journal of Politics* 17: 3–18.

———. 1959. "Secular Realignment and the Party System." *Journal of Politics* 21: 198–210.

———. 1961. *Public Opinion and American Democracy*. New York: Knopf.

———. 1964. *Politics, Parties, and Pressure Groups*. 5th ed. New York: Crowell.

Kiewiet, D. Roderick, and Mathew D. McCubbins. 1988. "Presidential Influence on Congressional Appropriations Decisions." *American Journal of Political Science* 32: 713–36.

———. 1991. *The Logic of Delegation: Congressional Parties and the Appropriations Process*. Chicago: University of Chicago Press.

Kingdon, John. 1968. *Candidates for Office: Beliefs and Strategies*. New York: Random House.

Klinkner, Philip A. 1996. *Midterm: The Elections of 1994*. Boulder, Colo.: Westview.

Kramer, Gerald H. 1971. "Short-Term Fluctuations in U.S. Voting Behavior, 1896–1964." *American Political Science Review* 65: 131–43.

Kranish, Michael. 1995. "GOP Eyes Battles on Foreign Policy: Both Sides Look to Use Issue in 1996." *Boston Globe*, Apr. 3: 8.

Krasno, Jonathan, Donald Green, and Jonathan Cowden. 1994. "The Dynamics of Campaign Fundraising in House Elections." *Journal of Politics* 56: 459–74.

Krehbiel, Keith. 1998. *Pivotal Politics: A Theory of U.S. Lawmaking*. Chicago: University of Chicago Press.

Ladd, Everett Carll, Jr., and Charles D. Hadley. 1975. *Transformations of the American Party System*. New York: Norton.

Lazarsfeld, Paul F., Bernard R. Berelson, and Hazel Gaudet. 1948. *The People's Choice: How the Voter Makes Up His Mind in a Presidential Campaign*. 2d ed. New York: Columbia University Press.

Leal, David L. 1998. *Essays on Gubernatorial Elections*. Ph.D. diss., Harvard University.

Levitt, Steven D., and Catherine D. Wolfram. 1997. "Decomposing the Sources of Incumbency Advantage in the U.S. House." *Legislative Studies Quarterly* 22 (Feb.): 45–60.

Lichtman, Allan. 1996. "Report on Congressional District 3 and Bordering Districts, State of Florida." Submitted to the court in *Johnson v. Mortham* (N.D. Flar., 1996).

Lin, Tse-min, and James M. Enelow. n.d. "Equilibrium in Multicandidate Probabilistic Spatial Voting." *Public Choice*, forthcoming.

Lott, John. 1995. "A Simple Explanation for Why Campaign Expenditures are Increasing: the Government is Getting Bigger." Unpublished manuscript.

Lublin, David Ian. 1995. "Race, Representation and Redistricting." In Paul E. Peterson, ed., *Classifying by Race*, pp. 111–25. Cambridge: Harvard University Press.

———. 1997. *The Paradox of Representation*. Princeton: Princeton University Press.

Luntz, Frank I. 1988. *Candidates, Consultants and Campaigns: The Style and Substance of American Electioneering*. Oxford: Basil Blackwell.

Luttbeg, Norman R. 1995. *American Electoral Behavior 1952–1992*. 2d ed.. Itasca, Ill.: F. E. Peacock.

Lyons, William, and John M. Scheb II. 1992. "Ideology and Candidate Evaluation in the 1984 and the 1988 Presidential Elections." *Journal of Politics* 54: 573–84.

Maggioto, Michael. 1996. Report submitted to the court in *Johnson v. Mortham* (N.D. Flar., 1996).

Maisel, L. Sandy. 1982. *From Obscurity to Oblivion: Running in the Congressional Primary*. Knoxville: University of Tennessee Press.

Mann, Thomas E. 1978. *Unsafe at Any Margin: Interpreting Congressional Elections*. Washington, D.C.: American Enterprise.

Mayer, William. 1996. *The Divided Democrats*. Boulder, Colo.: Westview.

Mayhew, David. 1966. *Party Loyalty Among Congressmen: The Difference Be-*

tween Democrats and Republicans, 1947–1962. Cambridge: Harvard University Press.

———. 1974a. Congress: The Electoral Connection. New Haven: Yale University Press.

———. 1974b. "Congressional Elections: The Case of the Vanishing Marginals." Polity 6: 295–317.

McCarty, Nolan M. 1997. "Presidential Reputation and the Veto." Economics and Politics 9: 1–26.

McCarty, Nolan M., and Keith T. Poole. 1995. "Veto Power and Legislation: An Empirical Analysis of Executive and Legislative Bargaining from 1961–1986." Journal of Law, Economics and Organization 11: 282–312.

McKinney, Cynthia. 1996. "A Product of the Voting Rights Act." Washington Post, Nov. 26: A, 15.

MacRae, Duncan. 1970. Issues and Parties in Legislative Voting: Methods of Statistical Analysis. New York: Harper and Row.

Miller, Arthur, Warren E. Miller, Alden S. Raine, and Thad A. Brown. 1976. "A Majority Party in Disarray: Policy Polarization in the 1972 Election." American Political Science Review 753–78.

Miller, Warren E. 1955. "Presidential Coattails: A Study in Political Myth and Methodology." Public Opinion Quarterly 19: 353–68.

Miller, Warren E., and Donald E. Stokes. 1963. "Constituency Influence in Congress." American Political Science Review 57: 45–57.

Milyo, Jeffrey. 1997. "Electoral and Financial Effects of Changes in Committee Power." Journal of Law and Economics 40: 93–112.

Neustadt, Richard E. 1990. Presidential Power and the Modern Presidents: The Politics of Leadership from Roosevelt to Reagan. New York: Free Press.

Nie, Norman H., Sidney Verba, and John R. Petrocik. 1979. The Changing American Voter. Enlarged ed. Cambridge: Harvard University Press.

Ornstein, Norman J., Thomas E. Mann, and Michael J. Malbin. 1994. Vital Statistics on Congress, 1993–1994. Washington, D.C.: Congressional Quarterly Press.

———. 1996. Vital Statistics on Congress, 1995–1996. Washington, D.C.: Congressional Quarterly Press.

Pace, David. 1997. "Outsiders Fund 42 Percent of House, Senate Campaigns." Athens (Georgia) Banner Herald, May 11: 4A.

Page, Benjamin I., and Robert Y. Shapiro. 1992. The Rational Public: Fifty Years of Trends in Americans' Policy Preferences. Chicago: University of Chicago Press.

Patterson, Samuel C., and Gregory A. Caldeira. 1988. "Party Voting in the United States Congress." British Journal of Political Science 18: 111–31.

———. 1990. "Standing Up for Congress: Variations in Public Esteem Since the 1960s." *Legislative Studies Quarterly* 15 (Feb.): 25–47.

Petrocik, John R. 1996. "Issue Ownership in Presidential Elections, with a 1980 Case Study." *American Journal of Political Science* 40: 825–50.

Phillips, Kevin. 1985. *The American Political Report.* January 11.

Pomper, Gerald M., Ross K. Baker, Charles E. Jacob, Wilson Carey McWilliams, Henry A. Plotkin, Marlene M. Pomper, eds., *The Elections of 1976.* New York: David McKay.

Poole, Keith T., and Howard Rosenthal. 1991. "Patterns of Congressional Voting." *American Journal of Political Science* 35: 228–78.

———. 1997. *Congress: A Political-Economic History of Roll Call Voting.* New York: Oxford University Press.

Popkin, Samuel L. 1991. *The Reasoning Voter: Communication and Persuasion in Presidential Campaigns.* Chicago: University of Chicago Press.

Ranney, Austin. 1951. "Toward a More Responsible Two-Party System: A Commentary." *American Political Science Review* 45: 488–99.

Ranney, Austin, and Willmoore Kendall. 1954. "The American Party Systems." *American Political Science Review* 48: 477–85.

Rohde, David W. 1991. *Parties and Leaders in the Postreform House.* Chicago: University of Chicago Press.

Romer, Thomas, and James Snyder. 1994. "An Empirical Investigation of the Dynamics of PAC Contributions." *American Journal of Political Science* 38: 745–69.

Salant, Jonathan, and David Cloud. 1995. "To the 1994 Election Victors Go the Fundraising Spoils." *Congressional Quarterly Weekly Report,* Apr. 15: 1057.

Salmore, Barbara, and Stephen Salmore. 1989. *Candidates, Parties and Campaigns: Electoral Politics in America.* Washington, D.C.: Congressional Quarterly Press.

Schattschneider, E. E. 1950. "Toward a More Responsible Two-Party System: A Report of the Committee on Political Participation." *American Political Science Review* 44: 1–96.

Schneider, William. 1984. "Half a Realignment." *The New Republic,* Dec. 3: 19–22.

Schoenberger, Robert A. 1969. "Campaign Strategy and Party Loyalty: The Electoral Relevance of Candidate Decision-Making in the 1964 Congressional Elections." *American Political Science Review* 63: 515–20.

Sellers, Patrick. 1998. "Strategy and Background in Congressional Campaigns." *American Political Science Review* 92: 159–71.

Shannon, W. Wayne. 1968. *Party, Constituency, and Congressional Voting:*

A Study of Legislative Behavior in the United States House of Representatives. Baton Rouge: Lousiana State University Press.

Sinclair, Barbara. 1983. *Majority Leadership in the U.S. House*. Baltimore: The Johns Hopkins University Press.

———. 1985. "Agenda Control and Policy Success: Ronald Reagan and the 97th House." *Legislative Studies Quarterly* 10: 291–314.

———. 1995. *Legislators, Leaders, and Lawmaking: The U.S. House of Representatives in the Postreform Era*. Baltimore: The Johns Hopkins University Press.

———. 1997a. "Party Leaders and the New Legislative Process." In Lawrence C. Dodd and Bruce I. Oppenheimer, eds., *Congress Reconsidered*, 6th ed., pp. 229–45. Washington D.C.: Congressional Quarterly Press.

———. 1997b. *Unorthodox Lawmaking: New Legislative Processes in the U.S. Congress*. Washington D.C.: Congressional Quarterly Press.

Smith, Steven S., and Eric D. Lawrence. 1997. "Party Control of Committees in the Republican Congress." In Lawrence C. Dodd and Bruce I. Oppenheimer, eds., *Congress Reconsidered*, 6th ed., pp. 163–92. Washington, D.C.: Congressional Quarterly Press.

Snyder, James M. 1992. "Artificial Extremism in Interest Group Ratings." *Legislative Studies Quarterly* 17: 319–46.

Sorauf, Frank J. 1992. *Inside Campaign Finance*. New Haven: Yale University Press.

Sorauf, Frank J., and Paul Allen Beck. 1988. *Party Politics in America*. 6th ed. Glenview, Ill.: Scott, Foresman.

Stanley, Harold W. 1988. "Southern Partisan Changes: Dealignment, Realignment, or Both." *Journal of Politics* 50 (Feb.): 64–88.

———. 1996. "The Parties, the President and the 1994 Midterm Elections." In Colin Campbell and Bert A. Rockman, *The Clinton Presidency: First Appraisals*, pp. 188–211. Chatham, N.J.: Chatham House.

Stimson, James A., Michael B. MacKuen, and Robert S. Erikson. 1995. "Dynamic Representation." *American Political Science Review* 89: 543–65.

Stokes, Donald E. 1965. "A Variance Components Model of Political Effects." In John M. Claunch, ed., *Mathematical Applications in Political Science*, pp. 61–85. Dallas: Arnold Foundation.

———. 1966. "Some Dynamic Elements of Contests for the Presidency." *American Political Science Review* 60: 19–28.

———. 1967. "Parties and the Nationalization of Electoral Forces." In William Nisbet Chambers and Walter Dean Burnham, eds., *The American Party Systems: Stages of Political Development*, pp. 182–202. New York: Oxford University Press.

————. 1973. "Comment: On the Measurement of Electoral Dynamics." *American Political Science Review* 67: 829–31.

Stokes, Donald E., and Warren Miller. 1962. "Party Government and the Saliency of Congress." *Public Opinion Quarterly* 26: 531–46.

Sullivan, Terry. 1987. "Headcounts, Expectations, and Presidential Coalitions in Congress." *American Journal of Political Science* 32: 567–89.

————. 1990. "Bargaining with the President: A Simple Game and New Evidence." *American Political Science Review* 84: 1167–96.

————. 1991. "The Bank Account Presidency: A New Measure and Evidence on the Temporal Path of Presidential Influence." *American Journal of Political Science* 35: 686–723.

Sundquist, James L. 1983. *The Dynamics of the Party System.* Rev. ed. Washington, D.C.: Brookings Institution.

Swain, Carol. 1993. *Black Faces, Black Interests: The Representation of African Americans in Congress.* Cambridge: Harvard University Press.

Tufte, Edward R. 1975. "Determinants of the Outcomes of Midterm Congressional Elections." *American Political Science Review* 69: 812–26.

Turner, Julius. 1951. "Responsible Parties: A Dissent from the Floor." *American Political Science Review* 45: 143–52.

Ward, Daniel S. 1993. "The Continuing Search for Party Influence in Congress: A View from the Committees." *Legislative Studies Quarterly* 18: 211–30.

Wattenberg, Ben. 1995. *Values Matter Most.* New York: Free Press.

Weber, Ronald. 1993. "Turnout, Participation, and Competition in 1992 Louisiana Congressional Elections." Submitted to the court in Louisiana v. Hays (1996).

————. 1996. "Final Report on Liability Issues for Hearing in *Moon v. Meadows.*" Submitted to the court in *Moon v. Meadows*, C.A. No. 3: 95CV942 (E.D. Va., 1996).

White, Halbert C. 1980. "A Heteroskedasticity-Consistent Covariance Matrix Estimator and a Direct Test for Heteroskedasticity." *Econometrica* 48: 817–30.

Witt, Evans. 1983. "A Model Election." *Public Opinion Quarterly* 6: 46–49.

Wolfinger, Ray, and Michael G. Hagen. 1985. "Republican Prospects: Southern Comfort." *Public Opinion* 8 (Oct.–Nov.): 8–13.

Wright, Gerald C. 1978. "Candidates' Policy Positions and Voting in Congressional Elections." *Legislative Studies Quarterly* 3: 445–57.

————. 1989. "Policy Voting in the U.S. Senate: Who is Represented?" *Legislative Studies Quarterly* 14: 465–86.

————. 1993. "Errors in Measuring Vote Choice in the National Election Studies, 1952–88." *American Journal of Political Science* 37: 291–317.

Wright, Matthew B. 1993. "Shirking, Political Support and Agency Costs in Political Markets." *Public Choice* 76: 103–24.

Zaller, John. 1998. "Politicians as Prize Fighters: Electoral Selection and the Incumbency Advantage." In John Geer, ed., *Politicians and Party Politics*, pp. 125–81. New Haven: Yale University Press.

Zupan, Mark A. 1992. "Measuring the Ideological Preferences of U.S. Presidents: A Proposed (Extremely Simple) Method." *Public Choice* 73: 351–61.

References to tables and figures are in italics.